ADVERTISING EFFECTIVENESS

findings from empirical research

by Giep Franzen

NTC PUBLICATIONS LIMITED

First published 1994 by NTC Publications Limited
Farm Road, Henley-on-Thames, Oxfordshire RG9 1EJ, United Kingdom
Telephone: 0491 574671   Fax: 0491 571188

A CIP catalogue record for this book is available from the British Library

ISBN 1-870562-88-7

Translated by Wendy van Os-Thompson

Typeset by NTC Publications Ltd
Printed and bound in Great Britain by Biddles Ltd, Guildford and King's Lynn.

Contents

Acknowledgements

I should like to thank the following friends, acquaintances and advisers who have read the first draft of this book and have sent me their comments and a wealth of useful material.

Donald E. Bruzzone	President Bruzzone Research Company
Prof. Jan van Cuilenburg	University of Amsterdam, Chairman Communication Sciences Division
Tom van Hulst	VNU
Ria Kuip	Director Cebuco (Newspaper Advertising Bureau)
Uwe Munzinger	Director Strategic Planning & Research, BBDO Düsseldorf
Karen Olshan	Executivep Vice President Research, BBDO Worldwide
Paula Kay Pierce	Corporate Communications Director, McCollum Spielman Worldwide
Jan Stapel	Director NIPO
David Walker	Senior Vice President, ASI Research Inc.
Gordon Brown	Millward Brown Market Research Limited
Allan R. Kuse	Executive Vice President Basic Research Services, Research Systems Corporation

I should also like to thank the people whose day-to-day help has been indispensable. Without them this book could never have been written. The two FHV/BBDO documentalists: Clary Veenstra and Doortje de Haan. And Ilse Londema, who saw to it, day in day out, that my hand-written manuscript ended up as a neatly printed, and I hope, readable text – the result of which you have before you.

Giep Franzen

Introduction

Anyone who, like the present author, has spent his entire life in advertising is bound to be amazed at the slow progress of our understanding of how advertising works. This is certainly not caused by a lack of scientific interest; vast numbers of publications exist on the theoretical aspects and on laboratory experiments on the subject. Our lack of knowledge may, perhaps, be due to a lack of realism among some scholars . The majority of their publications focus on matters which people who are involved in advertising practice barely recognise. Moreover, few publications are based on scientific observation and research into 'real-life' advertising: how do the advertisements, commercials or campaigns, to which real consumers of the advertised products are exposed in natural circumstances, actually work? How are they perceived and processed? To what extent are they effective in influencing purchasing behaviour? And what more widely-applicable conclusions can be drawn on correlations, and on the effects of all manner of technical and creative variables?

Those who work in advertising are confronted daily with a jumble of questions, large and small, to which they have to provide the answers themselves, if they are to get anywhere. They will not find these answers in abstract theories or in the results of laboratory experiments carried out under unrealistic conditions. Practitioners constantly base their decisions on simple, practical assumptions – on which they invariably have differing opinions with other advertising people. That makes advertising both fascinating and difficult.

Empirical surveys

In the last five to ten years, advertising research institutes in the United States have been issuing the results of a number of large-scale empirical surveys and analyses of the connection between a great many variables and advertising recall and shifts in attitude (brand preference and propensity to buy). In what was formerly West Germany considerable empirical research has also been carried out into consumer's sensory perception of advertisements. This book aims to collect and open up the findings.

To prevent this leading to a disjointed accumulation of isolated facts, a model has been used which follows the course of advertising processes. It is a variation on the well-known 'hierarchy of effects' models. Step-by-step the known facts relating to the various stages in the model have been examined, with particular reference to the results of the above-mentioned empirical research. When appropriate, the theoretical views and results of laboratory research are quoted.

Although we have taken a theoretical model, an effort has been made to avoid producing yet another 'theory book'. Moreover, it has not been the intention to discuss the surveys as such, or to contemplate the research methods and concomitant issues. Anyone who is interested in those aspects can easily find his way to the sources, using the list of references. This book is primarily about advertising, not about advertising research. An effort has also been made to avoid subjective assumptions and opinions. We shall try to adhere as closely as possible to the findings of the surveys. This book is mainly intended to be a 'helping hand' for people working in advertising: it attempts to marshal the facts for them.

How advertising works

What we want to know with respect to how advertising works is the effect of all kinds of variables on the effectiveness of campaigns in the marketplace. What do people, who are exposed to advertising, do, individually. How do they react collectively, as a 'market'?

Individual advertisers may have this kind of information at their disposal, but little is actually divulged, and when information is published, for instance as EFFIE cases, it is hard to generalise on the contents.

In the decades to come we can probably expect an increase in large-scale single-source research which examines various facets of individual 'advertising behaviour' and 'consumption behaviour'. Harder facts on the connections at the level of the individual will gradually become available. The results of one of the first comprehensive analyses, based on 400 cases in the IRI (ARF, 1991) databank are included in this book.

However, the surveys which are reported in this book use measured changes in brand preference or buying propensity as the norms for effectiveness in influencing the choice process (persuasion). Of course, an obvious question in this context is whether what people say they are going to do is a good gauge of what they actually do later. This is one of the hottest issues in the world of advertising research.

A few of the surveys on which this book is based do use as a criterion the actual, established behaviour in a market. One is the recent ARF copy testing validity project. It confirmed that scores for 'attitude shifts', like brand assessment, brand preference and propensity to buy largely tally with the established effectiveness of the tested commercials in the market-place. Another is the analysis of IRI cases mentioned earlier, which actually found no connection between recall and attitude scores, and market developments! We shall, of course, be coming back to this later.

In the eighties 'split-cable' tests also became possible. This entails a group of consumers receiving a commercial, whilst a control group does not. Buying behaviour of both sample groups is ascertained, after which the differences in buying behaviour can be related to the scores for recall and persuasion. Comparison, in particular of ASI measurements of the awareness and attitude effects with actual buying behaviour, does show that a consistent correlation exists (Walker, 1990). Clearly the debate on the validity of recall and attitude measurements is not over yet.

Short-term effects

Consequently, we should bear in mind that the criterion of effectiveness in almost all the cited research is what people say they think and say they will do, shortly after they have been exposed to the researched advertisements. In other words, they are measurements of short-term mental reactions to individual advertisements, usually seen only once. No scientific conclusions can be drawn from them with respect to the longer-term effect of campaigns. The research methods and types of questions used may well lead to a preference for advertisements which produce short-term memory effects compared with those which are less effective in that respect, but may well be better with longer-term behaviour effects.

As we shall discover, the various tests suggest that mood commercials in some respects are less effective than commercials with a relevant and distinctive product message. The possibility cannot be ruled out that this is partly the result of the research methods.

However, few advertisers solely aim at long-term effects. As Fletcher (1992) states:

> *"no advertisers wait years for their advertising to take effect. Advertising must work both immediately and residually. It must generate response both today and tomorrow. It works both quickly and slowly. Unless short-term results are achieved the long-term benefits will never materialise. Advertising could not possibly work in the future if it did not work in the present."*

The best commercials are usually the ones which have both short- and long-term effects, and which are able to combine the communication of a relevant product message with the development of positive emotional associations with the brand. With this in mind, it is worth seeing what can be learnt from the results of the recently-released empirical research.

Not a strategy book

This book is not about the development of advertising strategies. So it does not deal with 'what' we should be communicating 'to whom' in order to make effective advertising. We shall be concentrating solely on 'how'. What is known about the way in which countless execution variables work? What is known about the effect of the size of an advertisement and the length of a commercial? What is known about the way in which copy is read and visuals work? How does humour work, and what happens when we use 'voice-overs'? How should we apply logos? What are the effects of 'warmth' and 'liveliness'? Many such aspects will be considered.

No magic spells

However, this book will not be supplying ready-made recipes for good, effective advertising campaigns. The secret of effective advertising is that it is always a little bit 'new' in some way. But everyone who is involved in developing and approving campaigns implicitly applies a number of assumptions as to 'how advertising works'. And there is invariably a tacit agreement not to be explicit about these assumptions . On the few occasions that does happen, they prove to be based on scanty factual knowledge.

The main aim of this book is to fill some of the gaps in our knowledge. There often proves to be a far greater supply of knowledge on many subjects than the average advertising person has managed to assemble during his/her studies or practical experience. If he compares his existing assumptions with this information, and possibly thoroughly revises them, he may conceivably have far better results.

Strategy most important factor of success

One should never forget that the effectiveness of advertising campaigns is determined by what we communicate, and by how we do it. Execution variables only explain part of the measured effects. In one of the major analyses on which this book is based 15% of the variance in measured recall, comprehension and persuasion is explained by execution variables (Stewart and Furse, 1986). In another analysis, these variables account for 48% of the variance in recall scores and 19% in persuasion scores (MSW executional analysis II, 1990). Moreover, the MSW analysis reveals great differences from one product category to another. So the message itself is almost always very important, sometimes even the foremost variable as regards the persuasive effect of advertising.

No Golden Rule

The facts which we shall be dealing with are not intended as official 'dos and don'ts'. You cannot claim that advertising does, or does not work. It always works a little. And sometimes a lot. So it is always a matter of a little more or a little less, or much more or much less. So, in practice, we have to weigh things up carefully. What would work better in view of the specific objectives and circumstances? What do the following facts mean which represent averages of countless examples of advertising for countless brands and products, in a specific situation?

Many of the surveys which we report are not target group-specific. They indicate how advertising is perceived and processed by a random sample of people. Regardless of whether or not they are interested in the advertised product or brand. The facts might well be quite different if we were to use smaller, specific target groups of very involved (potential) brand purchasers. However, in some of the surveys on which we shall be basing our arguments, the samples are indeed accurately attuned to the target groups.

Differences in testing methods

Although the terminology used in the processed analyses tends to be very similar, the testing methods differ considerably. 'Related recall' in one analysis often means something quite different in another. That means that it is impossible to compare automatically one set of analysis results with another. It could also be dangerous to draw any general conclusions. However, if we are not prepared to accept these scientific objections and do not wish to compare the findings of the individual analyses and see them in a wider context, we shall get no farther than general theories and isolated facts. Advertising practice is desperate for an all-encompassing and realistic model based on empirical observation. Although it often fails to supply conclusive evidence, it does manage to give a plausible explanation of how something works in a certain respect.

Those who are not prepared to accept the limitations of the available information or who feel that it is too risky to look for a connection with information from entirely different sources, can in fact stop here. They have little alternative than to 'go it alone' and find their own way in the dark.

Research references (summary)

The results of the following analyses have been included:

Author(s), year, title (if relevant)	Research institute (or principal)	Primary focus of analysis or research	Size of sample
Stewart and Furse, 1986	Research Systems Corporation	execution variables	1,059 tv commercials
Lukeman, 1989	ASI Market Research Inc.	attention brand linkage	647 tv commercials
Walker, 1990	ASI Market Research Inc.	execution variables	876 tv commercials
Walker, 1990	ASI Market Research Inc.	recall, persuasion, validation	230 tv commercials
Stewart and Koslow, 1989	Research Systems Corporation	execution variables	1,017 tv commercials
Jacoby, Hoyer, Sheluga, 1980	AAAA	understanding of tv commercials	2,700 respondents
FHV/BBDO	NIPO	length, likeability and irritation	1,778 tv commercials
Agres	ASI Market Research Inc.	emotions	168 tv commercials
Haley & Bruzzone, 1985	ARF	copy research validity	5x2 tv commercials/15,000 interviews
Aaker & Bruzzone, 1985	Bruzzone Research Company	irritation	524 tv commercials
Moldovan, 1985	SSC&B	factors of success	'hundreds' of tv commercials
Olson, 1985	Leo Burnett	effect on trial purchases	65 launch commercials
Biel and Bridgewater, 1990	Bruzzone Research Company	likeability	80 tv commercials
Aaker and Stayman, 1990	Bruzzone Research Company	ad perception and impact	80 tv commercials
Biel, 1985	Bruzzone Research Company	likeability	73 tv commercials

Author(s), year, title (if relevant)	Research institute (or principal)	Primary focus of analysis or research	Size of sample
Bogart and Stuart Tolley, 1988	Admar Research	product interest and recognition	534 newspaper advertisements/ 7,296 interviews
v.d. Molen and Robben, 1991	NIPO for VNU	size, place, colour	515 magazine advertisements
v.d. Molen and Robben, 1991	NIPO	size, place, colour	4,100 magazine advertisements
v.d. Molen and Robben, 1991	NIPO	length, length of break, place in break	2,803 tv commercials
Starch, 1989	Starch INRA Hooper	size, colour, place, place on cover page	7,500 magazine advertisements
Starch, 1989	Starch INRA Hooper	size, colour, place, place on cover page	618 magazine advertisements
Waring, 1986	Gallup and Robinson	execution variables	over 100,000 advertisements
'Seherqualität II', 1991	Hörzu and Funkuhr (newspaper)	recall tv	6,174 interviews
'Dagbladen binnen bereik', 1985	Cebuco	reading of newsapers, newspaper advertisements	12,809 newspaper advertisements
Klein, 1990	McCollum Spielman Worldwide	execution variables	4,564 commercials
Klein, 1990	McCollum Spielman Worldwide	execution variables	7,729 tv commercials
Saupe, 1992	GfK Marktforschung	testimonials	965 tv commercials
MSW, 1991	McCollum Spielman Worldwide	comparative advertising	348 tv commercials
Maier, 1991	GfK Marktforschung	testimonials	185 tv commercials
MSW, 1982	McCollum Spielman Worldwide	humour	500 tv commercials
Merz, 1989	KfK Marktforschung	humour	70 tv commercials
Kuse, 1991	Research Systems Corporation	strategic and execution variables	5,000 tv commercials

Part 1

How to gain and retain attention

1 Advertising effects and their interactions

1.1 AIDA

For almost a century advertising practitioners and market researchers have been trying to understand how exactly advertising influences a consumer's decision to buy. The first person to formulate an appropriate model was St. Elmo Lewis: he introduced AIDA as long ago as 1900, or thereabouts. AIDA stands for Attention-Interest-Desire-Action – the effects which advertising should provoke in order to get a consumer to buy.

Since then reams of variations have been suggested, mainly consisting of other categories of effects: perception, comprehension, evaluation, memory, retention, knowledge, judgement, acceptance, attitude, caution, trial, yielding, sale, adoption, conviction, satisfaction, legitimating, confidence (Barry and Howard, 1990). Although the original AIDA hierarchy, with the early variations, kept going until around 1970, no real agreement ever existed as to its components. Moreover, criticism has increased of the basic idea of the hierarchy as such, in which a succession of stages is supposed to be passed through, with each stage 'successfully' completed before the next begins.

1.2 Interactions

Meanwhile understanding of advertising processing, and of its connection with established attitudes and buying behaviour has grown. The conclusion now is that there is absolutely no succession of stages. There is more likely to be a constant, more or less simultaneous interaction between existing knowledge (association networks), attitudes and behaviour on the one hand, and the perception and processing of advertisements on the other. If some succession does exist, the sequence of effects may well differ from the one on which hierarchy-of-effects models were based originally (cognition-affection-cognation, or knowing-feeling-doing).

This ultimately led to the latest version of the models, which Preston and Thorson came up with in 1984: the expanded association model. With it they attempt to express the interaction between existing associations, evaluations and behavioural tendencies on the one hand, and the assimilation of advertising on the other. Although it was a big step in the right direction, the sequence of effects still generates criticism. Consequently Moriarty (1983) suggested abandoning this basic idea. She proposed that the effects be regrouped in another meaningful way, and emphasising their inter-relations. She differentiates between three main areas: (1) perception (2) learning and (3) persuasion. She makes subgroups within each area, in which there are, in turn, various levels, depending on the extent of involvement. She groups the areas in a semi-circle, which does however also have a beginning (arousal) and an end (behaviour).

A review of the relevant literature shows that it has been a never-ending tussle to position the various aspects acceptably in relation to one another and to ensure that well-known interactions are also expressed appropriately. Maybe a fully satisfactory solution will never be found.

> *"The way in which advertising influences consumer choice is not a tidy mechanistic process with a set order. It is an extremely untidy, often irrational and, in particular, a human process. It is not successive and there is no clear sequence of cause and effect. That makes it difficult to distinguish, measure and quantify the effects of a campaign"* (Elliott).

1.3   Practice-based system

It is not in fact the author's intention to add an 'nth' version to all the existing models. But if the results of empirical surveys and analyses are to be correlated relevantly, it is essential to have a classification of effects and an indication of their interconnections. However, the main thing is to have a model with no start or finish. We are always dealing with situations in which existing consumer attitudes, buying behaviour and usage experience have just as much influence on the effects of advertising as the reverse. Even with product launches. So we are dealing with a system, rather than with a hierarchy.

> *"In a system, every variable interacts with other variables, in such a way that cause and effect cannot be distinguished. A variable can be both cause and effect, at the same time. Reality cannot be split up. Everything is interconnected."* (Ferguson, 1989).
>
> Ferguson postulates, that *"in General Systems theory, a modern concept, each variable in any system interacts with the other variables so thoroughly, that cause and effect cannot be separated. A single variable can be both cause and effect. Reality will not be still. And it cannot be taken apart. Relationships is everything."*

Within this system we can observe several groups of effects. The extent to which individual effects will be combined in groups or expressed separately is more likely to be due, within the framework of this publication, to practical convenience than to scientific subtlety. We have used the following arrangement:

1. **attention:** the area of exposure to advertising, monitoring (scanning) and the levels of attention;

2. **advertising processing:** the area of the different levels at which advertising stimuli are processed, and the form of processing: cognitive, affective and visual/verbal;

3. **brand awareness:** awareness of the brand and the levels of brand consciousness;

4. **brand associations:** the categories of association and storage in the memory in association networks;

5. **brand positioning:** comparison of brands with one another, and the relative position in the memory of one brand compared with competing brands;

6. **brand evaluation and attitude:** inclusion of the brand in the brand repertoire, emergence of levels of brand preference (or rejection);

7. **brand behaviour and product experience:** purchases (trial and repeat), development of levels of brand loyalty, and product-usage experience.

Interactions exist between these groups of effects, and these interactions are shown in the diagram 'Interactions between groups of effects' on page 6. A brief explanation of the groups follows.

1.3.1 Attention

Attention for an advertisement is determined, amongst other things, by the existing attitude towards the product category and the brand. Confirmation is sought for the choice after it has been reached, and the choice is strengthened in that alternatives are then rejected. This mainly brings about selective perception. A person perceives what coincides with his or her own attitudes, ignoring advertising for products and brands which he considers uninteresting or even rejects.

Attention is also affected by the extent of product experience. Increasing experience reduces uncertainty and, in turn, accessibility for (new) information.

1.3.2 Advertising processing

Advertising is processed at different levels, from very superficial to very 'deep'. As is the case with attention, the advertising processing level is influenced by interest in the product, brand attitude and usage experience. As well as by existing brand associations. These create expectations as regards advertising content. The advertising is interpreted partly on the basis of these expectations. To some extent people perceive what they expect to perceive, and look especially for confirmation of what they already think.

1.3.3   Brand awareness

Brand awareness is formed by all the ways in which a consumer is exposed to the brand – probably mostly because he wears it, or has it in his home, and so encounters it or handles it every day. Obviously advertising can make a valuable contribution to brand awareness, thanks to the special way in which a brand is reflected in its advertising. And to the force and frequency with which that takes place.

At a minimum level of attention ('mere exposure') advertising can ensure a certain feeling of awareness of the brand, although the advertising stimuli are not consciously processed.

1.3.4   Brand associations

Brand associations are mainly occasioned by product usage experience and advertising processing. Brand attitude also influences the formation and intensity of associations. A positive attitude stimulates (positive) associations, and reinforces them.

Positioning would also seem to influence the forming of associations: the perceived differences with competing brands 'colour' the perception and interpretation of advertising.

1.3.5   Positioning

Positioning is the classing of a brand in a product group or subgroup, and its 'cognitive mapping' – its relative position compared with other brands, which is determined by the characteristic, important attributes of that group and is based on developed associations. Positioning is influenced to some extent by brand attitude. A positive attitude (overall assessment) contributes to a greater perceived difference in relation to other brands.

1.3.6   Brand attitude

Brand attitude develops from awareness, brand associations, usage experience and the perceived difference compared with other brands (positioning). So brand attitude is hardly ever only an effect of advertising as the original hierarchy-of-effects models suggested. It is always a response to all the impressions and experiences one has had of a brand, with usage experience playing a particularly important part.

Interactions between groups of effects

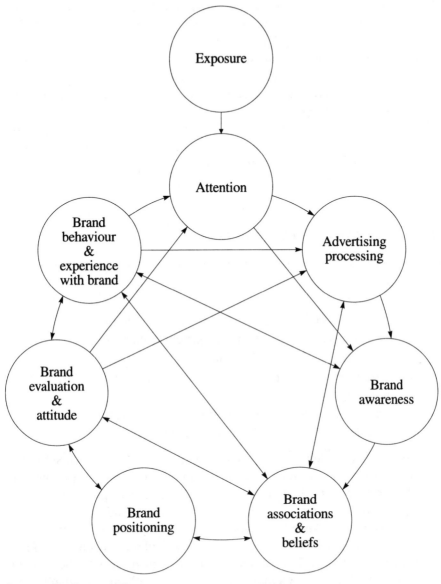

Source: Giep Franzen, 1992.

1.3.7   Buying behaviour and usage experience

Buying behaviour and usage experience are influenced by brand awareness, brand associations, positioning and brand attitude, amongst other things. But the presence of awareness and attitude does not necessarily precede buying behaviour. Joyce (1991) claims that, when there is only one measurement, there will always be a strong correlation between awareness, attitude and behaviour. However, successive measurements show that behaviour nearly always develops first. Ehrenberg, in particular, has provided substantial support for this claim. A (trial) purchase may proceed from a confrontation with the product or brand in the store, after which the consumer gets to know the product and develops an attitude towards it. After which advertising confirms and reinforces that attitude. However, a negative trial-experience may lead to non-perception of successive advertising.

Advertising is assumed to lead to 'lower order associations and beliefs'. 'Higher order associations and beliefs' allegedly develop from usage experience (Smith and Swinyard), and are subsequently confirmed and reinforced by advertising.

1.4   The criteria for effectiveness

Each advertising execution (advertisement, poster or television commercial) has to meet a number of criteria in order to be effective:
- it must be perceived with the senses;
- it must succeed in gaining and retaining our attention;
- it must succeed in getting us to register the brand well;
- it must be likeable and not irritating;
- it must contribute to the difference we perceive between the advertised brand and the alternatives;
- it must influence our choice in favour of the advertised brand;
- its central message must be stored in our memory.

By no means all advertising manages do meet all these criteria. Some, like brand 'registration', are more like decision premises. Nor are all criteria of equal importance for all products and brands. Sometimes pure attention will be more important than persuasion. At other times persuasion will have highest priority. And then, likeability is sometimes important, at other times not – though it is important not to cause irritation. We shall see later on that different 'advertising attributes' have different effects with respect to the different criteria for effectiveness. Humour, for instance, greatly affects attention, but affects choice less.

Each of these groups of effects will be reviewed in more depth in the following chapters. But more especially we shall examine what the aforementioned empirical analyses of large numbers of advertisements have taught us about the correlations between all kinds of advertising variables and these effects.

2 The communication society

Present-day society in the developed Western countries is sometimes termed an 'information society'. This means that it is mainly characterised by the production, diffusion and consumption of information, in all shapes and sizes. Unlike undeveloped societies, in which large groups of the population largely fill their days with activities geared to meeting the necessities of life, the majority of people in the West spend a large, and growing part of their time on communication. In an average American home the television is switched on for over 48 hours a week (so more than a full working week!). In 1965 it was still 'only' 41 hours and 53 minutes. The average American watched television for 2 hours and 41 minutes a day in 1967, in 1981 3 hours and 6 minutes and in 1990 3 hours and 36 minutes. American women even watched 4 1/2 hours a day in 1990! In addition, a considerable number of hours are spent on other forms of communication (Clark, 1988).

2.1 Growth in leisure time stagnating

However, communication consumption does have its limits – there are only 24 hours in a day – and they cannot be extended, as yet. We spend a great deal of our leisure time reading newspapers and magazines, and watching television. So it is useful to examine what is happening to our leisure time, how we experience developments and what we do with them. The shorter working week came about in the first half of the twentieth century. And meanwhile our working week has become shorter, with the increase in spare time in Western Europe mainly reflected in more days off. In West Germany, for instance, the course of weekly working hours was as follows:

	Hours
1950	50
1960	45
1970	41
1980	40
1990	38.5

Source: BAT Freizeitforschung 1990.

The daily amount of 'real' leisure time increased from 1.5 hours in 1950 (Allensbach 1952) to 4.1 hours in 1990 (BAT). Leisure time in the weekends rose from 1 1/2 days in the fifties to 2 days in the sixties, and holidays from 9 days in 1950 to 31 days in 1990. So in the past thirty years we have mainly acquired longer weekends and more holidays. In Germany daily leisure time only increased 3% between 1975 and 1985. So the great increase in leisure time occurred before 1970. Since then the German working week has decreased on average 2 1/2 hours – a drop of 'only' 6%.

In recent years, people in England with a full-time job have in fact been losing leisure time:

Spare time in hours/week	1986	1991	% change
Man with full-time job	39.1	35.0	−10.5
Woman with full-time job	32.2	22.8	−29.2
Woman with part-time job	34.8	37.8	+7.8
Housewife	36.1	38.2	+5.8
All (incl. unemployed)	**45.4**	**46.2**	**+1.7**

Source: The Henley Centre for Forecasting.

In the Netherlands, too, leisure time has decreased somewhat since 1975. The Central Statistics Office (CBS) has been measuring how the Dutch, from the age of 12 upwards, spend their spare time. In a period of 5 week-nights from 5.30 pm to midnight, Saturdays from noon to midnight, and Sundays from 8 am to midnight, the number of leisure hours rose 7.9 hours (33%) between 1955 and 1975. In the course of an entire week the Dutch have 46.7 spare hours in 1990. That was an hour less than in 1975. (Kraaykamp and Knulst, 1992).

Of the total of 'real' leisure time, 39% of all weekly leisure time (18.2 hours) is spent on media consumption. Since 1975 the share of reading in the time spent on media has dropped from 33% to 27% in 1990. In particular the time spent on reading magazines has decreased considerably in the past fifteen years.

Time spent on media in the Netherlands: hours per week*
Week-nights (5.30-12pm), Sat. (12pm-12am), Sun. (8am-12am)

Time spent on:	1955	1975	1985	1990
Total spare time	23.9	31.8	31.2	31.2
Media, (total)	8.4	15.1	15.2	14.6
of which:				
television	0.2	10.1	11.3	10.9
radio/audio	3.2	1.3	0.8	0.7
Reading, (total)	5.0	3.7	3.1	3.0
of which:				
books	2.4	1.0	0.9	1.0
newspapers	2.0	1.4	1.2	1.1
magazines	0.7	1.2	1.0	0.9
Other leisure activities	15.5	16.7	16.0	16.6

Notes: *12 year olds and older.   *Source:*   Socio-Cultural Planning Office.

Time spent on media in the Netherlands: hours per week (cont.)*
Primary consumption

Time spent on:	1955	1975	1985	1990
Total spare time	–	47.9	49.0	46.7
Media total	–	18.5	18.8	18.2
of which:				
television	–	10.2	12.1	11.9
radio/audio	–	2.2	1.4	1.2
Reading total	–	6.1	5.3	5.0
of which:				
books	–	1.6	1.4	1.5
newspapers	–	2.5	2.3	2.2
magazines	–	2.0	1.7	1.4
Other leisure activities	–	29.4	30.2	28.5

Notes: *12 year olds and older. *Source:* Socio-Cultural Planning Office.

2.2 How leisure time is experienced in the United States

Developments in the United States since 1945 have been quite different from in Western Europe: the average time Americans work had increased substantially in the past half century. That is largely due to the constant growth in the percentage of married women who are officially employed – from 20% in 1947 to 59% in 1989. That is by no means compensated by the decrease in the percentage of working men in the same period, from 89% to 77%.

The number of hours spent on housework has not dropped substantially either. The time saved by mechanisation on the domestic scene has been counteracted by higher demands as regards quality. Most time saved has promptly been spent on doing another wash, more cooking and baking, and more elaborate child care. The number of holidays, free days and days taken for sick leave have dropped in the past 10 years by 3.5 days a year. Schor (1991) produced the following estimates for the total number of hours worked in 1969 and 1987 (see 'Total hours worked per annum by people with a full-time job' on the following page).

She concludes that in 1987 Americans worked a month longer than in 1969! No wonder Americans constantly feel they have a chronic shortage of time. Working women, in particular, have that feeling – when they get home from work, they start their second job.

A survey in Boston (Schor, 1991) showed that women employed outside the home work 80 hours a week on average.

Total hours worked per annum by people with a full-time job

	1969	1987	Change
Hours in job:			
All	1,786	1,949	163
Men	2,054	2,152	98
Women	1,406	1,711	305
Hours doing housework:			
All	889	888	−1
Men	621	689	68
Women	1,268	1,123	−145
Total hours worked:			
All	**2,675**	**2,837**	**162**
Men	**2,675**	**2,841**	**166**
Women	**2,674**	**2,834**	**160**

Source: The Overworked American, J.B. Schor, Basic Books, 1991.

One in six American adults has a second job. And one in three has extra work in the evenings and in the weekends. Americans feel that they have less and less spare time. In 1990 Leisure Trends/Gallup calculated that Americans have 38 hours spare time a week, but when they themselves were asked how much spare time they had, they barely reached 20 hours. The difference lies in how leisure time is experienced: we fill our leisure time with things that give us a feeling of non-freedom. We 'have to' go to sport training, we 'have to' mow the lawn, we 'have to' pay social calls. In a 'time-values' study in 1991, Hilton encountered a pronounced feeling among people of not having enough spare time. And that in turn led to a feeling of stress:

- 29% feel permanently stressed;
- 33% cannot do what they intended every day;
- 38% try to sleep less in order to have more spare time;
- 31% think they spend too little time on the family;
- 27% feel they are trapped in the daily routine and;
- 21% have no time for fun any more.

48% of working mothers actually say they feel permanently under stress. Over half (54%) of Americans believe they have less spare time than in the past. Only 21% think they have more spare time (Business Week, 26-11-90). No wonder 68% want to slow down (Time CNN Survey, Time 4-8-91).

2.3   How leisure time is experienced in Europe

In Western Europe, too, the subjective feeling of having less and less 'spare time' is increasing. In West Germany no fewer than 53% of the 'working' population believe they have too little spare time (BAT). That is mainly due to the fact that they spend much of the time they are not formally 'working' fulfilling their obligations. Travel time to and from work has often increased drastically. And housework and the children make demands on their 'spare time'. For most people 'spare time' is only the time they can use as they want. In which they can do things they enjoy. And they feel that it is constantly decreasing.

2.4   Use of leisure time

What do we do in our spare time? Gallup researched it in the United States:

Time spent on leisure pursuits (USA), 1991

Watching television	34.4%
Sport/recreation	14.9%
DIY activities	10.4%
Social activities	9.6%
Reading	7.1%
Cooking/eating	4.6%
Shopping	4.1%
Games/hobbies	3.5%
Holidays/travel	3.3%
Visiting matches, entertainment	2.3%
Home studies	1.0%
Others (incl. culture, art)	4.8%
Total	**100%**

Source: Leisure Trends Inc./ The Gallup Organisation.

So Americans spend almost 42% of their spare time watching television and reading! In the Netherlands, too, much of the increased spare time between 1955 and 1990 has been filled with 'media consumption'. Between 1955 and 1975 the time spent on media in the above-mentioned periods rose from 8.4 hours a week to 15.1 – an increase of 80%! However, it has been dropping a little since 1975.

Most of the increased leisure time between 1955 and 1975 was (and still is) spent watching television. In 1975 hardly any more time was spent on other pursuits than twenty years previously. In 1990, in the course of one entire week the Dutch spent an average of 18.2 hours reading, watching television or listening to the radio or to music. That was a fraction less than in 1975. It takes up 39% of their total leisure time, about the same as in the U.S.

As we shall discover later in this book, time spent on reading dropped dramatically – by 40% between 1955 and 1990.

2.5   Television

The total supply of communication has increased exponentially, especially what takes place on the television screen. The number of channels that can be received in America grew 40% in the 1980-1990 decade. In 1991 Americans were able to choose between 12 over-the-air and 19 cable stations, on average.

In the Netherlands 90% of the households can receive cable television (1991), in the United States 62% (1992). The United States started out with 12 cable channels, but these days it is fairly normal to have a choice from 50 different channels. There are even plans to make the cable network suitable to receive 150!

Television now plays a dominant part on most people's lives in western society. Many are literally addicted. When Americans were asked about their favourite leisure pastime, 'watching television 'scored highest with 61% (Roper, 1990). The television set has become our foremost daily companion. But at the same time, television is going the same way as radio did some time ago. In 1979 25% of Americans said that television had a 'background' function. In 1989 the number had risen to 39%. In Western Europe, where the explosion in television 'supply' is very recent, this development can also be observed. The longer the television is on, the more it loses its fascination and its significance.

The number of possible leisure pursuits has increased considerably, which exerts increasing pressure on our spare time. Watching television gradually seems to be becoming a secondary pastime. It is acquiring a 'side-function', second or third to all kinds of other activities. A survey in West Germany (Opaschowski, BAT-Freizeit-Forschung Institut, in W&V 12/20 March 1992 – see 'What do we do whilst watching television?' on the following page) revealed that only 38% of television viewers did nothing else whilst viewing.

The percentage of viewers who watch a programme attentively dropped from 90% in 1986 to 77% in 1990.In addition, the number of viewers in the United States who do something else at the same time is continuing to increase:

	1965	1974	1981	1986	1990
Only watches tv	72%	53%	59%	61%	50%
Does something else at the same time	28%	47%	40%	39%	50%

Source: NAB 1990.

What do we do whilst watching television?

Only watch television	38%
Talk to other people	23%
Eat dinner	20%
Read	19%
Use the phone	12%
Do handicrafts	10%
Take a nap	9%
Iron	4%
Play with the children	4%
Attend to the pets	3%
Do homework	2%
Do odd jobs, repairs	2%
Attend to appearance	2%
Write letters	1%
Play games/do puzzles	1%
Other activities	6%

Source: BAT Freizeitforschungsinstitut 1992.

2.6   Information explosion

De Sola Pool et al. (1984) worked out the per capita annual increase in supplied communication. The following growth percentages were found for the United States and Japan:

	U.S.A.	Japan
1960–1965	9.9%	7.4%
1965–1970	6.1%	8.0%
1970–1975	6.3%	9.4%
1975–1980	4.6%	n/a

Every ten years the quantity of communication 'offered' via mass media to us personally doubles. Since 1960 it has octupled! And that does not include all the unaddressed items which fall into our letter boxes. Or everything we receive via our computer screens. In Japan they expect that total information production will rise from 100 index in 1989 to 470 index in 2000 – almost five times more in a little more than 10 years. (Nikkei, Tokyo 1990, in Van Cuilenburg et al. 1992). That relates to the total supply of information. In particular, communication outside the traditional mass media will boom.

The number of television stations transmitting over the air has risen in the United States from 668 in 1965 to 1403 in 1989 (NAB 1990).

And as we can all observe at news-stands, the number of magazines has also risen considerably in the decade. In the United States from 9,657 in 1975 to 11,239 in 1991. However, the average number of copies per issue rose even more.

	Average number of copies per issue	Average number of copies per 100 adults
1954	162,939,903	150.9
1974	250,749,387	173.9
1984	312,005,103	179.5
1989	363,194,636	199.6

Source: Magazine Publishers of America, in 1990-91 Magazine Handbook.

In West Germany the number of general interest magazines doubled between 1980 and 1990, from 267 to 545 titles. Copies sold, which is a better gauge of magazine consumption, increased by 30%, from 85 to 110 million.

In the UK the numbers of general interest magazines increased from 1,367 in 1981 to 2,373 in 1990. In the same period, the number of daily newspapers and (free) news-sheets) rose from 550 to 1,300.

In the Netherlands the amount of information available by way of books, newspapers and magazines rose around 30% between 1975 and 1988 (Van Cuilenburg et al., 1992). The average number of editorial pages in daily papers rose in that period from 13.8 to 17.2 – almost 25%.

As we have seen, the growth in audio-visual repertory has been even more tempestuous. Almost the entire population of the Netherlands can receive seven Dutch-language television stations – twice as many as ten years ago. More than half the population can also receive eleven or more foreign channels.

Total broadcast time of the Dutch transmitters has quadrupled in recent years:

	Transmitter	Hours broadcast each year
1983/84	NL 1+2	4,636
1986/87	NL 1+2	6,030
1988/89	NL 1+2+3	6,654
1990/91	NL 1+2+3 + RTL	7,813

This implies that, while total viewing time remains constant, average viewing in 1992 is only 25% of what it was 8 years ago.

Van Cuilenburg (1992) argues that an annual growth in information supply of 10% is not unrealistic for the Netherlands. It amounts to an increase by a factor of 2.5 in the year 2000.

2.7 Communication consumption

Per capita consumption of communication is also increasing somewhat each year, but it clearly cannot keep up with the growth in what is offered. De Sola Pool et al. (1984) calculated the following percentages:

Communication consumption annual increase

	U.S.A.	Japan
1960–1965	1.8%	3.1%
1965–1970	1.2%	0.7%
1970–1975	2.1%	3.0%
1975–1980	1.5%	n/a

From 1960 onwards per capita communication consumption increased 1.6% per annum, in Japan 2.5%. If we take a fairly optimistic estimate of an annual increase in communication consumption in the Netherlands of 3.5% between 1990 and 2000, this would increase by a factor of 1.4 in that decade. And assuming a simultaneous 'explosion' in supply by a factor of 4.7, only a very small amount (1 to 2%) of all available information would ultimately be consumed.

2.8 Communication overload

The growing discrepancy between communication supply and communication consumption has led to the phenomenon of communication overload – i.e. the share of communication supply which is not consumed. If a newspaper contains 75,000 words and we read 3,750 (5% of the total), the overload is 95% (see the diagrams 'Supply per capita' and 'Consumption per capita' on the following page).

De Sola Pool et al. used this approach to calculate roughly the communication overload in the United States and Japan, while Kroeber-Riel came to an average of 97% in what was formerly West Germany. The results were as follows:

	U.S.A. (1980)	Japan (1975)	West Germany (1988)
Television	99.1%	98.6%	96.8%
Radio	99.9%	99.8%	99.4%
Newspapers	98.0%	96.0%	91.7%
Magazines	95.0%	91.6%	94.1%
Average	**99.6%**	**n/a**	**97%**

Supply per capita, all media

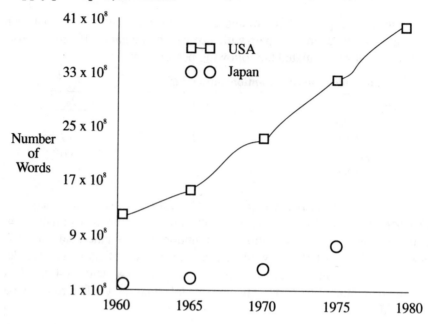

Source: I. de Sola Pool e.a., 'Information flows', 1984.

Consumption per capita, all media

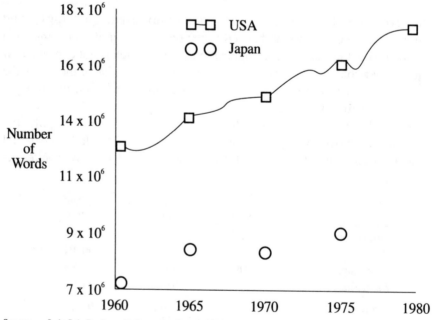

Source: I. de Sola Pool e.a., 'Information flows', 1984.

The percentage of broadcast television programmes 'consumed' in West Germany has meanwhile dropped to below 2%.

	Total trans-mission time (min./day)	Index	Viewing time (min./day)	Index	Percentage transmission time viewed
1985	3,168	100	147	100	5.0%
1986	3,900	123	149	101	3.8%
1987	4,440	140	154	105	3.5%
1988	5,754	182	152	103	3.0%
1989	7,122	225	153	104	2.1%
1990	7,890	249	156	106	2.0%

Source: GfK Marktforschung.

2.9   Increase in commercial communication

Another important fact is that the quantity of 'commercial communication', to which advertising belongs, is also increasing. Hard facts are hard to track down. Calculations in the United States show that the number of advertisements and commercials which are being printed or broadcast rose 103% between 1967 and 1982. This amount is expected to double once more between 1983 and 1998. Back in 1965 Weilbacher worked out that the average individual only 'processed' about 25% of the advertisements or commercials to which he was potentially exposed. In 1992 that percentage must be considerably lower.

Of the 48 hours that an average American household has the television switched on per week, the individual watches, on average, 3 hours 36 minutes per day. In that time he sees 83 commercials, i.e. about 20% of all commercials broadcast whilst the television is on. During the other 80% he is not in the room, or else he avoids them by making coffee, going to the lavatory or chatting to other people.

In West Germany the number of minutes of advertising transmission time rose by a factor of 4.4 from 1985 to 1990, although viewing time only rose 6%.

	tv commercials broadcast (min./day)	tv commercials watched (min./day)	Percent of tv commercials watched
1985	51	4.5	8.8
1986	108	4.6	4.3
1987	119	4.9	4.1
1988	144	5.3	3.7
1989	190	6.2	3.3
1990	223	7.1	3.3

In 1985 an individual actually saw 9% of the television advertising, in 1990 only 3%.

In all, 32,859 products were advertised in W. Germany in 1980. The number had risen to 47,336 in 1991 – an increase of 44% in 11 years (Nielsen, S&P). The total number of insertions and spots also rose 42%, from 1.8 to 2.55 million. In the United States the number of minutes of tv commercials per hour of transmission time is also increasing from year to year. Since 1985, there has actually been an increase in advertising minutes of 28% on prime time!

	Number of minutes advertising per hour transmission time (prime time)	
	Minutes	Index
1985	8.9	100
1986	9.3	104
1987	9.7	109
1988	10.0	112
1989	10.4	117
1990	10.7	120
1991	11.0	124
1992	11.4	128

Source: Commercial Monitoring Report; MSW.

As a result of the increase in 15-second commercials compared with longer ones, the number of commercials per hour has risen even more than the figures suggest. The average number of commercials per hour progressed as follows:

1982	21.7
1983	22.5
1984	23.0
1985	23.6
1986	24.0
1987	24.7

Source: Sami/Burke, 1988.

The average length of the transmitted commercials was 25 seconds in 1989. That means 27 commercials per hour of viewing time. In view of the average of 3 hours and 36 minutes that Americans watch television per day, that works out at 83 commercials a day, 581 a week and 30,200 a year!

In England the number of pages of advertisements rose from 269,000 in 1982 to 360,000 in 1991 – an increase of 34% in 9 years. In the same period the number of tv commercial minutes rose from 2,420 to 8,589 a month (not including satellite television). A growth with a factor of 3.55 in 9 years. (AMV/BBDO).

In the Netherlands advertising expenditure per inhabitant was 2.6 times higher in 1989 than in 1959 (in constant prices). But as no satisfactory figures are available on media inflation, the increase in volume cannot be calculated (Alsem et al., 1991).

2.10 Far-reaching consequences

At the end of this century we will find that consumers are being inundated with communication, commercial and non-commercial. The growth in total advertising volume will probably not be the worst threat, but the sheer amount of communication as such.

Even now consumers are being supplied with thirty times more information than they process. And the difference is still growing, with far-reaching consequences:

- Consumers must be increasingly selective in what receives their attention: they avoid more and more communication which they do not consider to be interesting or relevant.
- They have increasingly less attention for communication: they break off contact sooner, in order to switch their attention to the following item of communication.
- They process communication at a shallower, more superficial level.
- They are starting to 'consume' more pictures, at the expense of words.
- These developments are having considerable consequences for advertising. It is becoming more and more difficult to reach people (to ensure that advertising is there, when they are viewing, reading or listening) and to gain and retain their undivided attention.

Kover (N.W. Ayer, 1991) also points out that consumers focus their attention for ever-shorter periods.

"A great many television viewers give a commercial only three seconds to prove that it is worthy of their attention, if it is not they zap to another channel", he maintains.

It is not surprising that people try to avoid this communication overload. Not only do they do so passively, allowing their attention to wane. They avoid contact actively, literally dodging communication.

People also are becoming more cynical about the content of everything that comes their way. What are they supposed to do with it, what can they do with it? And that not only applies to advertising content. The same goes for most of what governments and politicians have to say. Kover suggests that we should start applying a resistance model. In order to overcome their resistance, we must give readers and viewers a good reason to favour us with their undivided attention. As we shall see later in this book, the relevance of information is still their foremost criterion. We must provide them with relevant information in a way they appreciate.

In 1985 Cebuco in the Netherlands conducted a large-scale survey with newspapers and came to the conclusion that there was a strong connection between the 'seeing' of advertisements and the extent to which readers subsequently rated them as 'useful' and 'interesting':

Judgement	Percentage of advertisement seen
Useful and interesting	59%
Not useful, but interesting	44%
Useful, not interesting	38%
Neutral, neutral	28%
Not useful, not interesting	23%

Source: Cebuco "Newspapers within reach", 1985.

Obviously we shall have to try, more than ever, not to irritate readers and viewers. Not because irritating advertising may not be penetrating, but because consumers can shut us off, merely by pressing their remote control. Why should they expose themselves to irritating advertising?

Under the influence of the ever-growing communication overload, advertising is generally being processed at an increasingly shallow level. This is mainly apparent in the drop in recall and recognition scores. Viewers are having more and more difficulty remembering the last commercial they saw. Spontaneous recall is decreasing faster than aided recall, which proves that some processing occurs, but it is becoming increasingly difficult to find the traces in the memory.

Burke (1990) registered the following development in spontaneous recall:

Can spontaneously remember the last commercial

1965	18%
1974	12%
1981	7%
1986	7%
1990	4%
1995 (forecast)	2%

Source: Burke Market Research.

The scores for related recall are also dropping (Fleschig, 1988):

1975–1979	24%
1980–1984	23%
1985–1987	22%
1988	21%

Source: Burke Market Research.

NIPO scores for the Netherlands also show a drop in the eighties, especially as regards spontaneous recall:

	Spontaneous recall	Aided recall
1975–1979	29.2%	62.4%
1980–1984	25.0%	58.2%
1985–1989	24.4%	59.6%

N.B. These NIPO scores are averages for all commercials, regardless of length.

On average, spontaneous recall drops 3% every 10 years, both in the United States and in the Netherlands.

A German survey (Seherqualität II, 1991) reveals that spontaneous brand recall with television commercials at similar broadcast times (early evening, Monday to Friday) is now only 16% of what it was in 1979. The drop in aided recall is again less dramatic, with scores of 75% compared with those in 1979.

Not only is recall of a certain commercial or advertisement measured, it is also quite common to measure whether a person remembers having seen (heard or read) advertising for a certain brand recently. This 'advertising awareness', which we shall be discussing in more detail later, is also on the decline. Average advertising awareness of 150 campaigns which GfK followed in West Germany, has developed as follows:

	Average advertising expenditure in DM 1,000 per month	Advertising awareness in target group
1985	700	18%
1986	700	17%
1987	730	17%
1988	700	15%
1989	680	14%

Source: GfK Marktforschung.

The drop in recall scores is not solely a problem of television. The same applies with magazine advertisements. NIPO measurements in three different periods with women's magazines show the following averages:

Full page recall score (Margriet and Libelle)

	1965–1970		1980–1985		1986–1991	
	(%)	index	(%)	Index 1965/70 = 100	(%)	Index 1965/70 = 100
Black and white:						
Advertisement seen only	31.9	100	28.8	90	26.1	82
Also read partially	21.7	100	10.6	49	10.7	49
Perceived fully (recognized)	53.6	100	39.4	74	36.8	69
Read partially in % perceived	44.0	100	27.0	67	29.0	72
Aided recall (NIPO impact)	11.3	100	9.7	86	8.9	79
Full colour:						
Advertisement seen only	36.8	100	37.0	100	36.1	98
Also read partially	25.9	100	15.3	59	17.1	66
Perceived fully (recognized)	62.7	100	52.3	83	53.1	85
Read partially in % perceived	41.0	100	29.0	71	32.0	78
Aided recall (NIPO impact)	14.5	100	15.0	103	15.4	106

So the scores for 'noting' (recognising) advertisements in Margriet and Libelle have been dropping constantly since 1965/70, on average, around one per cent a year over the past 20 years.

The drop in average recognition score for a full page in black and white is around 30% (from around 54% to around 37%), for a full page in full colour around 15% (from around 63% to around 53%).

However, the reading of advertisements dropped even more. With black and white full page ads reading was almost halved, with full colour advertisements it was a third less.

This means that, to an increasing extent, people only look at advertisements. Reading as a percentage of 'noting' dropped with black and white ads from 40% to 29%; with full colour from 41% to 32%.

The scores for aided recall with black and white ads dropped about 20% (from 11.3% to 8.9%). With full colour ads it remained fairly constant.

Newspapers, too, are undergoing a drop in 'noting' ('seeing') scores. If we compare the average recognition scores which Cebuco recorded in 1966 and Cebuco's recognition scores in 1985, we can note a decrease of 14 to 23%. This is approximately ca. 1% a year.

Noting of advertisements in newspapers

	1966	1985	% change
1500 mm	47%	36.2%	–23.0%
2500 mm	53%	42.5%	–20.0%
3500 mm	55%	47.5%	–13.6%

N.B. Percentages for 1985 are based on projected graphs, questions do not match.

Sources: Survey 'Geen dag' (Not one day), 1966;
Survey 'Dagbladen binnen bereik' (Newspapers within reach), 1985.

3 The pre-attentive stage

People are confronted, through their senses, with a constant stream of stimuli from their environment. Obviously they need to reduce all this sensory information. If we were constantly aware of the overwhelming quantity of stimuli which are coming at us, we would be permanently and completely confused.

The first protective mechanism we use is that of 'mechanical avoidance'. We switch off the television set, throw the advertising brochures into the dustbin, unseen. The second is 'physical avoidance'. We leave the room when the television is on. The third mechanism is performed by our own senses. We do not see or hear what is going on around us: our senses are 'doing something else'.

The latter selection is made by our brain, which filters sensory perceptions. We process most stimuli unconsciously. We only pay conscious attention to a small part of what our eyes see and our ears hear. Advertising needs to take a great many hurdles if it is to be perceived and processed consciously.

3.1   Pre-attentive perception

Attention is preceded by a stage which is termed 'pre-attentive'. That is where processes take place, subconsciously and automatically, which govern much of our daily activity. We walk, drive, eat and do most other everyday things outside our conscious attention. To some extent the same happens when we watch television and 'read' newspapers.

These pre-attentive processes are, in fact, the focus of our conscious attention. This can best be visualised as a permanent sensory registration of stimuli from our environment at a subconscious level, from which our consciousness is activated under certain conditions.

'Attention' and 'consciousness' are words which are closely related. Some people even view them as synonyms (Mandler, 1982). Consciousness is a state in which our brain interacts with the stimuli from our environment. This interaction can consist of various processes – cognitive (which includes the interpretation of the stimuli, activation of certain associations and visual images) and emotional (such as the evoking of certain emotional reactions).

3.2   Avoiding advertising

Television viewers and magazine readers cannot possibly pay attention to all the advertising these media bring into their homes. They switch off the set, use the remote control to zap to another channel or wind the video recorder on to the next programme. They switch their attention to something else in their surroundings, give their thoughts free rein, or leave the room where the television is running, to make a cup of coffee.

This not only happens during the commercials. Programmes, too, are followed with less and less attention. Burke (1990) established that in 1980 10 out of 100 'viewers' were only in the room by chance, but were not watching television themselves. In 1986 the figure had risen to 25 out of 100, and of those who were watching, 50% were doing something else at the same time. In 1965 that percentage was still only 28 (Bogart and Lehman, 1983).

Only 23% of all television viewers concentrates fully on the programme and does nothing else. The percentage in a survey in Germany in 1992 was practically identical (Seherqualität II). But that was already the case in 1979 (Seherqualität I).

A survey in Britain (BSB) supplied the following breakdown of television viewers' activities when they were not concentrating on the screen:

	Man (%)	Woman (%)
Reading	28	16
Snoozing	6	5
Leisure	6	21
Housework	5	10
Drinking/eating	19	19
Talking	15	14
Toilet	3	2
Others	19	15

As can be expected, recall score for commercials drop dramatically when people combine viewing with another activity.

Correct recall of brand of last commercial seen

	1965	1974	1981	1990
Only watching tv	20%	15%	9%	6%
Watching tv and doing something else	10%	10%	4%	2%

Source: Recall of last television commercial, Newspaper Advertising Bureau.

3.3   32% of viewers lost

It is not difficult to register whether or not the television is switched on, but it is certainly not easy to check people's physical behaviour from one moment to the next. So the combined effect of mechanical and physical avoidance cannot be adequately established.

A number of surveys in the United States show that a television set is switched on for 18% of the time, on average, with no-one in the room. During commercials an additional 22% of the viewers are doing something else – in other words, altogether 40% non-audience (Abernethy, 1990). But even among those who continue viewing, an estimated 10% are lost for the commercials because they zap to another channel. A survey in Italy (Denon 1985) showed that 12% of viewers zapped to something else at the first commercial, and 8% at the second or third. Audiences for commercials in the United States are assumed to be over 30% (22% + 10%) smaller than for actual programmes. So only 68% remain who do see the commercials – and that may well be an optimistic estimate.

Another survey (TV Dimensions 91, Media Dynamics Inc.) shows that in the United States 40-50% of people viewing a programme also pays attention to the commercials. 15-25% only had divided attention for the commercials and 35-45% manage to avoid them. So we can conclude that of the approximately 85 commercials to which Americans are exposed each day, around 60 are actually seen.

In a German survey (Compagnon Marktforschung, 1988, in W&V, 1988) television viewing behaviour was determined between 5.30 and 8 pm, by means of video recordings. In homes in which sets were on during the commercials, no more than 32% (ARD) and 36% (ZDF) were actually watched. Those who were assumed to have been viewing had either left the room or were doing something else.

3.4   Zapping and zipping

Dish aerials and cabling mean that television viewers can receive ever-growing numbers of channels. In the United States an average of 30; 62% of viewers have cable tv (1990) and can receive far over 30 stations. This gigantic supply generates extremely impatient viewing behaviour. Many people especially try to avoid the commercials. They use their remote control to zap to another channel. Or use the fast-forward button to wind on the video recorder past the commercials: 'zipping', as it is called.

On 2 March 1988 R.D. Percy followed television viewing in 1,000 homes in New York (Kinealy, 1988). He established that:

- in 18% of the households people 'zapped' more than once every 2 minutes;
- in 35% of the households they 'zapped' one to three times every 6 minutes; and that,
- in 46% of the households they switched channels every twenty minutes.

On average channel-switching took place every 3 minutes and 42 seconds. According to IRI, people switched most frequently in the first and last five minutes of a programme, and during the first five seconds of a commercial break.

Heeter and Greenberg (1985) reached the conclusion that there are different types of viewers, ranging from the non-zapper, who is loyal to his station and the superzapper, for whom viewing resembles a game – he may zap twice to three times a minute.

A Nielsen survey showed that 50% of people owning video recorders 'zip' through the commercials and that 25% of people who record programmes ensure they do not include the commercials. Readers Digest discovered that 65% of VCR owners use the fast-forward button during the commercials when they watch pre-recorded programmes. A survey by Cronin and Menelly (1992) came up with practically identical results: 6 out of 10 commercials were completely or partially 'zipped', and with 9 of the 10 advertising avoidance was specifically given as the reason. But since the viewing of pre-recorded programmes only accounts for a very slight percentage of total viewing time, this does not much influence the reach of commercials.

Ted Bates agency in London (currently called BSB) researched the reasons for zapping:

	Score
To see what's on the other channel	2.4
To avoid the commercials	2.1
They're boring	1.8
For a change	1.5
To see several programmes	0.9

4 = almost always
0 = hardly ever.

So to some extent zapping has the same function as scanning when people read newspapers and magazines. Readers or viewers allow their eyes to range over the pages or through the channels to see if perhaps there is something that interests them.

Hofstede (1990) believes that the main motive for zapping is the 'adventure' it entails. With your remote control you can go around the world. Curiosity is a basic human trait, and zapping helps you to embark on a voyage of discovery.

Zapping is also, to some extent, deliberate advertising avoidance. The viewer has become the editor. The viewing process has changed from passive tolerance to active censorship. These days viewers use their fingers to 'vote' with (Horsley, 1986). The loss in viewers caused by zapping was estimated to be 20% in the first commercial break on German television, but by the second break it has risen to around 40%, and it is continuing to increase. In a recent survey Germans admitted that during the commercials they do the following:

	1991	1992
I switch to something else for a moment	44%	53%
I leave the room for a moment	33%	43%
I do something else for a moment	20%	26%
I watch the commercials	38%	32%
Other reactions (e.g. switch-off sound)	2%	10%

Source: Opaschowski, 1992.

3.5   Viewing loyalty

In 1990 zapping and commercial-avoidance were researched in Spain by Tiempo/BBDO. They proved to correlate strongly with cable connection (or not) – so whether people are able to receive private channels – and to the possession of remote control. The following range was noted:

	Loss of 'viewing loyalty'
All homes	15–20%
Homes with cable link-up	20–30%
Homes with cable link-up and remote control	25–35%

'Viewing loyalty' should be interpreted as whether or not people leave the station they have been watching, and possibly return to it later. The reach of commercial breaks is constantly changing. Viewers are switching away from certain channels all the time, whilst new viewers are switching to those channels from others. To some extent the latter were only 'absent' temporarily, in order to avoid the commercials. Some of the 'leavers' do not return, but they are replaced by 'newcomers' – viewers from other channels. Lost viewers mainly return at the end of the commercial break, and at the start of the next programme.

3.6   Escapism

The longer the commercial break, the greater the 'escapism'. It is considerably less with short breaks. Some viewers display absolute advertising-avoidance: at the start of a commercial break they immediately escape. Others are greatly influenced by what precedes or follows the break. Lowest viewing density is recorded in the middle of longer commercial breaks, especially when they are between two different programmes. When the first programme ends, a number of viewers leaves the station. That continues at the start of the commercial break. Some of these 'old' viewers return towards the end of the break, in order to see the following programme. And then entirely 'new' viewers join in who also wish to see the programme. In the middle of the commercial break the leavers have already left and the 'joiners' have not yet arrived or returned. As is to be expected, advertising-avoidance zapping is greatly influenced by the nature of the previous and the following programmes, and by the programmes on other channels.

Zapping is less during commercial breaks in the middle of programmes, as most viewers want to continue watching the programme in question. Magazine-type programmes increase the tendency to zap. But zapping is less in continuing programmes like sports events and films. Of all the factors which influence zapping, the duration of the commercial break is the most important. Viewing loyalty is almost 100% with breaks of less than one minute, but if the break lasts longer than 4 minutes, loyalty is less than 85% (this does depend on many other factors).

Zapping and zipping are stimulated by the ever-increasing number of breaks for the networks' own announcements and for commercials. The time between programmes is often too long. Sometimes a good nine minutes are filled with trailers, acknowledgements, announcements, commercials and all the rest. Moreover, breaks of that type are predictable, and viewers know how much 'time off' they have before the next programme. We have become 'grazers' – the more we zap, the less we are involved. Viewers are becoming increasingly difficult to reach and display increasingly superficial viewing behaviour. (Nakra, 1991). Television has even become a game for super-zappers, rather like squash or table-tennis.

3.7   Attention

Attention is the process with which the subconscious processing of the flow of stimuli from our environment is interrupted. The pupil dilates, the lens focuses, orientation-response occurs. Attention means that there is contact between the stimulus and the receiver. It has been defined as the 'concentration of mental energy on a stimulus' (Van Raay, 1991). Certain stimuli are allowed into our consciousness and our brain becomes actively involved with them. We focus our attention on them. Attention can also be defined as the assignment of our analytical capacities to a limited number of stimuli from our environment (Mandler, 1982).

Our attention has direction and duration. The direction indicates on which stimuli our mental activity is focused, and the duration tells how long it is fixed there. The terms 'primary' and 'secondary' processes are also used. Primary in the sense of subconscious processing. Secondary in the sense of processing which takes place in our consciousness (Earner, 1974). The duration of the initial attention which we pay to a stimulus is often less than one second. In that short period we decide to continue or discontinue our attention. In next to no time we ask ourselves: is this information of any use to me? If it is not, we continue our 'scanning'. We are highly selective in the allocation of our mental energy.

We only have limited control of the course of these processes. The 'mobilisation' of our cognitive and affective capacities when we process stimuli is also largely beyond our control. A great many different factors play a part in the selection of what, from the constant stream of pre-attentive 'processings' of surrounding stimuli, is to be consciously processed.

3.8 Activating attention

There are three different groups of variables which are responsible for activating attention. They are person-specific, task-specific and stimulus-specific factors. The person-specific factors are by far the most important. They primarily relate to a consumer's lasting personal interests, value system, needs and desires. They determine the subjective relevance of a constellation of stimuli. For example, if someone is interested in photography, information on photographic equipment and films is very important. Consumers are activated, from inside, to perceive and process this information.

3.9 Attention and product-interest

The dominating influence of personal interest on the attention a person pays to advertisements is apparent from an analysis carried out by Starch (1966) in the V.S. (one of the institutes which have been measuring the viewing and reading of advertisements).

In a special survey among 11,000 households, the personal interests of men and women were measured. They were given a long list of possible interests and were allowed to select the three they particularly preferred.

The results were compared with the recognition scores for 8,000 full-page advertisements. In 1966 Starch's results were as follows:

| | **Women** | | **Men** | |
	Index of interest	Index of advertising recognition	Index of interest	Index of advertising recognition
Books	93	92	80	100
Business and finance	27	27	113	97
Cars	–	–	227	200
Cinema	153	203	200	183
Furniture	167	137	27	64
Household Interiors	40	90	–	–
Travel	73	104	113	130
Women's fashions	153	193	13	41

Source: Starch INRA Hooper.

The conclusion was that interest for different products varies greatly from one individual to another, that it differs in general between men and women and that the differences largely correlate with the perception of advertisements measured by means of recognition.

Bogart and Stuart Tolley (1988) found the following average recognition scores per product group, for half-page newspaper ads in the United States:

	Women (%)	Men (%)
Restaurants	54	40
Women's shoes	54	16
Women's clothing	51	20
Supermarkets	45	22
Jewellery	30	16
Furniture	30	18
Domestic appliances	29	19
Medicines	27	16
Financial services/banks	25	24
Floor-covering	22	19
Men's clothing	20	34
Sports goods	16	35

Source: Bogart and Stuart Tolley, 1988.

They also noted that interest in newspaper advertisements is closely connected with whether or not the respondent expects to purchase the advertised product within a year. Interest in the average advertisement proved to be 74% higher among this group of prospects than among non-prospects. Moreover, if the advertiser was the prospects' first choice, 87% were interested in his ad.

Only 18% of non-prospects or those who felt the advertised store or brand was an unlikely choice, were interested in the advertisement in question.

Interests in advertising

Preference for store or brand	Prospects (%)	Non-prospects (%)
First choice	87	47
Possible choice	75	37
Unlikely choice	45	18

Interest in advertised products proves to differ greatly among prospects from one product category to another. For babies' nappies it was 96%, for cigarettes 52%.

Zinkham and Gelb (1986) also concluded from surveys that there is a fairly strong connection between Starch scores and brand attitudes on the one hand, and measured inclination to buy on the other.

In the Netherlands advertising recognition scores prove to have considerable correlation with the question whether the person in question uses the brand or not. Admedia's RRO survey produces the following correlations:

	Uses product		Uses brand	
	Yes	No	Yes	No
Saw ad	61	50	66	52
Identified category	54	40	60	43
Identified brand	45	32	54	36
Identified product	41	26	44	27

Source: Admedia.

With television commercials the spread of attention appears to be less than with print advertisements. This suggests that selective perception has less extreme effects with television viewers than with readers of newspapers or magazines. It is easier to turn over the advertisement page than to avoid a commercial completely. ASI, one of the institutes in the United States which performs standardised measurements of the effect of commercials, obtains the following average recall score with women for 30-second commercials (1991):

Household products	45%
Food	44%
Beverages	42%
Services	41%
Toiletries and cosmetics	40%
Cleaning agents	39%
OTC pharmaceuticals	37%

A magazine reader can easily skip over advertising material in order to continue reading editorial matter 'uninterrupted' as it were. As we shall see later on, high involvement in articles tends to reduce the recall of accompanying advertisements. For a highly-involved television viewer it is more difficult really to avoid commercials, and continue viewing the programme without interruption. We shall see, that the higher the involvement in television programmes, the higher the recall score for commercials also tends to be. The editorial contexts of magazines and television programmes seem to have opposite effects on the attention levels for accompanying advertising material.

How medium contact leads to attention being paid

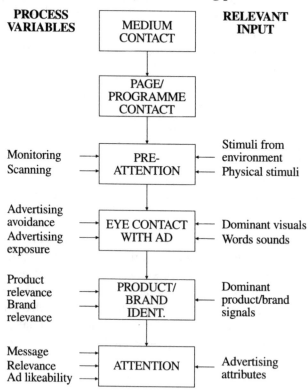

3.10   The nature of the stimuli

If a consumer is not himself motivated to pay attention to a constellation of stimuli, attention will be mainly aroused by the activating characteristics of the stimuli as such. These characteristics can be physical, emotional or cognitive. Emotional characteristics can, in particular, have a greatly activating effect. People are social beings. Their attention often proves to be activated by other people, especially by the portrayal of their faces and hands (Busnel, 1935). Eyes, in particular, have an activating effect.

Erotic stimuli also nearly always activate attention very strongly. As does the portrayal of small children and animals. It is not for nothing that they have frequently been used in advertising over the years – but not always functionally.

3.11   Physical attributes

Physical characteristics include:
- size: the bigger the more attention;
- colour: attracts more attention than black and white, and some colours attract more attention than others. Red signals danger and blood, and is eye-catching. Green has a moderate and blue a week activating effect;
- sound;
- intensity: loud sounds or bright colours attract more attention;
- movement: moving stimuli attract more attention than stationary;
- direction: the eyes follow every sign which indicates a direction.

Physical characteristics greatly influence the activation of our attention, the decisive factor being the extent to which the stimuli stand out from other stimuli in their surroundings. Important parts:
- **position:** a commercial in a break with 15 others will attract less attention than one in the middle of a football match;
- **contrast:** people pay more attention to stimuli which contrast with their past experiences;
- **isolation:** a few stimuli in a relatively large space attract attention.

Cognitive characteristics of stimuli which activate attention are especially those which set our perception unusual tasks. Berlyne sums them up as 'collative' variables. They include:

- novelty;
- complexity;
- surprise;
- incongruence;
- uncertainty;
- conflict;
- alienation;
- deviation from what is familiar.

They are closely connected. A surprising image, for instance a car driving up a ski jump has a stronger activating effect than one to which we are accustomed, like the same car in a traffic-jam. A deliberate contrast between visual and text can also have a cognitively activating effect. New, incongruent stimuli are noted faster than those to which we are accustomed. The stimuli need not be entirely new, but rather familiar things which are portrayed in a new and unexpected way. And they should represent meaningful information.

In general, pictures have a greater effect than words. People are activated by the first seconds they perceive – and that is nearly always one picture. As we shall be seeing, in 90% of the cases people first look to the visual part of an advertisement, before going on to the words.

Gestalt psychologists have shown that moving, changing stimuli, and stimuli which are new within an existing context, are perceived as 'figure', which is detached from the 'ground'. Advertising should, in fact, always work as the 'figure', and so try to stand out from its environment or 'ground'.

3.12   Avoid clichés

In advertising considerable use is still made of clichés or stereotypes. Car advertising rarely manages more than the depiction of a (usually widely known) type of car, with the customary headline and body text below. Sometimes page after page. Or else we are confronted with cheerful people, doing something together (eating, drinking, talking), pictures of plates of food which are far from exciting, or attractive young ladies who stare out at us vacantly. They generally belong to the 'stereotypes' category, and suffer from acute ordinariness – and so run the risk of not being 'provocative' enough. They generally get below-average scores with recognition and recall measurements. However, distinctive advertisements and commercials are remembered better than non-distinctive (Beattie & Mitchell). It really should be a key objective to produce advertising which differs from the stereotype – be it a general advertising stereotype or a specific product-category stereotype. And, of course, that is even truer for low-interest products than for products in which people are spontaneously interested.

Bogart and Tolley summarise matters relating to the activating effect of advertising stimuli on consumers' attention as follows:

"The extent to which an advertisement gets attention depends on what the advertisement transmits to the receiver, as well as what the receiver transmits to the advertisement".

3.13   Primary affective reaction

The great majority of stimuli which confront us do not penetrate into our consciousness. They go no farther than the level of pre-attentive processing.

Something in our minds decides to pay them no attention. It may be because of the nature of the stimuli or because of other stimuli in our environment which 'demand attention'. But sometimes, suddenly, something comes along which we find worthy of our attention. Van Raay called this the 'primary affective reaction'. Our capacity for the conscious processing of stimuli is extremely limited. Consequently we are permanently dividing up and allocating our available attention. And that invariably involves primary and secondary tasks. Primary tasks relate to the stimuli which receive our specific attention. The secondary variety are tasks requiring attention, such as other people's conversations, day dreams, music and other stimuli from our environment, which we process at the pre-attentive level. We can scan with one of the senses (the hearing, say) and focus with another (the sight). We read an article and at the same time scan the sounds we are receiving. But we cannot focus on two things at the same time.

3.14   Mere exposure effects

Advertising which is present in our field of perception is largely processed at the pre-attentive level. Numerous surveys have shown that stimuli which are only processed at the subconscious, pre-attentive level can, with repetition, still produce an affective response. They arouse a feeling of familiarity, a subconscious attraction, a positive attitude which is not occasioned by cognitive processing of stimuli and assessment processes, but purely by 'mere exposure' (Zajonc, 1968).

The very absence of cognitive processing can prevent counter-arguments: evidently people cannot oppose stimuli if they are not aware of them. People prove capable of recognising vast numbers of photographs after extremely brief exposure times (PARM study 1955, Ralph Norman Haber, 1978).

Bornstein (1986) analysed the results of 208 tests which had been carried since 1968 on this subject. All kinds of stimuli were used, like meaningless words, photos, drawings, paintings, names, objects and pictures of people. He noted that, with repeated short exposure, the effect increased. Even exposures of 5 milliseconds prove, a week later, to produce preference for these stimuli rather than those to which respondents had not been exposed (Seamon, 1983). Bornstein established that, in general, after 10 to 20 exposures a ceiling was reached. It was not necessary for the stimuli to be recognized. Exposure to subliminal stimuli generally in fact produced stronger effects than short exposure to stimuli which could be recognized afterwards.Bornstein puts this down to the occurrence of counter-strategies, such as denial and rationalisation. He believes than subliminal and supraliminal exposures might produce the same effects, but the receiver tends, with supraliminal exposures, to neutralise the effects.

We cannot be sure to what extent these experiments truly reflect an important part of the effect of advertising in everyday life. Nevertheless, we can assume that mere exposures that are only processed subconsciously do contribute to the development and perpetuation of the affective response to the brand in question. There are indications that affects which are formed subconsciously continue for a long time, meaning that they are stored in the long-term memory.

3.15   Brands on the scanning route

Advertising is, to an increasing extent, experienced ('processed') at the low, pre-attentive level. Something remains in our visual memory. We cannot recall it spontaneously, but we do recognise it when we are confronted with it again. In view of the magnitude of this phenomenon, it is crucial to include a brand prominently in an advertisement, so that subconscious perception can be ensured as far as possible. With print advertising this will nearly always require locating the brand in the extremely short scanning route which the eyes cover, in a dominant way compared with the surrounding visual stimuli. In a central place in the picture, in the headline, or as a logo. With television advertising, this must be achieved by properly integrating the brand in the auditive stimuli, and ensuring that it is also pictured conspicuously once, or several times. As we shall discover, repetition within the same advertisement/commercial can be an important aid to having the brand 'registered'.

Anyone looking at present-day advertising with understanding of these processes, is likely to conclude that these principles are more often ignored than followed. That must be the result of the general overestimation of the level of attention at which advertising stimuli are processed. Or of ignorance of the fact that most advertising contacts are processed solely at the subconscious, pre-attentive level.

3.16 Fluctuating intensity of attention

All the available research in this field indicates that people take a brief moment to 'decide' if something is worth giving more attention, or not. With press advertising this takes place with short 'fixation' on a few critical aspects of the visual stimuli offered. An average of 0.3 seconds is needed for fixation on a stimulus (Kroeber-Riel, 1990). That means that a decision is usually taken within one second whether or not it is worthy of the 'reader's' attention. With television advertising the starting seconds of every commercial are decisive for getting and retaining attention. Viewers immediately switch off mentally, often even physically, when the start of the commercial is unable to activate their attention.

Herbert E. Krugman discovered in a test of pupil dilation involving 160 60-second commercials that viewers' attention in the first 4 to 10 seconds correlated for 83% with attention over the entire 60 seconds. If a commercial does not succeed in activating attention in the initial period, the viewer reverts to the pre-attentive level and switches his attention to other stimuli from the environment or from his own memory.

Research by Stewart and Furse (1986), in which the test results of 1059 television commercials were analysed, also showed that if excitement, surprise, expectation ('queries') or drama are evoked in the first 10 seconds of a commercial, it affects the ultimate score this commercial makes for attention, recall and persuasion.

3.17 Newspaper reading behaviour

Not everyone reads a newspaper. The percentage of people doing so is on the decline. In 1990 in the Netherlands 29% of people of 12 and older no longer read a newspaper. Those who do read newspapers, do so in their own way. 15% say they read only the headlines and a few lines of text, spending 20 minutes a day on it. 14% say they read almost the entire paper, which takes them 42 minutes a day. The others are somewhere in between. They only read what interests them (38%), or other things (32%). Young people spend less time reading the newspapers than older people (Cebuco, 1985). The readers of newspapers do not see all the pages either. On average 74% of the pages are 'seen'. And more editorial pages (85%) are seen than pages with ads (67%). Nor do people see everything on a page.

On average they see 44% of the editorials and 31% of the advertisements. The latter depends on all manner of factors, as we shall be discovering.

	All regular readers of newspapers (%)	18-34 years (%)	35-55 years (%)	60-69 years (%)	Average reading time minutes	Pages as a % of total pages
Reads only headlines & sometimes a few lines	15	16	17	6	20	66
Reads only that of interest	38	45	34	36	28	72
Reads other things	32	30	33	36	38	76
Reads almost entire paper	14	8	15	21	42	85
Average reading time	**32min**	**26min**	**33min**	**42min**	**–**	**74**

Source: Cebuco "Newspapers within reach", 1985.

In the United States an analysis of video recordings and E.E.G.s taken when people were reading newspapers, followed by interviews, led to the following conclusions (Bogart & Stuart Tolley, 1988).

Every reader has a highly individual pattern of newspaper 'consumption'. Every reader has specific interests for certain editorial and 'advertising' topics. And every reader tries to avoid certain editorial and advertising topics. They try not to open the pages containing those topics, or turn the page after initial fixation and analysis. Readers are aware that they only have limited time available and so follow a scanning procedure, in order to make efficient use of their time. Generally they first scan the entire newspaper, or part of it, and then the material on a page. Initial scanning is based on visual elements. With only a few fixations, progressing in leaps from the top of the page to the bottom, a person determines whether it contains something sufficiently relevant or interesting to warrant his focused attention. This scanning is primarily based on distinguishing characteristics of the dominating stimuli: size and contrast on the one hand, content on the other. Mental activity (measured with E.E.G.s) varies tremendously over short time spans of several seconds. Arousal of the left (rational, thought) and of the right (feelings) hemisphere of the brain proves to be largely parallel. The scanning and reading of advertisements is closely connected to their size and content.

If we define 1 to 3 fixations per advertisement (0.30 to 0.90 seconds) as scanning, and 4 fixations or more as 'reading', the following connections with size and subject emerge (N = 81 ads).

Advertising processing	1/2 page or larger	Smaller than 1/2 page
Didn't look at all	5%	23%
Scanned (1-3 fixations)	58%	61%
'Read' (4 fixations or more)	37%	16%

Source: Bogart and Stuart Tolley, 1988.

The reading of advertisements is very closely connected to the attitude to the brand or store. Advertisements for brands and stores in a person's own 'selection repertoire' score three times higher for reading than those for brands or stores which are felt to be an unlikely choice.

	Brand/store choice		
	First	Also	Unlikely
Didn't look	12%	19%	17%
Scanned (1-3 fixations)	50%	52%	71%
'Read' (4 fixations or more)	38%	29%	12%

Source: Bogart and Stuart Tolley, 1988.

3.18   Television viewing

Some researchers (Anderson, Alwitt, Lorch and Levi, Hale, G.A., and Lewis, M., 1979) once examined how children divide their attention over television viewing and other stimuli in their immediate surroundings, such as other children, pets and toys. They determined what was the focus of attention every 3 seconds with 60 children aged between 3 and 5. The children proved to follow what was happening on television partially and at a low level of attention, largely with television sound as their guide. In this way, they could intensify or slacken their attention as they wished. Whenever the sound indicated that the content of the programme was changing and so new stimuli were presented, as it were, some children lost interest, whilst others actually turned their attention to the television.

The general view was that this was passive viewing behaviour, at a low level of attention. Attention was focused and intensified when it seemed as if something interesting was about to happen on the screen.

Anderson et al. established that children who watch television focus 150 to 200 times an hour on the screen, and then on something else in their surroundings. Over 60% of the times they focused on the television it was for less than 5 seconds (when watching Sesame Street). A glance focused on the screen for longer than one minute is an exception. Viewing behaviour of students hardly differs from that of young children. Anderson et al. pinpointed three main principles for viewing behaviour: (1) attention is influenced by understanding what is taking place on the screen, (2) when people are not watching they are monitoring the programme by means of the sound, and (3) inertia of attention ensures that breaks in programming are spanned.

3.19 'Understandability' essential

Understanding of what is seen and heard plays a fundamental part in attention. This is not at all consistent with the technical scope of the medium (all manner of video tricks). Neither children nor adults are inclined to pay attention to incomprehensible video 'fireworks'. They immediately switch off mentally when the pictures no longer represent anything meaningful.

Anderson's research also revealed that children's visual attention largely coincides with the presence on the screen of a recognisable, topical object or activity, and that attention flags or shifts when items are featured which are removed in place or time from 'here and now'.

'Viewers' mainly allow sound, voices, words and phrases to decide whether something is worth their attention. These are signals, as it were, of whether what is happening on the screen might be worth looking at. Once a person is looking at the screen, he is inclined to continue watching. This is sometimes called 'attentional inertia'. It is particularly prevalent after the first 12 to 15 seconds in which a programme part is followed visually. However, when there is a break in the programme, viewers also tend to cease watching. 'Attentional inertia' ensures that viewing is 'suspended' for some time – and that the break is spanned in this way.

3.20 First seconds crucial

This principle is important for the way in which commercials work: attention at the start of the commercial is determined partly by the attention for the programme component (or commercial) preceding it. The viewer gives the commercial a moment's opportunity to prove it is worthy of his attention, as it were. Clearly this must take place in the lead-in seconds of the commercial, otherwise the inclination to break eye contact will prevail. This start can also be a signal for other viewers, whose attention is still focused on other things in their surroundings, to start watching the screen.

Television advertising can no longer count on viewers' spontaneous and automatic attention. It must succeed in activating it, as is the case with advertisements in newspapers or magazines. Nor is attention retained automatically: most 'eye contact' with the screen lasts no longer than five seconds.

The fluctuating levels of attention during the viewing of programme components and commercials are not only caused by the nature of the stimuli themselves, but are partly the result of the mental and physical impossibility of maintaining attention at a constantly high level. Attention is constantly ebbing and flowing, also when we read the newspaper or a magazine. We would seem to allow our attention a moment's rest as we leaf through, and then embark with renewed attention, on something which appears worth while.

View-Facts, in the United States, tests the effect of commercials on a moment-to-moment basis. They have discovered that the best-scoring commercials are those whose 'likeability factor' (more about that later) remains high throughout the presentation of the information. A few seconds and a simple reaction along the lines of 'I like it' make a world of difference between a commercial with higher selling effects and one with lower (Jim Spaeth, ARF Workshop).

4 Physical variables

4.1 Physical variables

In the years before and just after the second world war, advertising researchers were particularly interested in the influence of mechanistic variables on attention for advertisements. What is the influence of the size, and of the place of the advertising? They realised that attention was not automatic, but had to be 'obtained'. With the advent and growth of television advertising, interest in the foregoing faded. It was assumed that there was more or less automatic contact with television audiences. Interest switched to the question which variables in particular influenced viewers' recall and choice.

However, magazines and newspapers are still very important media in many countries, and so the question of the influence of mechanistic variables on attention for advertisements is still relevant. A great deal is known on the subject, thanks to research, amongst others by Gallup and Starch in the United States, NIPO in the Netherlands and Infratest in Germany. For years they have been investigating whether people have seen an advertisement, read it completely or partially, whether they can still remember it after a certain time (usually after 24 hours), and to what extent they are inclined to go out and buy the product in question on account of the advertisement.

4.2 Recognition a good criterion

The main question is whether it really is recognition that is measured, or the respondent's assessment of the probability of his having seen the advertisement in question when he first read the paper. Recognition is based on what is present in our memory. So the next question is whether each eye contact is registered and stored in the memory. Comparison of recognition scores with observations by others during the reading process always produce differences.

Stapel (1972) reports on an experiment in which the match between recognition and observation was only 70%. 23% of the differences could, however, be explained by the fact that the observed viewing time was only 0.75 seconds or less. When registered viewing and recognition did tally, viewing time averaged 2.75 seconds.

So there is a clear connection. But advertisements are also recognized although no eye contact was recorded. Similarly, some advertisements were not recognized, although there had indeed been eye contact.

Lastly, Hess (1976) carried out a comparative test into perception of 2-page advertisements (sample 2736 perceived advertisements) and noted a 76% match between contacts recorded with a video camera, and recognition measurements after a few days. In 10% of the cases recognition was 'measured' without eye contact having occurred. In 14% eye contact had taken place, but the advertisement was not recognized a few days later. We must bear in mind that very short contacts might not be stored in the memory. In addition, some memory loss occurs within a few days. Consequently, recognition measurements do prove to be a reasonably reliable methods for measuring the 'seeing' of advertisements. Stapel (1976) draws the conclusion that the establishment of page contact using recognition measurements mainly results on an underestimation of physical reality. On the basis of the statement "I have not opened this page at all", an average page exposure of 79% was established for a certain issue of Margriet women's weekly. The average score for users of the advertised product was 91%, but for non-users only 72%. The divergence for non-users ranged from 57% to 86%, for users from 88% to 93%. In view of these facts, actual page contact with this particular issue of Margriet will have been about 90%.

4.3   Recognition from 0.75 seconds perception onwards?

Non-users of a product or brand decide, in the initial scanning phase of the pre-attentive stage, 'not to look at' this page (with ad). Later, they state that they have not opened that page of the magazine. How long did that first pre-attentive 'perception' last? 0.3 seconds, 0.6 seconds, 1 second? When does perception lead to subsequent recognition? Other surveys also reveal that very short, mechanically-recorded contact with advertisements lasting 0.75 seconds or less do not result in subsequent recognition. At 0.75 seconds, 'minimum' perception probably takes place, and incipient communication. That is why tests based on recognition of advertisements measure advertising perception rather than physical page contact.

Having sorted through all the information and ideas on this subject, Zinkham and Gelb (1986) came to the conclusion that there is, in fact, little difference in opinion as to whether the recognition method is a good way of determining whether an advertisement has at least received minimum (i.e. longer than 0.75 seconds) attention.

Back in 1932 Dr. Daniel Starch introduced a method, based on recognition, for determining to what extent readers had noted advertisements, associated them with the appropriate brand, and what percentage had read 50% or more of the text ('read most'). And Starch INRA Hooper Inc. are still examining about 100,000 different advertisements from 700 different issues of about 100 magazines in much the same way every year.

Finn compared the various 'Starch scores' with current views on information processing. He concludes that the scores are suitable for determining the different processing levels which are differentiated in the information processing theory (Finn, 1988).

When we analyse Starch scores and try to find connections with physical variables of advertisements, we must distinguish between 'ambient' factors, such as the place of the advertisement in the medium, editorial or programme 'environment', and variables within the advertisement itself, such as the amount of copy.

4.4 Size

Over the years, the relative size of advertisements has been the most important physical factor in generating attention. Not the absolute size (number of square centimetres), but the size of the advertisement in relation to the other stimuli in the immediate surrounding area. This determines whether the advertisement has a chance of being perceived at the pre-attentive stage, and consequently whether it is 'effective' in the very first phase of advertising processing.

A Starch INRA Hooper analysis of 7,500 full-page and spread advertisements in business journals (Business Week, Forbes, Fortune and Manhattan) in 1987 and 1988 showed that the average score for 'noting' of full-page black and white ads was 29%, and for double spread pages 34%. With full-colour ads the scores were 42 and 52%, respectively. So double the size produces an increase in 'noting' of the ad of 17% with black and white, and 24% with full colour.

Analysis of double spreads full colour in women's magazines had similar results; they were noted 26% more than single page full colour.

Stapel and Van Doorn (1991) noted the following averages for recognition of black and white advertisements in magazines (averages over the period 1965/1970; as we saw earlier since then the scores have dropped):

	Lowest	Highest	Average
Half page	7%	76%	44.7%
Full page	15%	82%	53.6%
Double spread	36%	79%	63.0%

Infratest in Germany calculated averages based on the test results of

18,161 advertisements (Rehorn, 1989). As we have already seen, scores for recognition and recall have been dropping considerably in the last decade. Consequently, it is not wise to compare absolutes, relating to different periods. If we index the data on the basis of full pages black and white, we obtain the following figures:

	1/2 page		1/1 page		2/1 page	
	b/w	fc	b/w	fc	b/w	fc
Opened page (*RRO Netherlands 85-90*)	84	107	100	122	–	144
Recognized ad (*NIPO Netherlands 65-70*)	83	–	100	119	120	128
Recognized ad (*Infratest Germany 69-70*)	69	115	100	146	138	164

There is no obvious explanation for the rather large differences between the Dutch and German scores. The testing method probably plays a considerable part. Admedia made the following connections between size and colour, based on the RRO (recognition) survey:

	1/2 page		Full page		Double spread
	b/w	fc	b/w	fc	fc
Opened page	38%	48%	45%	55%	65%
Identified category	31%	37%	36%	46%	55%
Identified brand	21%	29%	28%	40%	48%

Source: Admedia.

So, with increasing sizes, we see a diminishing return for noting of the ads, with recognition as the measure. The same applies with newspapers. Average scores for advertisements in the Dutch newspaper Het Parool over the 1965-1970 period (Stapel 1972) were as follows:

Het Parool 1965-1970

	Recognition	Index
< 250mm	24.5%	
250– 562mm	29.8%	59
563– 937mm	38.8%	–
938–1,312mm	42.2%	84
1,313–1,625mm	44.5%	–
1,625–2,000mm	45.8%	90
2,000–2,250mm	48.7%	–
2,250–2,750mm	50.5%	100
2,750–3,375mm	54.8%	–
3,375–5,000mm	56.7%	–
5,000mm+	63.0%	120

Source: NIPO

Respondents who are able to tell something about an advertisement they have seen are registered as readers. In the sixties that proved to be about 40% of those who had seen the advertisement – with both magazines and newspapers. With very large sizes in newspapers (3375 mm) the percentage was slightly higher (around 47%). In the eighties the percentage of readers had dropped to about 30% of those who had seen an advertisement.

4.5   The power of size

Besides looking at averages for all advertisements, we can also examine the highest scores per size. They reflect a kind of 'ceiling': the maximum that can be achieved with a very good advertisement for a very interesting product. This maximum proves to be around 70% for a full page in a magazine. It is interesting to note that 1/3-page ads get higher maximum scores than half-page ads. Horizontal 1/2 and 1/3 pages also achieve higher maxima than vertical.

Highest 'noted' scores in business journals

	Black & white	Full colour
1/3 page vertical	40%	43%
1/3 page horizontal	45%	47%
1/2 page vertical	32%	37%
1/2 page horizontal	34%	49%
2/3 page vertical	42%	55%
Full page	70%	73%

Source: Starch INRA Hooper.

The Dutch averages are almost identical to those which Starch had ascertained in the United States. If the percentage of 'noters' is said to be 100, the scores for brand linkage and reading are as follows (Laufer, 1986)

Noted advertisement	100
Saw brand	89
Read (half the) text	40

Source: Laufer, 1986.

These figures apply to all readers of a magazine. If we only consider those who are interested in the product, we reach the following averages:

Saw advertisement	100
Saw brand	91
Read (half the) text)	46

Source: Laufer, 1986.

The average score for 'saw advertisement' is 24% above the average for all readers of the magazine with people who are interested in a product.

In other words, if someone is interested in a product, the chance of him noting the advertisement is 25% higher. The number of readers increases slightly more than proportionally, but on average is still below 50% of the 'noters'.

4.6 Colour

Colour has a greater effect on the extent to which advertisements are noted than size. Starch (1989) presents the following correlations for business magazines (Business Week, Forbes, Fortune and Manhattan):

Average noted

	Black & white	Full colour	Increase full colour compared with black & white
1/3 page	21%	25%	19%
1/2 page	22%	32%	45%
2/3 page	24%	35%	46%
Full page	29%	42%	45%
Double spread	34%	52%	53%

Source: Starch INRA Hooper.

So with full page, full-colour advertisements 'noting' is 45% higher than for full page black and white, and 53% higher with double spread. A combination of size and colour leads, with double spread full-colour ads, to 79% more 'noting' than with full page black and white.

The Dutch RRO survey produced the following differences between black and white and full colour with full page ads (based on measured recognition):

		Full page black & white	Full page full colour
Opened page		45%	55%
Identified product		36%	46%
Identified brand		28%	40%
Ad reaction	positive	35%	37%
	neutral	40%	41%
	negative	16%	15%

Source: Admedia RRO survey.

Another survey reveals that colour, in particular, has a 'signal effect'. Black and white advertisements and those with spot colour are recognized on average by 29% of readers, full colour by 39% (so a third more) (ESOMAR/Wapor Congress 1973). Yet colour proves to generate hardly any more 'reading'. NIPO discovered that 43% of people who had noted a full-colour advertisement in Margriet women's weekly, read something in it, compared with 41% with black and white. Colour does not produce a longer reading time either. The Dutch RRO survey also reveals that appreciation for colour ads is hardly any higher than for black and white.

All this data should not allow us to lose sight of the fact that averages are involved. Comparison of Starch scores for advertisements which were used in both black and white and in colour leads to the conclusion that the effect of colour is greatest when it is used to reinforce the impression of the product. If colour is only used to gain attention, in a way which is not related to the product, it can even have a negative effect.

4.7   On the left or on the right

Beside the relative size of an advertisement and the use of colour, the place in the medium is also important in deciding whether or not it receives attention. However, the findings with respect to location on the left- or on the right-hand page are not very consistent. Kiss and Wettig (1973) and Steur (1985) reach the conclusion that there is scarcely any difference. The scores of Admedia's RRO survey and of NIPO research do not produce any appreciable differences:

		Left-hand page	Right-hand page
Admedia RRO survey:			
Opened page		79%	78%
Looked at ad		55%	55%
Identified product category		46%	47%
Identified brand		40%	41%
Identified product		31%	32%
Ad reaction	positive	35%	44%
	neutral	44%	31%
	negative	16%	16%
NIPO survey:			
Total noted		52%	51%
Read some		16%	15%
Spontaneous recall		6%	5%
Aided recall		25%	24%

Sources: Admedia RRO; NIPO.

However, Jeck Schlottmann (1987) conducted an experiment using eye-tracking, and came to the conclusion that the right-hand pages had a consistent advantage in the overall process of perception and processing over the left-hand pages. And Andresen's research confirms this (1987).

All these mechanistic factors help to decide whether an advertisement is perceived by the senses. Processing can be stopped at this earliest moment, or else the reader can 'continue' and then analyse what the advertisement is about – which product, which brand?

4.8   Place in the magazine

Advertisements at the front of a magazine receive a little more attention than those at the back. Analysis of Starch scores (1989) produces the following correlations for full page full colour ads:

Page location	Noted	Associated with brand	Read most
Trade journals:			
First part of magazine	46%	39%	11%
Second part of magazine	43%	37%	10%
Third part of magazine	41%	36%	10%
Women's magazines:			
First part of magazine	53%	47%	12%
Second part of magazine	50%	44%	12%
Third part of magazine	49%	44%	12%

Source: Starch INRA Hooper.

In Starch's tests 'noting' and brand linkage drop considerably the farther back in the magazine the ad is located, but the effect on reading is much less. Laufer (1986) found a far greater connection between the location, and recognition and recall with the ads that he tested in Der Stern (Germany).

Index: scores for ads in first 20% of mag. = 100	Recognition		Recognition	
	All ads	fp/fc*	All ads	fp/fc*
In first 20% of mag.	100	100	100	100
In second 20% of mag.	100	102	97	100
In third 20% of mag.	94	92	91	89
In fourth 20% of mag.	82	90	75	83
In fifth 20% of mag.	78	94	72	89

Note: * Full page, full colour advertisiments.   *Source:*   Laufer, 1986.

The Dutch RRO survey reveals the following connections:

Location in:	1st part mag.	2nd part mag.	3rd part mag.
Opened page	81%	77%	78%
Looked at ad	57%	54%	55%
Identified category	47%	46%	47%
Identified brand	40%	39%	42%
Identified product	32%	31%	32%

Source: Admedia.

NIPO recall score show an even stronger correlation, as do Laufer's. This suggests that a little more time might be spent on advertisements at the front of the magazine, when readers are still 'fresh'.

	Quarter of the magazine			
Position in	1st	2nd	3rd	4th
Total noted	55%	52%	50%	50%
Read something	17%	16%	15%	14%
Spontaneous recall	7%	6%	5%	5%
Aided recall	28%	25%	22%	23%

Source: NIPO.

Starch has analysed these connections further, according to product group, as well as comparing the scores of identical ads. It turned out that averages were partly influenced by the type of advertiser. Large brands, which usually succeed in making the most attractive advertisements, are located nearer the front, with less known and smaller brands at the back. That may be deliberate policy of the larger advertisers, but it may also be caused by unconscious preferences of the magazine make-up people.

Comparison of the scores for 'noting' for each advertiser show that they scarcely decline at all:

	Cars percent noted	Toiletries & cosmetics percent noted
First part	48%	49%
Second part	50%	49%
Third part	49%	45%

Source: Starch INRA Hooper.

When identical advertisements were compared (a very small sample) the differences completely disappeared. Starch's conclusion was: a good ad is noted, regardless of its location in the magazine. Advertisements on the inside or outside cover of magazines are an exception (Starch 1989). Advertisements on the inside of the cover score on average 29% higher for 'noted'; those on the back page score 22% higher and those on the inside of the back page 6% higher. Averages vary only slightly from one magazine, and one reader category to another. A second exception is the location beside the list of contents in magazines. The 'noted' scores of ads in those locations is 24% higher on average than for ads inside the magazine (Starch 1990).

4.9   Location alongside editorial

People often think that a location beside an editorial article is preferable to one beside another advertisement. But that is far from true. Starch (1990) found the following correlation for full-page advertisements:

			Index
	Noted	Linked to brand	Read most
Located beside editorial article	100	100	102
Located beside other full-page ad	110	106	109

Source: Starch INRA Hooper.

Not everyone is interested in the same editorial topics. Some readers deliberately avoid certain subjects, and so easily miss the advertisements beside them. Others, who are highly interested in a certain subject, may not want to be distracted by an advertisement when they are reading the article. In a laboratory experiment by Norris and Colman (1992) involvement in magazine articles was without exception negatively correlated with recall, recognition and global memory for accompanying advertisements. The result of the experiment showed unambiguously that the more readers felt they had concentrated, been absorbed in and paid close attention to the articles, the less they remembered about the accompanying advertisements. Also the more entertaining, interesting and enjoyable the readers rated the articles, the less they remembered about the advertisements. Deep involvement in an article is likely to be accompanied by a narrowing and focusing of attention and a consequent lack of attention for distracting stimuli like advertising material. The noting of advertisements beside other advertisements is partly influenced by the reader's interest in those other ads. Readers do not only read a magazine for the editorial content, but also for the advertisements which they consider to be interesting. Location alongside another ad which is interesting can help to increase the chance of being noted compared with a location beside an uninteresting article. Even location beside an editorial article on the same subject as the ad, or one which is related to it, proves, on average, to have no effect on the scores for noting and reading:

			Index
	Noted	Linked to brand	Read most
Located beside related article	100	100	98
Located beside unrelated article	100	98	100

Source: Starch INRA Hooper.

4.10   Number of pages in a magazine

The number of pages in a magazine appears to have a limited negative influence on page exposure, but a stronger negative influence on the time spent on a page (ESOMAR/Wapor Congress, 1973). Page exposure varies between 80 and 90% of the readers of a magazine. Contact with advertisements is lower than contact with pages. It would also appear that the more pages a magazine contains, the lower ad contact will be. But Laufer (1986) cannot find a significant correlation for advertisements in Der Stern.

4.11   Advertising volume

The advertising volume in a magazine has a strong correlation with the time spent on advertisements (ESOMAR/Wapor Congress, 1973). An average reading duration of 6.2 seconds was established with a magazine with 21 advertisements, and 1.7 seconds with one containing 45 advertisements.

NIPO also confirms a strong connection between the number of advertisements and noting, reading and recall. Especially women's weeklies with fewer than 20 advertising pages achieve substantially higher scores:

Average score	Number of advertising pages			
	−20	21-40	41-60	60+
Total noted	59%	53%	50%	50%
Read something	23%	16%	15%	15%
Aided recall	37%	26%	22%	24%
Spontaneous recall	11%	6%	5%	5%

Source: NIPO.

4.12   Television

4.12.1   Number of commercials

As can be expected, for television there is a strong correlation in commercial recall between the number of commercials in one break. In particular, scores for spontaneous recall drop substantially the more commercials there are in a break. After the commercial channel RTL 4 started up, the length of commercial breaks on other Dutch channels was cut, and consequently since then average recall score have risen.

Average score	Number of commercials in break					
	1–6	7–8	9–10	11–12	13–14	15+
Spontaneous recall	38%	35%	31%	27%	25%	23%
Aided recall	71%	68%	65%	62%	61%	57%
Extra aided recall	75%	71%	72%	70%	68%	68%

Source: NIPO.

Seherqualität II survey in Germany (1991) found the following connection:

	Number of commercials per break				
	Average	1-5	6-10	11-15	16+
Spontaneous recall	100	216	156	89	75
Aided recall	100	79	111	89	103
(Index: average = 100)					

Source: Seherqualität II, 1991.

4.12.2 Length of television commercials

Similarly, there is a connection with the length of commercials. NIPO scores for aided and spontaneous recall and extra aided recall produce the following correlations:

	Length of commercials in seconds				
Average score	15	20	30	45	60
Spontaneous recall	20%	21%	28%	40%	39%
Aided recall	55%	56%	63%	70%	70%
Extra aided recall	62%	66%	79%	70%	71%

Source: NIPO.

We can conclude from this that the connection between the length of a commercial and perception thereof (measured by means of aided recall) is not very great. But longer commercials do establish themselves better in the memory, meaning that spontaneous recall of 45-second commercials is almost double that of 20-second commercials. Commercials lasting 15 seconds obtain almost the same scores as those of 20 seconds, and those of 45 seconds score much the same as those of 60 seconds.

4.12.3 Location in the break

The location in the break greatly influences recall score. The 'Seherqualität II' survey in Germany (1991) produces the following correlation:

	Location in spots in the break					
	First Average	One of first 3 spot	Other in the spots	One of last 3 middle	Last spots	spot
Unaided recall	100	161	118	82	143	150
Aided recall	100	113	114	98	97	94
(Index: average = 100)						

Source: Seherqualität II, 1991.

The first three spots make appreciably higher scores, and those in the middle considerably lower.

Back in 1930 Ebbinghaus and Witasek observed that items in the middle of a series are not remembered as well as those at either end – the primacy and recency effect, as it is called.

4.12.4 Location as regards programme

The programme in which or after which a commercial break is broadcast affects recall score. In the United States analyses of Burke and ARS data bases indicate that recall score for commercials in breaks between two programmes are about 25% lower than those which interrupt a programme. An analysis which Burke conducted in 1978 into recall score showed the following connection with the type of programme:

Type of programme	Spontaneous recall
Films	26%
Drama	23%
Comedy	20%
Variety	20%
News	16%

Source: Burke, 1978.

In Germany the Seherqualität II survey (Hörzu and Funkuhr 1991) produced the following averages:

| | Av. | **Type of programme** | | | | |
		Film	Sport	News	Series	Quiz
Unaided brand recall	100	143	168	93	68	114
Aided related recall	100	57	160	125	44	155
(Index: average = 100)						

Source: Seherqualität II, 1991.

Selective attention does allow a viewer to ignore commercials, but a viewer who is deeply involved in the programme is unlikely to zap and is therefore likely to pay attention to the commercials in a break. An uninvolved viewer by contrast, is more likely to change channels, or 'mentally' zap the commercials.

5 Creative variables

A reader who 'decides' to continue with an advertisement after initial visual perception, fixes his gaze on several elements within the advertisement. He analyses, from a single visual element and a single word, what the advertisement is about. This occurs very fast. Each fixation lasts about 0.3 seconds.

The size of the illustration proves to be a particularly important variable for product recognition, and so for the extent to which the advertisement now receives focal attention. This is not really surprising, considering the extremely short time readers spend on advertisements; Kroeber-Riel concludes from his many studies that it averages 2 seconds. 50-75% of this time (1 to 1.5 seconds) is spent analysing the visual stimuli. Ninety per cent of 'readers' first fix on the dominant, visual elements before going on to elements in the text.

| | Place of advertisement | |
Average score 'noted' with:	Among editorial content	On ordinary advertising pages
No illustrations	17%	23%
Illustrations less than 50% of advertisement space	22%	32%
Illustrations more than 50% of advertisement space	33%	40%

Source: Cebuco "Newspapers within reach", 1985.

So advertisements in which illustrations formed more than 50% of the space are 'seen' by almost twice as many readers as ads which consist of text alone. This is partly due to the fact that pictures become fixed in our memories better than texts. The fact that something 'has been seen', as is registered in recognition research, in fact means 'seen and stored in the memory'. Textual advertisements may be 'seen' just as often, but invariably very briefly. And a text which is seen is often not stored in the (visual!) memory. In tests a day later, readers no longer recognise the space which is filled with letters.

5.1 Visual focal point essential

Not only is the size of the visual stimuli important for their processing, but also, and especially, the structure. Simplicity, realism, closeness of what is depicted and dominance of the elements determine the extent of processing. The number of illustrations (or illustrative elements) has a negative correlation with recognition scores. Both Marplan and Starch reach the conclusion, after analysing test results, that one dominant visual focal point is by far the most important creative variable by which attention is gained (Hendon, 1973).

The initial, very rapid analysis of the visual elements can lead to a higher level of understanding as to what the advertisement is about, and to continued and intensified attention. The headline can now be dealt with, plus the end-line, logo and several words or sentences from the text.

Experiments show that mental processes which enter our consciousness are very short and relatively transient. Our attention is more likely to be in the form of individual units or frames, which enter the conscious states one at a time, rather than a smooth, continuing process.

During 'conscious' processing of external stimuli, internal memory contents are evoked, with which the external information can be interpreted and combined. This is then returned to the memory, in its new state. For example, our memory tells us 'this is about Safeway's peas'. If this does not activate our interest, our attention shifts to the next constellation of stimuli.

5.2   More words mean less attention

That is the way we might envisage advertising processing – at least if a reader has reached the stage of conscious attention, interpretation and processing. It is, in fact, rather a haphazard process. The reader definitely does not get round to reading texts 'properly' from top left to bottom right.

The recognition of (and consequently attention for) advertisements proves to increase when they contain fewer words. (These figures largely originate from the years when television was still an 'emerging' medium.) In fact this conclusion applies to all the words in an advertisement. The number of words in the headline, the length of the headline, and the number of lines of which it consists correlate negatively with measured attention.

In an analysis of a great many post-tests, Starch found the following correlation between the measured recognition of advertisements, the reading thereof and the number of words in the ad:

	Index: fewer than 25 words = 100	
Number of words	Noted/associated	Read most
Fewer than 25	100	100
26– 50	99	69
51–100	91	39
101–150	89	35
151–250	81	32
251–500	79	32
More than 500	74	30

Source: Starch INRA Hooper.

Alpers (1976) tested recognition of 2,762 full-page advertisements in Der Stern. He also concluded that those with little text obtained higher recognition scores. This was again confirmed in later findings by Laufer (1986). For advertisements in Der Stern he found the following correlation between the amount of text and recognition of ads:

Index: average score for ads with little or no text = 100		
	Recognition	Recall
Advertisements with little or no text	100	100
Text up to 1/3 of space	86	82
Text 1/3 to 1/2 of space	77	73
Text 1/2 to entire space	60	61

Source: Laufer, 1986.

Admedia analysed the RRO scores for advertisements in Margriet, as regards the percentage of the area that the text takes up in the entire advertisement space. Again, the conclusion is: The greater the percentage of text, the lower all scores.

Average scores	Text as a percentage of ad space				
	0-20%	21-40%	41-60%	61-80%	100%
Opened page	79%	78%	79%	77%	71%
Saw ad	57%	55%	55%	51%	40%
Identified category	47%	46%	46%	43%	33%
Identified brand	40%	39%	39%	38%	31%
Identified product	32%	32%	30%	30%	24%
Ad reaction positive	41%	48%	43%	38%	39%
neutral	39%	35%	37%	36%	34%
negative	15%	11%	17%	19%	24%

Source: VNU RRO survey.

NIPO had the same findings when they analysed the Impact test. Only 40% of people who note (ascertain via recognition) an advertisement, also read something of it (analysis NIPO scores). It turns out that six out of ten people who subsequently recognise an advertisement, have only glanced at it briefly. After this analysis reading as a percent of noting has even decreased to approximately 30%.

Average scores	Text as a percentage of ad space			
	9-20%	21-40%	41-60%	60%+
Total seen	55%	51%	45%	43%
Read some	16%	16%	14%	14%
Spontaneous recall	6%	5%	4%	4%
Aided recall	27%	24%	20%	20%
Assessment nice	49%	46%	37%	28%
irritating	18%	20%	23%	30%

Source: NIPO.

The striking thing about these analyses is that, the more space in an ad is taken up by text, the less it is appreciated.

The conclusion is obvious: short, sweet and simple works far better than long, complicated and detailed. The more you omit, the greater your chance of getting conscious attention for the ad. Obviously that does not mean that you should never make ads with longer texts. Sometimes there is highly relevant information for a very involved target group. That puts a different complexion on the matter. But for products which everyone knows, about which there is little new to say, and for which no-one is desperate for information, it is wise to be keep the amount of text within very modest proportions.

5.3   Two seconds per advertisement

With print advertising a reader's attention is mainly reflected in the number of seconds he spends on an advertisement. Various institutes in the former West Germany carried out tests using videotaped eye contact to examine how magazine advertisements were processed. Kroeber-Riel and his staff at the University of Saarland have been particularly prolific in their publications on the subject. Their brief conclusion is that a reader devotes about two seconds to an advertisement (the average with black and white and full-colour advertisement). The size of the advertisement plays a substantial part, which confirms Starch's earlier findings. The averages for the various ad sizes are:

Double spread	2.8 seconds
3/4 and full page	1.9 seconds
1/2 page or less	0.6 seconds

Source: Kroeber Riel, 1990.

The connection between size and reading time is linear, to all intents and purposes: as the size of an advertisement increases, there is an almost proportionate increase in perception time. The second variable which has a marked influence on perception time is the product category to which the advertisement relates. Averages for full pages for the various product categories were as follows (Kroeber-Riel, 1990):

Category	Perception time (secs.)	No. of ads tested
Airlines	2.0	9
Fashion, clothing	1.9	18
Cameras	1.9	8
Cars	1.8	15
Banks and savings banks	1.7	9
Alcoholic beverages	1.6	21
Cigarettes	1.3	22

N.B. At least 50 video recordings were made for each advertisement.

Andresen (1987) conducted tests, using eye-tracking methods, into the processing of advertisements. 100 subjects (mainly students) were asked to glance through a magazine (Der Spiegel and Der Stern) from start to finish to begin with, and then to read it the way they normally would. During the first stage (glancing through) the following advertising contacts were recorded:

	Der Spiegel	Der Stern
Contact with the ad	66%	81%
Contact with the visual	62%	77%
Contact with the headline	28%	29%
Contact with the body copy	13%	10%

Source: Andresen, 1987.

The advertisements were 'looked at' for less than 1/3 of a second by 14% of the subjects on average. Average duration of contact with advertisements, measured over both stages (glancing through and reading) proved to be 1.6 seconds for Der Stern and 1.2 seconds for Der Spiegel. During the reading stage absolutely no contact occurred with an advertisement in an average of 24% of the perceptions. And when contact was recorded, it lasted on average 2 seconds with Der Stern and 1.8 seconds with Der Spiegel. This corresponds with earlier findings of Kiss and Wettig (1972) and Kroeber- Riel (1990).

The dispersion of contact duration in relation to the type of stimuli which were processed, produced the following pattern:

Duration of contact, Der Stern

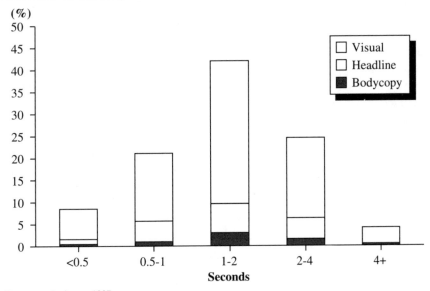

Source: Andresen, 1987.

Only a very small percentage of readers (2% for Der Spiegel) had contact with the advertisement for 4 seconds or longer. Findings were not much different for advertisements in Der Stern: there too only 5% of the subjects spent 4 or more seconds on an advertisement. In both cases 88% of the stimuli presented in the ads were not perceived. People barely got round to contact with body copy in particular.

Stimuli not perceived

	By all respondents		By those looking at the ad	
	Spiegel	Stern	Spiegel	Stern
As % all presented stimuli	98%	96%	88%	88%
Visual	87%	73%	41%	26%
Headline	95%	93%	54%	48%
Bodycopy	100%	99%	93%	93%

Source: Andresen, 1987.

Contact with an advertisement is almost always restricted to contact with the visual component. The vast majority of respondents had no contact with headlines in this test. This means that visual components should communicate the message as much as possible, and that headlines should have a supporting or complementary function. An advertiser will be taking very great risks if the central message can only be understood out of the body copy.

5.4   Contact generally broken

Of the 2 seconds spent on average on an advertisement, 1 to 1.5 seconds is usually devoted to the visual elements and 0.5 to 1 second on the copy. Most of this is, in turn spent on the headline; only a fraction of a second is left for the body copy. Clearly readers' perception time has very different allocations. However, it happens only sporadically that more than 5% of readers spend more than 10 seconds on an advertisement (Kroeber-Riel, 1988). Of course, 'involved' readers spend slightly more time on ads, particularly in special interest magazines, yet rarely more than four to five seconds, on average, per advertisement.

The publishers of the German 'Ärzte Zeitung' carried out eye-tracking research with doctors who read the journal, and reached the following results:

Size of advertisement	Average seen by	Average reading time
3/4 page and larger	89%	5.0 sec.
1/2 page – 3/4 page	67%	2.4 sec.
1/4 page – 1/2 page	52%	2.1 sec.
Smaller than 1/4 page	47%	1.5 sec.
Average		**2.8 sec.**

Source: Von Keitz, 1985.

This survey also illustrates how the relative size affects the actual reach of advertising. Not only do small advertisements get less attention, but they are also seen by fewer readers.

Supply of information in ads in Der Stern (required contact time)

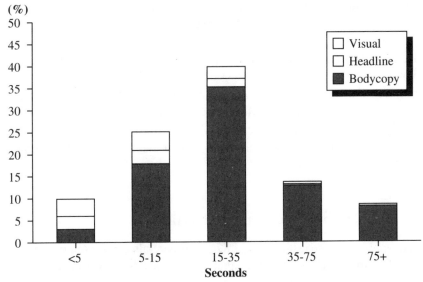

Source: Andresen, 1987.

Kroeber-Riel (1990) relates the time people spend on advertisements to the time needed to process the information offered. He concludes that, on average, 35 to 40 seconds are needed to read the copy contained in an advertisement. He observes that an average of 65% of the visual content is processed and a mere 2% of the verbal content. The conclusion is obvious: communication in advertisements greatly depends on the visual component. Before the average reader reaches the body copy, he has broken contact with the advertisement.

5.5   Irritating commercials are zapped away

We know of no empirical record of the perception time of television commercials: how long does someone watch a commercial, when does he zip or zap, or when does he switch his attention to other stimuli in his environment ('psychological zapping')?

A laboratory test of the phenomenon (Olney, Holbrook and Batra, 1991) shows that viewing time per commercial greatly depends on its characteristics. There is more likely to be a direct connection with its uniqueness (something which will be discussed in more detail at a later stage) and with the feelings it succeeds in evoking, than with the factual information it contains.

The attitude of consumers to advertisements or commercials is often abbreviated in scientific circles to Aad (Attitude towards the ad). Advertising researchers refer to 'likeability', which is generally measured on a 5-point scale. We shall discuss this in more detail later. The Aad or likeability has an important effect on the viewing of a commercial and so on its reach. The assumption that a television commercial can count on viewers' automatic attention is by no means valid. Boring or irritating commercials are 'zapped away' by growing numbers of viewers, who either use their remote control or reach a decision (in their own minds) to switch their attention to something else.

5.6   People make no effort for advertising

An analysis of the test results of 876 commercials carried out by ASI and reported to the ARF by David Walker in 1990 leads to one clear, concise conclusion: everything that requires cognitive effort, both visually and auditively, from viewers, diminishes their attention. Of the commercials which are out to make viewers think, 82% score lower than average. And 80% of commercials without those characteristics achieve higher than average scores.

Levels of attention are greatly influenced by the basic creative form. Voice-over commercials make the lowest scores for attention, followed by consumer and user testimonials. Commercials which use on-screen dialogues or compères score markedly better on average.

The general conclusion is that people who talk on the screen, either directly to the audience or to one another, are better able to catch and hold attention than voice-overs. On the whole they are easier to follow than 'pictures with commentary'. Stewart and Furse's (1986) research into the effectiveness of 1059 American television commercials also reveals the negative effect of all kinds of elements which demand more cognitive effort.

The comprehensibility and recall of commercials are (according to Henderson Blair, Kuse, Furse, Stewart, 1987) adversely influenced, amongst other things, by:

- graphic displays;
- use of animation, story-board concepts, stills, cartoons and rotoscope;

- situations which have no connection with the product;
- complicated product demonstrations;
- too high a level of informative content: information on product composition, components, ingredients, raw materials, or on nutritive value;
- too many people in the commercial who do not play a central part, but only serve as a background. They do not contribute in conveying the central message, and so are a distraction;
- too many propositions, confusing viewers.

5.7   Attention-inhibiting characteristics

These findings coincide with the general conclusion on the essence of what restricts attention: all these elements require more cognitive effort from viewers. If we want to hold their attention, we must have a simple, cohesive story, in which one scene follows another logically, with the smallest possible number of breaks, the amount of information must be limited to one or a few claims, without too many distracting details.

As we shall be seeing, it is also important not to be too abstract. Animation and cartoons are usually an abstract reflection of real life, and consequently require greater effort for interpreting and understanding them. A dialogue or a good presentation is usually easier to follow.

Levels of attention are also affected by variables in execution. Attention is limited by distracting visual movement, like fast-changing scenes, objects flying across the screen, visual distortion and, in fact, everything that is hard to follow or understand.

Another variable which restricts attention is text on the screen: viewers evidently have a resistance to reading on the screen (this applies in the United States, but might well be different in countries which are accustomed to subtitles).

Commercials with pervasive use of loud music also tend to have lower attention scores. That does not relate to simple jingles, musical pay-offs or light background music, but to loud, aggressive music which dominates the commercial.

A number of graphs follow which reveal the connection between measured attention and certain characteristics of 30-second commercials. They have been derived from David Walker at ASI Market Research. 'measured attention' means, in this context, that the commercials have been perceived to such an extent that something has been retained in the memory. It is not the same as 'related recall', with which a viewer also correctly remembers the brand. The white bars indicate the dispersion of commercials in the data set. So, successively 20% of all commercials score lower than 30% for measured attention 20% score between 31-37%, 20% score between 38-43%, 20% between 44-49% and 20% higher than 50%. The black bars represent the dispersion of the commercials with a specific characteristic. It is evident that of the commercials in which humour is used, only 8% score below 30%, and 28% obtain over 50%.

Measured attention – Humour

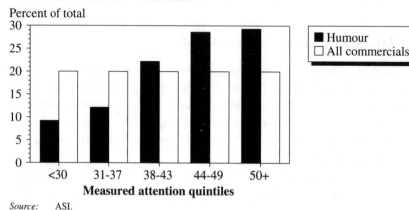

Source: ASI.

Measured attention – Celebrity identified by name

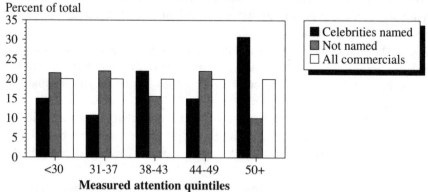

Source: ASI.

Measured attention – Mood

Percent of total

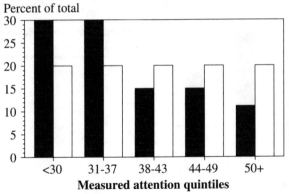

Source: ASI.

On-screen dialogue

Percent of cases

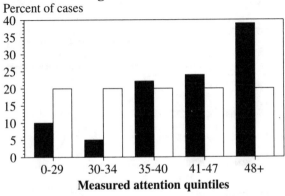

Note: n = 133.
Source: ASI.

On-screen dialogue plus humour

Percent of cases

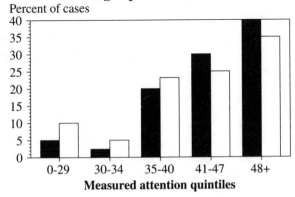

Note: n = 83.
Source: ASI.

On-screen dialogue plus cute character

Percent of cases

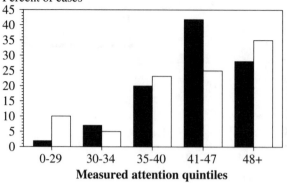

Measured attention quintiles

Note: n = 30.
Source: ASI.

Voice-over plus on-screen text

Percent of cases

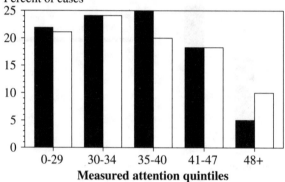

Measured attention quintiles

Note: n = 61.
Source: ASI.

Voice-over plus visual text

Percent of cases

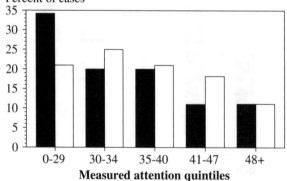

Measured attention quintiles

Note: n = 103.
Source: ASI.

5.8   Attention-stimulating characteristics

Humour is a variable which proves to augment attention substantially. Moreover, 'sweet' subjects (like cute pets, small children and babies), a pleasant, cheerful tone, a continuing personality (advertising property), celebrities, well-known sports people, television, music or film personalities (particularly when their names are mentioned) all have a positive effect on attention. The basic form and execution variables together have a dramatic influence on attention scores. When humour is added to on-screen dialogues, the chance of getting attention greatly increases. When distracting visual movement is combined with voice-over the opposite happens.

5.9   Visual concept commands attention

McCollum and Spielman Worldwide (Klein 1990) also analysed the effect of variables on awareness scores with 7,729 television commercials which had been pre-tested in the nineteen-eighties. This entails recall, measured about 20 minutes after exposure to a commercial in a controlled environment of programme components and other commercials. 123 different 'advertising characteristics' were catalogued, 28 of which proved in the analysis to be of influence on awareness scores. Together they accounted for 48% of the variation in these scores.

Four variables were in fact of decisive influence:

- unique visuals;
- mood (slice-of-life and lifestyle);
- music;
- brand identified in the first five seconds.

There was a distinct shift, compared with commercials which had been tested in the nineteen-seventies, and which had been analysed in a similar way in 1976. At that stage commercials in which the brand was only identified in the last five seconds also scored well. This illustrates the ever-diminishing attention span for television commercials. Animation, jingles and 'presenter concepts' also managed to activate viewer attention better in the seventies than in the eighties. In both decades a unique visual concept, in which the brand and the central message are well integrated, proved the be by far the most important attention-generating variable. The influence of 'mood' and emotional appeals on attention for commercials prove to have increased appreciably in the eighties. In a world of harsh realities, there may well be an increased need for emotional satisfaction. Commercials which succeed in linking emotion to the product or brand as an expressive or central value, also manage to activate attention better than in the past. This may result in more profound processing and identification. Moreover, it takes little or no cognitive effort. In the past decade music, too, gained ground as a means of activating attention, especially with its possibilities for evoking moods and emotions.

Part 2

How people process advertising

6 Levels of advertising processing

People deal with advertising in different ways. Some forms are perceived with the eyes only, without the brain being actively involved. The perceived stimuli are stored away in the memory 'unprocessed', as it were. Other forms require application if they are to be understood, processed and fitted in with one's existing knowledge; or even for the person concerned to have an opinion on them. Sometimes the process is mainly cognitive, sometimes the concomitant reactions are primarily emotional.

There are a great many theories on advertising processing. We shall suffice with outlining them, in order to put the empirical findings in their context.

We can distinguish between three dimensions:

1. The levels of advertising processing
2. Cognitive and affective processes
3. Processing of visual and verbal stimuli.

6.1 Involvement, opportunities and capacities

Advertising processing comprises several 'levels' which relate to:
- the intensity of attention paid to an advertisement;
- the extent to which existing associative networks in the memory are activated and used to decode the presented stimuli;
- the depth of understanding of the presented stimuli, and;
- the way in which new information is fitted into existing 'knowledge structures'.

There are three factors which greatly influence this process:
- the involvement of the receiver of the presented stimuli;
- the circumstances in which the stimuli are presented, and;
- the personal capacities to process the stimuli.

We shall look at these different factors briefly later.

6.2 Primary and secondary tasks

When we look at the levels of advertising processing, we should always bear in mind that it involves a division of our attention among the various 'tasks' which present themselves. All kinds of things are happening at the same time, in our minds, and in our physical and social surroundings. Time and again we have to select which stimuli are to receive our attention. We decide to read the newspaper, whilst listening with half an ear to the television. Or else we sit behind our steering wheel, carefully watching the pedestrians on the zebra crossing, whilst 'seeing' a billboard out of the corner of our eye.

This involves what are termed 'primary' and 'secondary' tasks. Primary tasks are those which receive our conscious attention, secondary tasks relate to what our senses register, and are usually stored in our memories, but with which our brains are not actively occupied.

6.3   Processing levels

Frequent reference is made to 'information-processing levels'. which in fact means the 'depth' at which our senses and brains are occupied with the stimuli. If we only perceive the stimuli through our senses and code them perceptually, this is described as 'superficial'. If we further analyse the information we are offered, add to it or even distort it, and form an opinion on it, that is termed 'in-depth' processing.

'In-depth' should be considered as a metaphor. Entire conferences have been devoted to deciding exactly what it means. Does it relate to a sequence of stages in which stimuli are processed? Or to the extent of cognitive processing? Or to the cognitive effort what is made? Or to the degree of semanticity and abstractness? Treismann (1979) has demonstrated that it is far too simple to suppose that there is a chain of consecutive or even hierarchical steps. The crux of the matter would seem to be the extent and complexity of the interaction between our sensory perceptions on the one hand, and the wealth of information contained in our memories, as anchored in our cognitions, emotions and behavioural tendencies on the other.

Craig, who was the first to formulate the 'levels-of-processing' concept, believes that two central assumptions are involved. With deeper processing, coding is apparently more significant, and it is retained longer in the memory.

6.4   Forms of processing

In general, we can distinguish between the following forms of cognitive processing:
- **Pre-attentive perception:** the stimuli in our environment are scanned; this is an unconscious, automatic process. Very general, rough characteristics of stimuli are analysed: to what extent do they diverge from what is 'normal'? Does something change in our environment? Should we be paying attention to something?

- **Sensory coding:** we pay more specific attention to a stimulus constellation. We focus our gaze for several fractions of a second on several of its elements (usually the visual component). We analyse the constellation superficially. What is it? What is it about? We now pay attention to the striking features: contours, colours, contrasts, sounds and structure. The stimuli perceived in this way are retained very briefly in our senses to start with, and then stored 'temporarily' in our short-term memory.

- **Cognitive elaboration:** we integrate the meaning of the perceived stimuli in our existing knowledge structures (associative networks).

- **Semantic analysis:** we analyse the factual meaning of the stimuli. What are the abstract, symbolic features? We form hypotheses about it and look for confirmation. Semantic analysis, in turn, has various levels, various degrees of meaning.

- **Attitude-formation:** we form an opinion on the newly-acquired knowledge. This new knowledge may coincide with our existing attitudes, thus reinforcing them. But there may also be some conflict. Then we shall have to try to eliminate it, by adjusting our attitude to the new knowledge. Or else we resist the new information. We develop disbelief, which we try to support with the existing knowledge in the memory.

The results of research into the effects of the various forms of processing on the storage of stimuli in our memory are not unanimous. Not only would the 'depth' of the processes seem to have an effect, but also their nature and duration. The extent to which processed stimuli differ from other stimuli in the same category which have already been stored in the memory, also influences storage in the memory. This could be one explanation for the fact that we remember pictures more easily than words and sentences: on the whole they are more distinctive. Almost every picture has something unique, pages with copy all look alike.

6.5   Multiple Resource Theory

Wickens (1984) developed an interesting new theory on the processing of stimuli which Smith and Buchholz (1991) adapted for the processing of television commercials, in particular. Wickens assumes that we have several 'attention resources', which, in theory, work independently. That is why he refers to Multiple Resource Theory (MRT). He differentiates between:

1. **The processing stage:** which he divides into three stages or levels:

a. *Sensory coding:* the pre-attentive processes and the analysis of structural characteristics of stimuli. It is mainly based on pictures, colours and sounds. Words are not processed yet.

b. *Central processing:* in which 'reading' can take place. The series of letters which constitute the words are compared with codes in the memory, helping to identify these words. They are then combined into sentences. At the same time visual stimuli are processed in depth in our brains. Now large sections of the left hemisphere of the brain start operating. The significance of consecutive sentences is integrated and the significance of the passage which has been read is interpreted and related to the knowledge already stored in the memory. After that the up-dated knowledge is rearranged in the memory.

c. *Response processing:* this entails forming opinions and reacting in words, with facial expressions and sounds, gestures and actions.

2. **Processing codes:**
   a. *spatial*, instinctive, emotional, 'holistic', and/or;
   b. *semantic*, analytical, during which interpretation of the stimuli takes place, by means of the verbal codes stored in the memory. Visual stimuli are also used to develop a verbal concept, for example of a brand, and to develop verbal 'beliefs' about it.

3. **Input and response modalities:**
   a. *visual*, (via the eyes – printed text is also processed visually);
   b. *auditive* (via the ears).

Wickens' theory implies that, if different resources are needed for two simple tasks, it is quite possible to perform them efficiently at the same time (parallel processing). But if several complex tasks have to be dealt with at the same time and the same resources are needed, we have to make a choice. We have to allocate our resources to one or other assignment and give it priority. If we have to apply several resources simultaneously in order to execute a difficult assignment, other tasks, which have to be carried out at the same time, suffer.

6.6   Involvement

When involvement is low, advertising stimuli are mainly only decoded perceptually. During perception, our brains 'do' little or nothing with the stimuli reaching us. We store them away directly and unprocessed, as it were. And we are perfectly capable of performing a second task at the same time, bringing different resources into play. For example, we might be thinking about things we have to do tomorrow. Because we do not analyse or interpret the presented information further, auditive-visual unity is not necessary. We process both types of stimuli in parallel, but in fact separately.

However, with high involvement, we have to use several resources simultaneously in order to process the proffered stimuli. In that case, we process both the visual and the auditive stimuli at a central level. We relate them to existing knowledge, supplement them with what we already know, and possibly also form an opinion on them. We will often make use of all the processing resources at our disposal. The effectiveness of this processing will depend on the congruence between visual and auditive stimuli. If that is not present, different types of information are, in fact, being offered – one sort via the ears, the other sort via the eyes.

That overburdens our resources. Central processing suffers. We need so much capacity to interpret the different stimuli we are receiving that we do not get round to 'considering' and 'structuring'. And then the simultaneous perceptual coding of different types of presented stimuli thwarts their central processing. If congruence does exist between the proffered visual and auditive stimuli, they can be processed as an integrated unit. The interpretation of the auditive stimuli is not thwarted by that of 'incompatible' visual stimuli. We need less processing capacity and so it can be used for the central processing of the information – we still have sufficient capacity available to analyse what it means and even to have some 'view' on it.

6.7   Metaphor

So in fact we should not refer to 'information-processing levels'. But in everyday advertising practice we need to simplify complicated psychological processes and so we shall continue to use Craig's original metaphor. But, how many 'levels' should we define? Some authors stick to four (Greenwald and Leavitt, 1984), others prefer six (Macinnis and Jaworski, 1989). We have opted for the latter number: two levels of secondary processing, three of primary processing and one of divided processing.

Secondary   1. Pre-attentive processing.
                 2. Minimal secondary processing.
                 3. Divided processing.
                 4. Passive primary processing.
                 5. Active primary processing.
                 6. Primary processing with identification.

6.7.1   Level 1: pre-attentive processing

This level has already been discussed at some length in this and in earlier chapters. Here stimuli from our environment are processed unconsciously. Our eyes and ears do pick up the stimuli, but our brains are barely activated. Only minimum, rudimentary analysis takes place – just enough in order to proceed to the next processing level, if appropriate. For example, when someone calls our name, or if something suddenly changes in our surroundings (we suddenly lose something, for instance). At this level our senses 'register' very briefly the proffered visual and auditive stimuli, and our brain processes them automatically and unconsciously.

It would seem possible for repeated pre-attentive processing of the same stimuli to generate a slightly positive attitude to the stimuli. We are more inclined to select a brand which is vaguely familiar than one which is totally unknown. But it will be clear that the advertising effect at this level is minute. Even with the recognition method it may well prove impossible to pinpoint the advertising effect. That might in fact be a form of subliminal advertising – not deliberately carried out by advertisers, but effected by consumers in their own minds, as a kind of self-defence.

6.7.2   Level 2: minimal secondary processing

Involvement in the advertisement is again still very slight. Our attention is primarily focused on another task. Our senses do perceive the advertising stimulus as a secondary task (this is also described as 'focal attention'), but the decoding level is still minimal. We merely process several general characteristics which force themselves upon us because they are very dominant or stand out obviously from their surroundings. They may be large, bright, colourful, or very different in shape, for instance. Repeated processing of stimuli at this level leaves its mark in our memories. We perceive a yellow sign with heavy black lettering, and recognise Kodak. The more often we have perceived the same stimulus, the faster this 'analysis' will be.

6.7.3   Level 3: divided processing

Now attention is divided between two tasks, for instance an advertisement and another task. Our ears and eyes perceive a television commercial, but our thoughts are also on what has happened during the day.

This kind of situation occurs when we are very occupied with something else, and our motivation to process the proffered advertising stimuli is slight. We do identify what it is about. A minimum level of understanding is involved. We relate the stimuli our senses perceive to what is stored in our memories. We see a fat man, made up of car tyres, and think: "Oh, Michelin". At the same time we are remembering a difference of opinion with a colleague. We only get as far as the processing of several prominent signals in the advertising. We are only half aware of what is going on.

Advertising processing at this level does lead to the formation of associations in the memory, or to reinforcement of existing associations. But these associations are not very structured. And much repetition is needed to get the associations well embedded. If we receive the same stimuli a little later, we recognise them. "Yes, I've seen that advertisement before."

6.7.4 Level 4: passive primary processing

Something happens on the television that attracts our attention. It is about a product we use regularly and that interests us a little. Or else someone we know is in the commercial, and that gives us a nice feeling.

Our attention is now focused primarily on the commercial, but at the same time our senses continue registering other stimuli from our environment. Admittedly, we do process the stimuli produced by television commercials primarily, but passively and rather superficially. We now understand roughly what the commercial is about, and what it is intended to convey. We think: "Oh, Pampers. Now they evidently have different nappies, for boys and girls".

Many television commercials and print advertisements for low-involvement products are probably processed at this level. We only process several elements from the information offered us. We look at a photograph for a few seconds, a few fractions of seconds at several words in the headline, see the brand and turn to the next page. Our 'two seconds per advertisement' are up. With a little help (aided recall) we can still remember the advertisement a little later on.

6.7.5 Level 5: active primary processing

Our attention is focused primarily on the advertisement. We are interested in the presented information. The rough analysis which took place at the last level is now extended to the processing of more details. We check what we read or see against the information we have already stored in our memories, and derive fresh significance from it (cognitive responding). We think: 'Hey, didn't McDonald's always have beef hamburgers? Now they've got something with chicken. What could that be?' We pay focused attention to the commercial for a little longer. We add chicken to our associative network on McDonald's. We integrate the new information on McDonald's with what we already had stored away.

At this level an attitude often comes about regarding the processed information (affective responding). We either agree or disagree with it. We find it interesting, or it leaves us cold. We are amused, or not. We relate the information to our own problems and our own values. And that may also cause a boomerang effect: our attitude changes in the opposite direction to what the advertiser had intended.

Processing now also leaves a distinct mark in the memory. A day later we can usually still describe what we have seen, read or heard. And this can be measured with spontaneous recall questions. "Do you remember what commercials you saw yesterday before the news?" Yes, the McDonald's commercial spontaneously springs to mind.

6.7.6   Level 6: primary processing with identification

Our attention is again primarily focused on the advertisement. The commercial is about something with which we certainly have some involvement. ('A new kind of jam, with very few calories!') And we identify with what takes place in the commercial. We see a child making breakfast. All kinds of things go wrong. After a whole carry-on, the toast and the tea are ready. We know what it is like. It happens to us regularly. Will the jam taste good? Often low-calorie jams have less taste. Perhaps it might be worth trying it?

Advertising now is not only neutral, abstract information for us. We interact with what happens in a commercial. It relates a little to our own lives (self reference). We assimilate the new information and integrate it with what we already knew. We might plan to look out for the product sometime.

For a moment there has been nothing other than this advertising in our life. For a moment we shut ourselves off from all other stimuli and put ourselves into the actions of the actors. For a moment we played their parts with them, and learnt from their experience. For a moment we had the same feelings as they did. If we are asked the next day what advertising we can remember, this might be the one that first springs to mind – what is termed 'top-of-mind' recall.

6.8   Recognition and recall depend on processing level

Laboratory research by Saegert (1979) with print advertisements, and by Reid and Soley (1980) with television commercials shows that there is a strong correlation between the level of advertising processing and later recognition and recall of the advertisements. If deep processing takes place (levels 5 and 6 in this arrangement), recognition and recall are better than if advertising has been processed at a more superficial level. Deeper 'processing' probably provides a more distinctive coding with respect to other contents of the memory, making it easier to find it and recall it in the 'memory store'. Processing at superficial levels 2 and 3 can probably only be ascertained with the recognition method or with extra aided recall.

7 Cognitive and emotional processing

We tend to assume that people have a cognitive system and an emotional (affective) system which is also sometimes termed 'non-cognitive'. Emotions are said to be the consequence of cognitions. We perceive something with the senses, identify it cognitively, and sometimes react to it with an emotion. There is still some debate as to whether there are two systems, and whether the emotions always have cognitive roots or whether they might also be direct reactions to stimuli. To some extent it is related to the definition of the word 'cognition'. Cognitions can be unconscious and irrational. One thing is certain: people think and people feel. Thoughts are not divorced from feelings, and vice versa. *"Affective and cognitive aspects of persuasion are intertwined rather than separate"*, according to Burke and Edell (1989). It is more like a two-coloured single-lane road, rather than a double-lane road. Reactions to advertising are always a combination of the two. A piece of advertising which consists solely of verbal information can evoke a feeling of boredom. Another, which is seemingly purely emotional in content, can teach us that we can record precious moments immediately with an 'instant' camera. So there is no point basing our arguments on a dichotomy. Cognitive (informative) and emotional reactions should, in fact, be seen as two components of one system.

The sequence of thinking and feeling is not particularly important for the processing of advertising either. The main thing is the extent to which the two occur as reactions, and how each affects our attitudes and behaviour independently. When is each of the two relevant?

For many years there has been little interest in consumer psychology for the emotional aspects of advertising processing. Affective reactions, such as the development of preferences, were considered to be merely the results of the cognitive processing of rational information. And that was the case almost throughout cognitive psychology. The 'Handbook of learning and cognitive processes' (Estes, 1975), a 2,133-page, six-volume work only mentions the words 'affect' and 'attitude' once!

This is probably due to the fact that it is difficult to contemplate emotional processes analytically. Everything that is rational and logical can be analysed, measured and structured. It is far more difficult to do so with emotions and feelings. That applies for primary emotions, like fear and joy, which have been the main focus of scientific attention and about which a great deal is now known, thanks to the work of Nico Frijda and Robert Plutchik, amongst others. But it is especially true for the whole gamut of more specific feelings, which are used so much in advertising.

Attempts to catalogue, classify and describe these specific feelings only really began around 1980 in the United States. All these 'systems of feelings' are based on dictionary definitions: their foundations are semantic representations of feelings as found in (American) dictionaries. They are then grouped according to subjective assessments or using sorting techniques and cluster analyses.

In the United States a series of measuring techniques has meanwhile been developed to establish the nature of emotional reactions to advertising. They use words which represent feelings, or 'facial' expressions. An example of this is BBDO's Emotional Measurement System (EMS), which makes use of the latter. However, all these systems are relatively new and still do not belong to standardised advertising research, as supplied by research institutes. Consequently, as yet scarcely any empirical data is available on the effects of certain emotions. Most available information comes from laboratory tests, carried out by universities. That has helped to provide better insight into the wealth of human emotional reactions which advertising can arouse. But we are still a long way off obtaining a good idea of how exactly our cognitive and emotional systems interact in the processes of advertising processing and product and brand choice.

7.1   Categories of emotions

Russel and Starkman produced a list (based on earlier inventories by Holbrook and Batra, amongst others) of 26 different categories of emotions and more specific feelings (see table 'Emotional adjectives' on the following page).

A perceptual chart has been drawn up, by means of BBDO's EMS. It is based on two dimensions: *active-passive* and *positive-negative*. The chart comprises eight clusters of emotions:

Source: BBDO Worldwide.

Emotional adjectives

Category	Descriptive synonyms – (emotional adjectives)
Joy	Joyful, Happy, Delighted
Surprise	Surprised, Amazed, Astonished
Sadness	Sad, Unhappy, Depressed
Anger	Furious, Angry, Enraged
Disgust	Disgusted, Revolted, Repulsed
Contempt	Scornful, Contemptuous, Disdainful
Fear	Fearful, Afraid, Frightened
Shame	Ashamed, Embarrassed, Humiliated
Guilt	Guilty, Remorseful, Regretful
Affection	Loving, Affectionate, Friendly
Activation	Aroused, Stimulated, Excited
Hypoactivation	Bored, Unexcited, Disinterested
Competence	Confident, Assured, Competent
Helplessness	Powerless, Helpless, Weak
Surgency	Playful, Entertained, Lighthearted
Scepticism	Sceptical, Suspicious, Distrustful
Pride	Proud, Superior, Worthy
Serenity	Restful, Serene, Comfortable
Conflict	Tense, Frustrated, Upset
Desire	Desirous, Wishful, Hopeful
Duty	Virtuous, Honest, Dutiful
Faith	Reverent, Worshipful, Spiritual
Gratitude	Grateful, Thankful, Appreciative
Innocence	Innocent, Pure, Blameless
Interest	Attentive, Curious, Interested
Distraction	Distracted, Preoccupied, Inattentive

Source: Russel and Starkman.

Edell (1991) has produced a structure of four different categories of emotions which can be aroused by advertising:

1. *upbeat*: cheerful, playful;
2. *warm*: affectionate, hopeful, calm;
3. *uneasy*: anxious, uncomfortable, tense;
4. *negative*: bored, disgusted, dubious, disinterested.

7.2   Intensity of emotions

Apart from differentiating between categories, we can also differentiate between levels of emotions; it might be better to refer to intensities or modalities. Stout and Leckenby (1986) distinguish between:

1. **Descriptive feelings:** relating to recognition of the emotion which is expressed by the advertising, for example by the people it features. We may see that someone is happy, for instance. We understand what we perceive, what people in the commercial are feeling., but we ourselves do not have a happy feeling. This reaction is, in fact, more of a cognition than an emotion.

2. **Empathic feelings:** we can relate to the people in the advertising. We have the same feelings as they do.

3. **Experiential feelings:** these are, in fact, authentic emotional reactions to stimuli. They are not the same feelings as those expressed by people in the advertising. For instance, we do not feel happy in the way they do, but very bored. The happiness they express strikes us as exaggerated and unreal, and we react to it with negative emotions.

Psychophysiological instruments, like the E.E.G. and the skin resistance meter, have been available for some time for measuring the intensity of feelings. As far as we know, they have not been used in advertising practice. Laboratory tests (Thorson, 1991) have shown that the heart beats faster when people see emotional commercials, and slower with commercials which are primarily cognitive. Learning is better with a faster heartbeat; moreover, attention drops with commercials which do not succeed in evoking a measurable emotional response. It would seem that people are able to process new information more efficiently and in greater quantities with moderate stimulation, as compared with slight stimulation (boredom) or extreme stimulation, for instance if feelings of great fear are generated. So now we can measure what kind of emotional reactions people have to advertising, and also establish the intensity of these reactions. But we are still a long way off empirical knowledge as to how emotional reactions work. This is a considerable gap in our knowledge of how advertising works. Let us take a look at what we can find out from laboratory tests.

7.3   Emotions and attention

In the unconscious process in which we scan stimuli in our environment, our attention is particularly activated by biologically-important stimuli, notably including those which express the emotions of others.

Even a small amount of emotion depicted in advertising will increase our attention for it (Lang, 1990). Kroeber Riel used the eye-tracking method to establish that the more emotional elements advertising contains, the greater the number of fixations. Viewers also focus their attention on these affective elements – especially people's faces.

Other tests suggest that the greater the intensity of the emotional reaction, the greater the chance that viewers will continue to watch the commercials. Pieters and Warmerdam (1990) established a connection between the intensity of emotional reaction and recall of advertising. Brewer (1988) also concludes that stimuli producing an emotional response are remembered better, particularly if the emotion is positive and intense.

Thorson and Friestad (1985) worked out and tested a model on the effect of memory. This was also said to demonstrate that the more intense the emotional experience when a commercial is viewed, the stronger the engram (trace) which remains in the brain, and the better it is remembered later on. However, other tests suggest that recall drops with very strong emotions. The highest recall score are achieved with advertising in which cognitive and affective components interact the strongest. As we shall discover later, a differentiating product message is one of the most important variables for recall scores. R.S.C. (Rosenberg 1991) analysed 5,000 tested commercials for 1,300 brands in 200 product categories. Emotional appeals as such proved to be neither more nor less effective in influencing brand choice than rational appeals. But the use of an emotional approach to communicate a differentiating message with a brand produced the highest persuasion scores, on average.

7.4 Positive and negative feelings

People like positive feelings, and strive to prolong them. They also tend to back away from things which arouse negative feelings. Consequently, advertising mainly appeals to positive feelings. Negative emotions do not represent values to which we aspire either. Feelings of guilt and shame are generally strong emotions, but definitely not values. If we make use of negative feelings that is usually to stop people from doing something – like wearing furs or polluting the environment.

If branded articles use negative appeals it will be because the product can solve or help to prevent those negative things. The result is often a 'problem-solving' approach. "You have an annoying problem, let our product solve it for you."

7.5   Emotions and ad likeability

Depicted emotions and our emotional reactions to them influence ad likeability. As we shall see later in this book, this can, in turn, affect brand likeability. A test conducted by Stuart and Leckenby (1988) with 50 commercials and 1,498 respondents shows that readers have greater appreciation for the advertisement and the brand when the ad has evoked an emotional response (descriptive, empathic or experiential) than for advertisements which generate no feelings.

7.6   Emotions and brand likeability

The path of emotions towards a positive attitude to a brand does not always or only proceed via Aad or likeability. When people have to select a brand, they are invariably faced with a daunting task. Sometimes because they perceive too little difference between the brands. Sometimes because the products involved are complicated, and they know too little about them, or else have difficulty assessing them. And then they are inclined to follow their feelings, and just choose a brand which makes them 'feel good'. When a good feeling is evoked by advertising it reduces the need to process its cognitive content. People are also less inclined to resist the arguments it contains. And someone with a good feeling usually also has positive thoughts. The 'good feeling' can be associated direct with the brand, and start to function as a selection variable. This would seem to be most prevalent with so called 'parity products'.

A famous saying in the advertising world is: "If you don't have anything to say, sing it". Music and song do indeed have a direct and often acute effect on our feelings. A more scientific way of expressing the same thing would be: "If you don't have anything to say, create a good feeling".

When commercials of that type are made, it is as well to weigh up the balance between the primarily negative and subsequently positive feelings that are activated. If stimuli which evoke negative feelings last too long, attention will be cut off before the brand has had a chance to reverse them into positive feelings.

Another test (Thorson, 1991) reveals that when people have experienced an emotion strongly, they are more inclined to say that their choice has been influenced positively, that they are less cynical about the commercial, and that they appreciate the advertisers more.

7.7   Emotions as product values

Often product values are primarily emotional. To a growing extent we are not basing our choices on what products 'do' for us in a functional or an instrumental sense, but on the emotions they arouse in us. We often drink coffee because of the caring and togetherness feeling it gives us, beer to relax and to feel cheerful, tea because of the feelings of serenity is represents. The primary task of emotions in advertising is often to express the emotions we associate with the use of the advertised product. Because these feelings are linked to products, they are not really suitable for differentiating brand perceptions. They are, in fact, mainly used by brand leaders with large market shares. Coca-Cola, Douwe Egberts coffee, Kodak, Pickwick tea. Their message is: the feelings you expect when you use this product are best embodied in our brand. The values concerned are almost always impressive and central.

7.8   Emotions as differentiating brand associations

When advertising constantly activates certain, specific feelings in conjunction with a brand, they will ultimately be associated with that brand. This process takes place according to the principle of classical conditioning. In its simplest form this means that when the perception (processing) of an conditioned stimulus (brand) is paired repeatedly with another unconditioned stimulus, the conditioned stimulus will start to assume the associations of the unconditioned stimulus.

Classical conditioning – Timotei

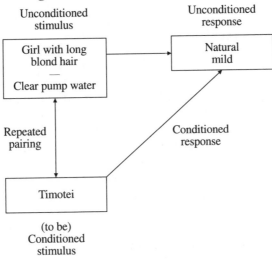

When we repeatedly pair the brand Timotei with the picture of the girl in the white dress with the long blond hair, washing her hair with clear water from a pump in the open air, the time will come that Timotei evokes the same association: natural, mild and unspoilt. And, if McDonald's repeatedly shows children having a good time in their hamburger restaurant, together with their parents or grandparents, the feelings of enjoyment and togetherness which that evokes will eventually be linked with McDonald's.

Advertisers have learnt to handle cognitive information in a fairly disciplined way. They know that, in order to develop strong associations, they must greatly restrict the amount of information and repeat it often. The same probably applies to an even greater extent for emotional stimuli.

If an emotional association is to be developed, you must:

- develop a strong stimulus, which immediately and unequivocally calls forth this emotion;
- always link the brand to this stimulus;
- do so frequently, for a long time. Laboratory tests suggest that a minimum of 20 repeats are needed to develop the association;
- coincide with existing emotional associations, which usually came about over the years and are based on countless stimuli (brand use, other users, etc.); consumers must be able to repeat the experience of the feelings;
- be consistent as regards media;
- ensure that the feelings really are linked with the product or brand: so they must always be very much in evidence.

Brands which are successful with this strategy continue to make the association as strong and intense as possible for decades.

7.9   Messages recalled better

As we have seen, laboratory tests have repeatedly shown that cognitive stimuli processed in situations in which people are also stimulated emotionally, leave deeper marks in the memory than stimuli which are only processed cognitively. The stimuli are remembered faster and in more detail. This has also been found with advertising. Cognitive advertising messages are remembered better and longer if the viewer also experienced an emotional reaction during viewing. But this does vary with the type of emotion. Agres (1987) conducted a special analysis, based on 168 commercials tested by ASI, comparing the effect of commercials with and without emotional stimuli. The commercials were divided into a successful group, with above-average scores for recall and persuasion, and an unsuccessful group, with below-average scores. The following correlation was found:

Commercials with:	Percentage commercials successful as regards persuasion
Rational (instrumental) benefit only	21.5%
Rational and explicitly emotional benefit (value)	29.4%
Rational and implicitly emotional benefit (value)	36.7%

Source: Agres, 1989.

Commercials with an emotional benefit linked to the instrumental benefit (value) proved to be considerably more successful. It would seem that the implicit processing of emotional benefits is more effective than the explicit mention of them. It was striking that all but one commercial in the sample contained an instrumental benefit, but only 28% also contained an emotional benefit. It illustrates that advertisers in the United States believe there is a need for an instrumental benefit, but perhaps are not yet sufficiently aware of the fact that consumers choose many brands on account of the impressive, expressive and central values they represent.

The correlation between persuasion scores and emotions in viewer response came as a surprise:

Commercials	Percentage commercials successful as regards persuasion
Without emotional viewer response	32%
With humour prevailing	28%
With varying mood (at start and finish)	21%
With unchanging mood	10%

Source: Agres, 1989.

Commercials containing no emotional stimuli proved in this analysis to work better on average than those containing such stimuli! Many commercials containing humour proved to be recalled better, but were weaker as regards persuasion. Commercials with varying moods (usually starting off negative and ending positive) obtained average scores for persuasion. Commercials with unchanging mood were, on average, weakest in their effect.

By and large, these conclusions coincide with what Stewart and Furse had already observed in 1986: in their analysis humour mainly contributed to recall (the factor most influencing it), but not to persuasion. Feelings of warmth, relaxation and comfort even had a negative effect on recall and no effect on persuasion in their analysis.

In short, emotions greatly affect persuasion if they represent values, so are related to the product and the brand. But the positive effect on brand choice of emotions which are only activated in order to influence ad perception, would seem dubious, at the very least. The use of humour, for example with products associated with intimacy or with status, can then be counterproductive. We shall be returning to this later.

7.10 Functions of emotions

When we try to generate emotional reactions with advertising, we shall have to be well aware of the effect(s) we want to achieve. We must differentiate between a tactical and strategic use of emotions:

Tactical:
- more attention,
- extended attention,
- deeper processing of the message,
- better recall.

Strategic:
- greater likeability for the advertising with a view to establishing greater likeability for the brand,
- linkage of the brand to feelings that product use brings about,
- the development of differentiating associations with the brand.

It is essential to exercise great discipline when using emotional stimuli in the last two cases especially.

7.11 Emotions: the essence of communication

*"Emotions form the tie between individuals...A central human urge is the need for **contact**."* Pieters (1990).

Robert Plutchik refers, amongst other things, to the emotion of 'acceptance', the feeling of being close to someone, of having a bond with them. Ben Lazare Mijuskovic states it even more clearly, (having studied the relevant philosophy, psychology and literature extensively). He comes to the conclusion that a human being is fundamentally alone, isolated, and that his central motivation is: to have 'real' contact with another human being; to accept and to be accepted; to be 'intimate'. Research reveals that to show emotions, interpret emotions, and react to them is the central aspect of intimacy, of 'true' contact. On the one hand, a human being wants to be independent and self-reliant, on the other he wants to have a bond with others, be accepted. These very emotions are what bond us as human beings. Emotions are what make us human beings. Two answering machines, linked by a telephone cable, exchange information. Two people linked by emotions have contact. Ray and Batra once remarked that misunderstanding of the role played by emotions in advertising has probably wasted more advertising money than anything else. Research into the effect of emotions in advertising is, in fact, still in its infancy. According to Pieters:

"Our attention has been focused for far too long on the cognitive processes in advertising processing. Slowly we shall have to start catching up."

8 Visual and verbal processing

With the advent of television and the ever-increasing number of channels we can receive, society is becoming increasingly geared to audio-visual communication. Audiences are also becoming increasingly accustomed to processing visual stimuli. It is impossible to imagine life without printed communication, but it is undeniably losing relative ground to audio-visual communication.

De Sola Pool et al. (1984) worked out the following shares for printed and broadcast media in total supply and total consumption (measurements apply to the supply and consumption of words).

	Supply		Consumption	
	1960	1980	1960	1980
Print media	7.6%	2.3%	31.4%	17.0%
Broadcast media	92.2%	97.6%	58.3%	76.2%
Other media	0.2%	0.1%	10.3%	6.8%
Total	**100%**	**100%**	**100%**	**100%**

Source: I. de Sola Pool e.a., 1984.

In the United States electronic communication already made up 98% of total communication supply in 1980.

8.1 Reading on the decline

In the Netherlands, too, the trend is that reading will decline in the long-term. When television was in its infancy, considerably more time was spent on reading than is the case today. And with far less varied a selection of reading matter than is available nowadays. Research by the Socio-Cultural Planning Office in the Netherlands (Kraaykamp and Knulst, 1992) shows that between 1975 and 1989 average viewing time rose 18% and average reading time dropped 16%. The time the Dutch spend on reading has dropped from 6.1 hours a week in 1975 to 5.1 hours in 1990 (–16%). The reading of magazines, in particular, has dropped considerably: from 2 hours a week to 1.4 (–30%).

The decline in reading is mainly due to the ever-decreasing number of people who open a newspaper, magazine or book at least once a week. 9.5% of the Dutch population never reads these days, 29.2% do not read newspapers, and 28.6% do not read magazines any more. In addition, the amount of time spent on magazines is also dropping, from 144 minutes a week in 1975 to 118 minutes in 1990.

The following table shows the number of people who read books, newspapers and magazines in the course of one week (in autumn), as percentages of the population aged 12 and older.

Percentage of people who read books, newspapers and magazines

	1975		1990	
	Percentage of people who read (%)	Minutes per week per person that read	Percentage of people who read (%)	Minutes per week per person that read
Books	49.4	194	43.6	206
Newspapers	80.0	188	70.8	186
Magazines	83.3	144	71.4	118
Total reading	**95.7**	**382**	**90.5**	**331**

Source: Socio-Cultural Planning Office.

The development varies considerably for different types of magazines and newspapers.

Percentage of people who read by type of publication

	1975 (%)	1990 (%)	Relative change 1975–1990 (%)
Total reading	**95.7**	**90.5**	**–5**
Books	49.4	43.6	–12
Magazines, (total)	83.8	71.4	–15
Women's magazines	40.7	29.7	–27
Family magazines	19.1	8.5	–55
Juvenile magazines	11.7	7.9	–33
News magazines	12.7	7.2	–43
Radio/tv guides	33.6	15.7	–53
Hobby magazines	42.4	30.5	–28
Door-to-door magazines	43.1	41.2	–4
Newspapers, (total)	80.0	70.8	–11
National quality press	15.7	13.9	–11
National popular press	37.2	25.5	–31
Regional newspapers	52.3	48.6	–7

Source: Socio-Cultural Planning Office.

8.2 Regular readership

In particular 'marginal' readers of newspapers and books have dropped out. A 'hard core' of regular readers has remained and they tend to read a lot. Per capita sales of newspapers and magazines among people aged 12 and older rose until 1980, but after that followed the trend of decreasing readership figures. Yet the trend in purchases is still ahead of the trend in consumption – so more newspapers and magazines are still being bought, but they are being read less.

This drop in reading is not only the consequence of the pull of the medium of television, but also of the increase in other possible pursuits, both in one's leisure time (sports and hobbies) and at work.

8.3 $2\frac{1}{4}$ hours of television a day

The pull of television is increasing, because of the growing challenge the medium represents. A wider choice of channels results in more viewing, as does the increase in hours transmitted. Possession of a video recorder also generates more viewing: 2 hours a week more in the Netherlands.

Between 1975 and 1985 use of television rose from an average of 113 to 135 minutes a day (23% of which was secondary use, alongside reading, talking, eating, working, etc; these proportions prove to be stable).

The growth in television viewing compared with reading is particularly prominent among the younger generations and people with a lower education. Since 1975 reading has become more specifically a pursuit for older people and for those with a higher education. Amongst young people, reading has, in fact, become an unusual occupation. They have exchanged reading for the ever-growing possibilities of the screen.

The Socio-Cultural Planning Office established in 1990 that young people divide the time they spend on media – primary 'consumption' (expressed in minutes per day and recalculated by the author in hours per week) – in the following way:

Media consumption in minutes per day

	12–19 years of age		20–34 years of age	
	1975	1990	1975	1990
All media	153	140	145	129
Television	83	103	78	90
Radio	16	6	9	5
Listening to music	18	8	8	4
Print media	36	23	50	30
of which:				
Newspapers	7	4	25	12
Magazines	11	7	14	9
Books	17	12	12	9

Source: Socio-Cultural Planning Office.

In the 1985-1990 period young people's television viewing increased further. However, with older people the pattern seems to be stabilising. Especially among older people with a secondary or higher education the time spent on reading has continued to be stable over the last fifteen years.

Television viewing (primary) in hours per week

Age	Education	1975	1985	1990	Change 1975–1990
40 or younger	lower	11.3	13.3	14.5	+28%
	secondary/higher	8.4	11.6	12.2	+45%
Over 40	lower	11.7	12.7	13.0	+11%
	secondary/higher	9.2	11.1	10.9	+18%
Total sample		**10.4**	**12.0**	**12.3**	**+18%**

Source: Socio-Cultural Planning Office.

Reading in hours per week

Age	Education	1975	1990	Change 1975-1990
40 or younger	lower	4.5	3.2	–29%
	secondary/higher	5.6	4.5	–20%
Over 40	lower	6.1	5.1	–16%
	secondary/higher	7.3	7.2	–15%
Total sample		**6.1**	**5.1**	**–16%**

Source: Socio-Cultural Planning Office.

However, the obvious question is whether this might not be an ever-present phenomenon. In 1955 young people aged between 12 and 17 only spent 5 to 10 minutes reading the newspaper (Central Statistics Office, 1959). Now they are around 50 years of age. In 1985 they read the newspaper for 21 minutes a day, on average – which is about the same as people aged between forty and fifty did in 1955. Evidently people only develop an interest in newspapers as they grow older. Over the years young people prove to have less interest in reading than their elders. Yet the gap is growing all the time.

However, that does not alter the fact that there is a decline in reading in absolute terms. Research in West Germany, as it used to be, has shown that there has been a drop of over 50% in the reading of newspapers and books by young people aged between 14 and 29 since 1970.

8.4 Visual culture

Not only do people read less, but, more especially, they read *differently*. Reading consists more and more of processing several lines of text, to complete or explain photographic material. It differs less and less from watching television. So not only is there a gradual expansion of television, at the expense of newspapers, books and magazines, but, in particular, an increase in viewing pictures at the expense of reading text.

As we have already seen, of the two seconds, on average, readers spend on an advertisement, about $1\frac{1}{2}$ seconds are spent on processing pictures and only $\frac{1}{2}$ second on words. In a laboratory test based on eye-tracking with 17 advertisements and 77 respondents, Jeck Schlottmann (1987) reached the conclusion that readers preferred illustrations in almost all respects to texts. And that applied to people with high and with low involvement alike. In 75% of the cases the first fixation related to an illustration, in 20% it was a headline and in 5% of the cases something else. For those whose involvement is low, pictures accounted for 70% of all fixations, and with high involvement it was still 58%. With low involvement headlines account for about 20% of fixations and other elements only 10%. People with high and with low involvement prove to read very little of the body copy – the former only reached an average of 6 fixations on the body copy, and those with low involvement did not even manage more than one.

8.5   Visual communication

Laboratory research (Rossiter and Percy, 1978) has revealed that pictures have a greater effect on attitude formation than words. Mitchell and Olsen (1981) and Mitchell (1986) reached the conclusion, based on laboratory experiments, that the presence of illustrations not only contributes towards the development of cognitive associations (beliefs), but also to greater appreciation of the advertisement: a positive 'Attitude towards the ad' (or Aad). This may contribute to a positive attitude towards the brand.

Our visual memory is probably better developed than our semantic memory. We assimilate pictures at lightning speed, and can also recognise large numbers of pictures after very brief moments of perception.

Research has shown that:

- People's attention is primarily activated by pictures and sounds.
- Visual articles in magazines attract more readers and generate higher levels of learning and recall (Greenberg and Garfinkel).
- Pictures are processed first, before people get round to processing words. With an average processing time for advertisements of two seconds, 70% to 80% is spent on the visual part. People often only get round to processing an occasional word or sentence.
- A picture of average complexity takes only $1\frac{1}{2}$ to 2 seconds to be processed. In the same time only 7 to 10 words can be processed.

- Pictures can sum up a great deal of information in a simple way, leading to faster communication (i.e. better communication within the given processing time).

- Pictures can be communicated at a lower processing level than words: less cognitive effort is needed. (This does assume that pictures have spontaneous 'power of expression' and are not visual puzzles.) Words require extra conversion into meanings, especially when they are abstract;

- The order of picture-word works better than word-picture (Brainard, Desroches and Harve). So words which complement pictures communicate better than pictures which help explain words.

- Pictures which supplement words are remembered better than pictures alone (Edell and Staelin, 1983).

- Two pictures which are clearly connected (think of side-by-side comparisons) stimulate associative learning better than two pictures which have nothing in common as regards content.

- Concrete pictures work better than abstract – concrete meaning objects, persons and places which you can see, feel, smell, hear, taste. Abstract pictures are those which cannot be interpreted by the senses (Richardson).

- Brands and products which are integrated in the illustration are remembered better (Lutz and Lutz, 1977) than those which are not.

- Pictures usually activate emotions faster and better than words.

- Pictures can be more vivid than text, and so generally easier to remember (Taylor and Thompson, 1982).

- The long-term memory has an almost unlimited capacity for the storage of pictures.

- Visual recollections hardly fade either.

- Pictures have a direct effect on attitudes: when we see something, we often immediately know whether we find it 'attractive' or 'ugly', 'pleasant' or 'unpleasant'. Van Raay's 'primary affective reaction' is probably dominated by pictures.

- Pictures are very decisive for the attitude towards the ad – and consequently also indirectly influence the attitude towards the brand.

8.6   The functions of pictures

In advertising practice, verbal communication is still emphasised very strongly, and often one-sidedly. Much deliberation is given to every word. But the visual side by no way receives the attention it deserves. It is often dealt with very casually.

It is particularly important to consider the functions pictures can have in the effect of advertising. For example, pictures may be:

Tactical functions, which can

- stop the eyes in the scanning process;
- activate attention;
- support primary verbal communication;
- activate feelings; or

Strategic feelings, which can

- independently convey cognitive messages;
- convey feelings by means of emotional conditioning;
- fix the brand firmly in the memory, by means of 'inner' pictures;
- differentiate the brand from competing brands, by means of inner pictures;
- achieve a positive attitude towards the advertisement ('Aad'), apart from the communication content.

When pictures are only, or mainly used to get attention and have no other essential function in communication, there is a danger effective communication is only achieved with that (usually) very small section of the 'receivers' with high involvement with the product or brand, who are also prepared to read (longer) texts.

Most advertising is processed in a low-involvement situation, which greatly limits verbal communication in particular. This fact is often insufficiently evident from advertising research, since research conditions temporarily cause a high-involvement attitude in respondents. Advertising which is only processed at a pre-attentive or secondary level under normal conditions, is processed at a far 'deeper' level during an interview. It is, therefore, crucial for advertising research to approach as near as possible the natural conditions in which ads are processed, and to be very cautious about questioning people at length.

8.7   Visualising the central message

Analysis of more than 100,000 advertisements tested by Gallup & Robinson in the United States, shows that when communication of the message is primarily visual, test scores (recognition, communication of the message, favourable buying attitude) are around 32% above the average. If neither the product or the idea can be portrayed visually, these scores are 27% below the average (Waring, 1986). Especially when the product is the visual focal point of the advertisement, substantially higher than average scores are reached. This is often a problem when services are advertised, but it can be quite tricky for product advertising too.

If we have to rely on many words to communicate the central message, it is wise to consider whether print media is practical. The media consumption of the target group (age, education) and the interest and relevance of the message will be decisive.

Specific visual communication has to be 'steered' very carefully. The pictures should evoke the desired cognitive and/or emotional reactions almost independently. The main problem is that, on the one hand, they must also be sufficiently new, vivid, distinctive and 'stimulating' to work as 'attention-getters', while on the other, their function in specific communication may not be harmed.

8.8   Borrowed interest

It is frequent practice to use 'borrowed interest' in order to communicate ideas, especially in the approach used in institutional advertising. Borrowed interest relates to the depiction of a provoking event, thing or person, which attracts the attention and which ties in with the central message. This technique often lacks an obvious connection: the visual element does gain attention for a moment, but the subsequent cognitive effort required to understand the message means that the vast majority of readers give up before they have reached the message. 'Cute' subjects (children, animals) are also used to 'borrow' interest. We shall discover later on that borrowed interest certainly can contribute to attention and likeability. But it will only be effective in influencing brand choice if there is a clear connection with the product or message.

8.9   The processing of advertising copy

Research by Stern and Quick, amongst others, (Kiss and Wettig, 1972), has shown that, on average, 'readers' of general interest magazines only spend a few seconds on an advertisement (see Chapter 5). Most of the time (70-80%) is spent on looking at the illustrations; they spend an average of less than one second reading the text. Less and less 'reading', as learnt at school (tidily, from top left to bottom right), takes place when advertisements are processed. We primarily focus on the pictures – they are looked at and analysed first.

Is it about something that interests us or not? Generally contact will be broken after that. If the advertising relates to computers, for instance – a lot of people have no interest in that subject. But the initial analysis can also lead to further contact. What does the advertisement want to tell us? Our eyes pause for a few fractions of seconds at the words in the headline, and then skip over the text to the logo: whose ad is it? If we are still interested, our eyes will return to elements in the advertisement. They flit, as it were, from stimulus to stimulus. We fixate on each stimulus for 0.25 seconds. On average our eyes move four times each second. When something in our minds decides we have enough information, we move our attention on to the next advertisement, or to another constellation of stimuli. That occurs after about 7 fixations. The average reader never actually gets round to reading an entire sentence (a longer-than-average headline, for instance).

8.10   10 seconds is very exceptional

Obviously there are situations in which people spend more time on an advertisement, but these are 'exceptions to the rule'. As referred to earlier, research into how doctors read the advertisements in the German 'Arzte-Zeitung' singled out only one advertisement on which an average of 10 seconds was spent.

Even car ads in general interest magazines are given more than ten seconds by only a very small proportion of the readers. A survey among readers of 'Manager Magazine' into reading of an advertisement for an investment product also revealed that only 10% of readers spent more than 10 seconds on it – 45% spent less than 3 seconds (Kroeber-Riel, 1990).

8.11   Contact broken

So, as a rule: *contact with an advertisement is broken after a few (1-4) seconds.* Advertisements really should be arranged with that in mind. How can the essence of the message be communicated in two seconds? To start with, the number of words must be strictly limited. The basic principle these days should, in fact, be: no more words than are strictly necessary to communicate the central message.

Secondly, this requires a hierarchical set-up, as regards content. Whenever possible, visuals should be allocated a central role. The headline can support the visual component – together they should communicate the central message. If the central message is 'hidden' in the body copy, the vast majority of 'readers' will fail to process it. The copy should then be structured in such a way (heading, subheading, caption with an illustration, accents in typography) that the more seconds are spent on the advertisement, the more the information is 'offered' in order of importance.

Readers must be given the least possible opportunity to allow their eyes to wander through a text, because that inevitably leads to chaotic communication. The person who compiles the advertisement should lead the reader's eyes past the important stimuli, in a sequence which produces a smooth processing and understanding of the message. The main question here is: at what level is an advertisement processed (see Chapter 6)?

It is wise to assume that it takes place at a very 'shallow' level whenever newspaper or magazine advertisements are read. The higher our demands on cognitive processing and the energy that takes, the earlier people will break off contact. Later we shall see that this also happens with television commercials. And since the printed media have less scope for stimulation, there is no reason to expect print ads to do any better than television commercials.

8.12 Activating schemata

Advertising must take into careful account the schemata present in people's memories. We have distinct ideas about how things look, and we are familiar with certain words which have concrete meanings for us. We use them to help us interpret the pictures and words we perceive with our senses. The better they succeed in activating existing schemata (i.e. evoking images and meanings which are present in our memories), the faster and easier the interpretation process will proceed. The less successful they are, the more mental effort will be required for interpretation.

Words are speech codes. The word 'chair' is a code for something with legs, a seat and a back. It is an abstraction. The concrete aspect of a chair is what we perceive with our senses (sight, touch). The abstract code 'chair' always contains considerably less information than the fastest sensory perception of the physical original. If we look at a chair for 1 to 3 seconds, we process a large amount of information about it. If we are to convey the same amount of information in words, we are likely to need several sentences, which take ten or more seconds to process.

8.13 The more concrete, the better

So, generally speaking, the more concrete the information, the easier it will be to process. One's own experience of something is more concrete than a depiction. A depiction of something is more concrete than a description. A concrete description is better than an abstract description. Concrete words are those which refer to things, people and places, of which we have images in our memories.

By and large, advertising does not take much account of these principles. Pictures are often too abstract and too little subservient to the communicative content of the message. Texts are (far) too long and insufficiently hierarchically structured. The interaction between visual and copy is often far too complicated, or totally non-existent. Usually those who make the advertisements assume that a profound processing and considerable cognitive effort will take place, for which 30 seconds or more are required. That never occurs with low-involvement products, and only among very few readers as far as high-involvement products are concerned.

8.14   Headlines

After the visual, the heading is the element of an advertisement which receives most attention. Jeck Schlottmann's research (1987) shows that headlines account for 20% of all fixations (visual 70%). But that 20% only accounts for 1.4 fixations: on average, people do not read more than a couple of words of a headline. So headlines must be short, clear and concrete; not conundrums. Concrete headlines are to the point: if at all possible, they contain, together with the visual element, the central message of the advertisement. We must avoid forcing the reader to think about it (for a long time) when 'reading' it. When a reader has 'fixated' on the (main) visual and headline, and still does not understand what the advertiser wants to tell him, he will probably switch his attention to a following constellation of stimuli. That is why 'teaser' headlines, using double meanings and play on words, are dangerous.

Boastful headlines and exaggerated claims also put readers off. Analysis of the Gallup and Robinson scores shows that, with puzzles and boasting, advertising effect is 38% below the average (Waring, 1986).

John R. Rossiter analysed the so-called 'starch scores' (measurements of recognition, brand linkage and degree of copy reading) and compared the scores with the structural characteristics of advertisements, in particular the headings.

His findings were as follows:

1. Recognition is aided by:
    - headlines containing nouns (not verbs);
    - headlines containing a personal reference ('you');
    - the size of the illustration.

2. Brand linkage is aided by:
   - short headlines;
   - nouns in the headline;
   - adjectives in the headline;
   - product/brand as the 'object' of the headline;
   - the size of the illustration;
   - personal reference in the headline;
   - no question mark in the headline.

3. The reading of copy is stimulated by:
   - definite and indefinite articles ('the' and 'a') in the headline – probably because they suggest uniqueness;
   - adjectives in the headlines (like 'new' and 'special');
   - no imperatives in the headline.

These findings confirm opinions on the processing of pictures and texts derived from cognitive psychology. As Rossiter states: the recognition of advertisements is greatly determined by the visual component. Words can also be codes for inner visual images. The more concrete the words, the more they refer to things we have perceived with our senses and then have stored in our memories, as 'interior pictures'. Nouns and adjectives are generally more concrete than verbs and adverbs, and that explains their effect on the processing of advertisements.

Personal references in the headline stimulate the expectation that the message may be relevant for us.

9 Involvement, opportunities, capacities and understanding advertising

The level at which we process advertising is determined primarily by our involvement in that advertising. It decides the degree of our motivation to process the stimuli presented to us. And then, the circumstances in which the stimuli are presented play an important part. Lastly, our personal capacities determine how processing takes place. We have depicted the main variables which influence the level at which advertising is processed in the diagram 'Levels of advertising processing' below.

Levels of advertising processing

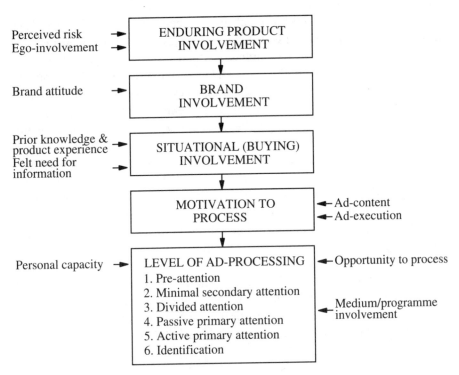

It starts with what is called 'enduring product involvement'. This relates to our general 'relationship' with the product, regardless of time, place and stimulus. It also partly depends on product interest, as encountered in Chapter 3. We have seen that recognition scores are very closely connected with measured product interest, especially with press advertisements.

9.1   Involvement

Involvement is sometimes defined as the number and intensity of the connections a person makes between a stimulus and his personal life. A number of factors can influence it: in particular, the risks a person runs when selecting a product, the subjective importance the product represents for the reader or viewer. But the subjective importance of the product, and interest in it, are antecedents for involvement – or facets or possibly different words for it (McQuarrie and Munson, 1992).

A person's knowledge and experience of the product, and the stage at which he is in the buying process, also effect involvement.

The brand, too, plays an important part. A brand can be like a good friend, but also like a person to whom you are indifferent, or whom you even dislike. You are always interested in a good friend. If you dislike someone, you try to avoid him if at all possible.

Product and brand involvement are not constants. They increase and decrease, depending on what stage in the buying process the person in question is. This especially applies to purchases which take place infrequently, and which entail greater ego-involvement and a greater perceived risk. Before we make up our minds about the purchase of a new car, our interest in what is new in the car field is heightened, particularly in the category in which we think we shall be buying. After purchase, our interest gradually declines again.

These factors determine our a priori interest in information which advertising offers us. We have already seen that involvement in a programme can also affect the processing of commercials. During films and important sporting events involvement is higher than during news broadcasts or magazine programmes. This greatly affects recall scores. But the foremost influence on involvement may well be exercised by the characteristics of the advertising itself. The results of the empirical tests which we shall be discussing in subsequent chapters tend to confirm this: does the advertisement or commercial manage to activate our attention, and does something happen with which we can really identify? Is the information presented in a purely cool, distant, rational, abstract way, or is it related to our personal lives? Is it about the product, or might it perhaps be especially about ourselves?

9.2   Circumstances

The circumstances under which the stimuli are presented also greatly influence the level at which advertising is processed. To what extent do they have a favourable or an unfavourable effect?

When we drive past a billboard at a speed of 30mph on our way to work, the effect will be different from when we are reading the Sunday Times magazine quietly at home on a Sunday afternoon (something which too many designers of billboards tend to ignore). When we see a commercial during a break in a film something different happens from when we see the same commercial sandwiched with 15 others into one 5-minute commercial break after the news.

An advertisement in a 30-page magazine is processed in a different way from one in a magazine with 130 pages. Numerous surveys have shown that the amount of information which has to be processed within a certain space of time greatly affects the level of processing. This applies just as much for a billboard which we whizz past as for a commercial break on television. A good illustration of this is the relationship between time spent reading magazines and the processing of advertisements, as depicted in the following table:

The influence of time spent reading magazines on impact scores

	Reading time in minutes			
	Up to 29	30 to 59	60 to 119	120+
Seen ad registered brand	29%	40%	43%	68%
Relevant response to	14%	17%	32%	34%
Message	13%	16%	25%	33%

Source: Rolf Speetzer, 'The Value of Media Exposure', Axel Springer Verlag, Hamburg.

The number of stimuli which are presented in one advertisement, in relation to the time spent on them, also influences processing. The more extensive and complicated the information, the more time we need to process it; and if we do not have that time, we process it less completely and more superficially. Information can be processed actively within the two seconds which are spent on average on an advertisement, provided that the ad does not offer too many competing stimuli.

9.3   Personal capacities

Intelligence, knowledge and experience are crucial in advertising processing. It is not only a matter of intelligence and the kind of education we have had, but rather of the product knowledge we have acquired and which is stored away in the association networks in our memories. That knowledge is often insufficient for us properly to understand and process the information confronting us. Even as regards simple things like detergents and toothpastes. But, of course, even more so for complicated products like photographic equipment, video recorders and personal computers.

Misunderstanding is tremendous when it comes to information offered to us. This is caused by a combination of the three factors we have already mentioned: involvement, opportunities and personal capacities, which ensure that advertising is generally processed at a very superficial level, which, in time, will become increasingly superficial.

9.4   Redundancy and overload

Früh (1980, in Windahl et al., 1992) points out that 'receivers' only want to expend a certain amount of energy in understanding a message. He reaches the conclusion, based on a survey into the reading and understanding of newspaper articles, that there are two limiting factors – redundancy (*the banality threshold*) and overload (*the complexity barrier*).

He has illustrated his theory in the following way:

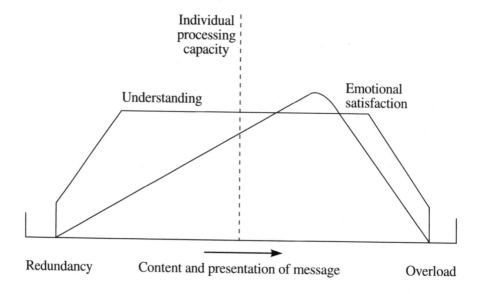

Source: Windahl e.a., 1992.

The extent to which the advertisement is processed is determined by the content and the presentation of the message, compared with the receiver's motivation. If the message contains no new or relevant information and the presentation is not interesting, processing is stopped in the initial stage. It does not cross the *banality threshold* (redundancy).

If the message is new and relevant, and its presentation is interesting, its processing gives emotional satisfaction. That means that the receiver is prepared to put more energy into its processing. But if the message or the presentation becomes too complex, the receiver reaches a point at which he no longer wants to go on. It would cost him more energy than he is prepared to expend on understanding the message. He has reached the *complexity barrier* (overload). Emotional satisfaction recedes and the receiver terminates processing. Effective advertising must keep these two factors in mind. It should not make use of widely-known information and present it in an uninteresting way. On the other hand, it must certainly not be too complicated, requiring too much cognitive energy.

9.5   Understanding advertising

The minimum requirement for most advertising to achieve the desired effect is that the central message be understood, and preferably the content of the other elements as well. However, what is actually communicated does not only depend on the content of the advertising itself, but also on the existing contents of the receiver's memory. 'Pure perception' does not exist. What we see is always a mixture of perception and interpretation. Whether advertisers like it or not, viewers and listeners filter, add, omit, interpret, distort and even reject. Advertising is very much a dynamic, interactive process. People do what they want with it. They remove what they want and adapt the information to their own established ideas and opinions. Quite often a packaging, a print advertisement or a commercial proves to convey something entirely different from what the makers had intended. A substantial percentage of users of Vidal Sassoon's 'Wash and Go' (Pert Plus) apparently do not see the product as a shampoo but as shower foam, and lather themselves with it from head to toe.

Anyone who is involved in advertising research has observed the phenomenon for himself: we are sometimes amazed that consumers misinterpret what we consider to be the simplest of stimuli. So communication without a degree of miscomprehension is unheard of. But to what extent does it occur? And what factors influence it?

9.6   The receiver as a 'sense-maker'

Receivers have been usually described as a group with common, objective, and in particular, socio-demographic characteristics. That meant that it was easy to lose sight of the individual receiver, especially as an active participant in the communication process. Particularly in the last decade recognition has been growing for the independent, active part played by individuals in the communication process. So really we should no longer refer to 'receivers of messages', but primarily see the people with whom we communicate as individuals who create their own meanings from the sensory stimuli they receive. They are striving to make sense of the world around them, and as such participate actively in the communication process. Derwin (1984) summarises the main points of this theory of 'sense-making' as follows:

- 'Sense-making' starts with the receiver. In that context the message is seen only in the way in which it crosses the path of the receiver.

- 'Sense-making' assumes the message has no autonomous impact, but that the receiver will decide for himself what impact a message will have on him.

- 'Sense-making' sees the characteristics of the context in which a message is received not as stimulating or inhibiting factors, but as contexts in which the receiver uses the message to make sense of the world around him.

- Information is defined as what is informative, from the receiver's point of view.

- 'Sense-making' is predicted from the receiver's situation.

Since every receiver is unique, it is difficult to steer the process of sense-making in a more or less uniform way for large groups. To a degree, everyone sees their own advertisements and their own commercials. But because they belong to the same group or subculture (for example, they are all 'real ale drinkers'), they do all have common experiences and views, which enable us to communicate with them meaningfully. However, there is a prerequisite: the 'sender' must get the feel of the subculture, in order to assess how the 'sense-making' process will generally proceed within that culture. Possibly the most important reason why the process of 'sense-making' does not go according to the sender's plan, is that he has not made enough effort to empathise with the target group; and that is what we call *miscomprehension*.

9.7   30% misunderstood

Jacoby (1977) carried out a survey for the AAAA into the 'miscomprehension' of television commercials which covered both commercials and clips of ordinary programmes. 'Miscomprehension' was defined as the evocation of a meaning which was not part of the message and which could not logically be 'derived' from it either.

'Standard' range of miscomprehension associated with product/service advertisements

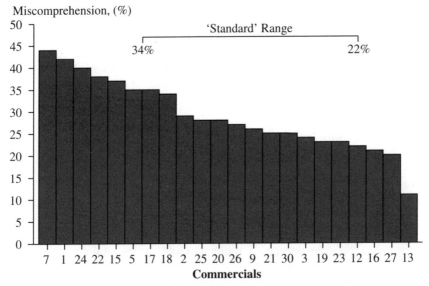

Miscomprehension, (%)

Source: Miscomprehension of Televised Communications, Jacob Jacoby, for AAAA 1980.

2,700 people were involved and 60 'communications', 22 of which were commercials. The question was: "What was the main idea of the commercial/film clip you just saw? What other ideas were in the commercial/film clip?" A comment of true/untrue was also asked for on 6 short statements which were derived from each communication.

The survey produced the shocking conclusion that 29.6% of the meanings derived from all the communications were incorrect. It varied from 11% to 50% for each item. The average was a little higher with programme clips than with commercials. Among the latter 29% miscomprehensions occurred. Over half the mistakes related to facts in the communications themselves. The other half related to the respondents' interpretation of them.

We must bear in mind that some of the correct answers were guesses. Further analysis of the results by Schmittheim and Morrison (1983), taking this fact into account, led to the conclusion that only 46% of the meanings were understood correctly, as opposed to the 70% originally stated.

In 1987 a laboratory test followed into the (mis)understanding of print ads. 1,350 respondents were asked to take as long as they wanted to read two advertisements and two items from articles. The test consisted of 108 items altogether (54 advertisements and 54 articles). Average reading time per item was 49 seconds. The respondents then had to state the main message of the communication, and what other things they had read. The test was deliberately organised so that all 'communications' received full, focused attention. It revealed that even under these optimum conditions only 65% of the advertising messages were correctly understood.

Nineteen per cent were wrongly understood, and 16% of the questions could not be answered. In view of the long time (49 seconds) spent on reading each ad, compared with the average of two seconds which people really spend on advertisements, it is reasonable to assume that the extent of miscomprehension of advertising messages must been much higher under real-life conditions.

9.8   Consequences of communication overload

Other small-scale tests have also uncovered high levels of miscomprehension. Surveys into the understanding of television news programmes (Robinson, 1982; Sahin e.a., 1981; Edwardson e.a., 1981) recorded miscomprehension scores of 38%, 60% and 72%.

In an analysis of recall score for 1,059 television commercials by Stewart and Furse (1986) the degree of understanding of the main message was established. The results are distorted because they in fact related to the central message, *as it was remembered*. Consequently there is a high correlation of 0.7 with the scores for related recall. The factors which influence related recall also largely coincide with those which influence the understanding of the central message. They will be discussed in detail in Chapter 15. They are closely related to activation of attention, relevance of the message, the cognitive effort required to follow and interpret the commercial, the amount and complexity of the information provided, and the presence of distracting and disturbing elements.

The number of different appeals which are used, the number of product attributes and ingredients, and the number of people taking part in the commercial have a more negative effect on understanding than on recall.

We are probably encountering the effects of the communicative overload in commercials, making it more difficult for people to pick up the central message. People can only process a very limited amount of information in a short time, especially if it is hard to understand and the level of attention is low because they are not very interested.

9.9   Audio-visual unity

Schlinger's research (1979) shows that viewers can become confused if there is a lack of audio-visual unity – if the picture does not communicate the same thing as the sound. The viewer has to divide his attention over two different kinds of stimuli. And, as we have said before, this is drastic for processing.

Attention is focused on the visual element and processing of the audio is then secondary, or vice versa.

Confusion can be aggravated by a high tempo, badly integrated elements, too many scenes, fast scene-switching, pictures which are not logically connected, and rushed dialogues. These findings were also confirmed in an extensive survey into miscomprehension among a representative sample of 1,978 Americans (Hoyer, Srivastava and Jacoby, 1984). Once more the simultaneous use of two processing modes, visual and auditive, for stimuli with different meanings, resulted in divided attention. It is particularly important to avoid depicting visual copy visually if it is not congruent with the other pictures or with the sound.

9.10   A priori expectations

The use of difficult or unknown words and complicated sentences also contributes to in/miscomprehension. The 'receiver' sometimes lacks the product experience to be able to interpret what it is all about. This would seem to occur especially with electronic goods. The information must be extremely simple, particularly when we want to address a wide audience.

A substantial amount of what is misunderstood is, however, due to the receiver's expectations as regards the message. Viewers and readers often have some idea of what the advertiser wants to say – and proceed to deduce this from the advertising, even if that is not part of the message. The problem with miscomprehension is widely underestimated. Advertisers should be aware of it, and take measures to keep it to a minimum. They should pay special attention to the interaction between visual and copy, and between visual and sound.

10 Brand linkage

It goes without saying that if advertising is to be effective, readers/viewers/listeners must be able to link it with the brand that is being advertised.

10.1   45% incorrect brand linkage

MSW measures recall of a commercial about 20 minutes after forced exposure in a controlled environment of other commercials and programme components. About 25% of the respondents can no longer remember the advertised brand, and 10% name the wrong brand. Another 10% only manage to name the product group.

However, analysis of 876 30-second commercials which ASI in the United States (Walker, 1990) tested for a number of dimensions, proves that of all the commercial exposures which people remembered after 24 hours (based in this case on related recall), 45% were *not* linked to the correct brand. Almost exactly the same conclusion can be drawn from a large German survey (Seherqualität II, 1991). Once more, based on related recall (in which the product is given as the stimulus) only 13.4% of viewers who had seen a 'block' of commercials could name a brand they had seen. 5.7% named the wrong brand. This also signifies an incorrect brand linkage of 43%.

The lack of correct brand linkage – either immediately during processing of the commercial, or because it has been lost in the memory shortly after the exposure – proves, according to ASI, to be independent of the attention the commercial has received.

The average level for measured attention (recall of the commercial), based on several specific stimuli, worked-out in the ASI tests at 41% for the 876 commercials. In another test with 1,059 commercials carried out by Research Systems Corporation and analysed by Stewart and Furse (1986), the average was 30%. The German survey (Seherqualität II) also produced an average aided recall of 30.8%. So the questions and the set-up of the test greatly influence the measured attention levels! An absence of correct brand linkage reduces the average effective reach of the commercials from 41% to 23% (.55x41).

Brand confusion was also researched in the Netherlands. Consumers were asked to take their time identifying advertisements from which the name and slogan had been removed (T. Hecker, M. Verhallen, 1988). Of all the advertisements which were recognised, 24% were attributed to the wrong brand. There was a decided correlation between the level of total recall and correct brand linkage.

	Advertisement recognition	Percentage of total ads recognised	
Brand	Total recognition of advertisement (correct *and* incorrect)	Brand correct	Brand incorrect
Robijn	97%	92%	8%
Pampers	95%	89%	11%
Dixan	84%	65%	35%
All	79%	77%	23%
Peaudouce	79%	75%	25%
Billies	79%	81%	19%
Libero	75%	75%	25%
Biotex	62%	89%	11%
Dobbelman	38%	66%	34%
Klok	26%	50%	50%
Average	**71%**	**76%**	**24%**

Source: T. Hecker, M. Verhallen, 1988.

Incorrect brand linkage is probably the factor which most reduces potential advertising effectiveness.

10.2   Linkage variables

The variables which cause brand linkage are different from those which influence attention.

With television commercials, brand linkage is mainly determined by the way in which the brand is assimilated in the commercial. Of commercials in which the brand is named within the first eight seconds and then repeated at least twice, 70% achieve above-average scores for brand linkage. With commercials in which this is not the case, 72% score lower than the average (Walker, 1990). Analysis of pre-test results of 7,729 commercials by MSW reveals that, whereas in the seventies identification of the brand in the last five seconds of a commercial was still sufficient to achieve good brand linkage, in the eighties identification in the first five seconds has become an important criterion for effectiveness. People would seem to need a 'hook' on which to 'hang' the processed stimuli in their memories. If they have no hook, they have a 'storage' problem, as it were. If the hook is presented too late, the 'hanging-up' process will have to take place afterwards, but by then the brain will be busy processing other stimuli, hampering correct storage of earlier stimuli.

The longer viewers have to wait before they know what brand is being advertised, the lower the average brand linkage scores as a result. And it is more important to hear than to see the brand name. Moreover, the total time that the brand or logo is on the screen also proves to increase brand linkage considerably.

Tests by Millward Brown show that viewers' attention fluctuates greatly during a commercial. If the brand is communicated at the very moment that attention has ebbed, brand linkage will suffer. This proves to be a frequent problem. The advertiser succeeds in intensifying attention for the actions, but at the moment that attention is at its peak, he forgets to say what the brand is. The result being that viewers can recount the commercial well, but do not have any idea what brand was involved. So whatever it is in the commercial that activates viewer attention, must be linked directly to the brand *and* to the message.

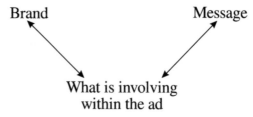

Brand   Message

What is involving
within the ad

Brown believes, probably correctly, that this is far more important than the number of seconds for which the brand is on the screen. It is a matter of 'creative highlighting' of the brand.

Clearly the product category which is being advertised also affects brand linkage. The more brands advertised in a category, the more difficult it is for viewers to link the right brand with the right commercial. Meaning that brands in small categories, or for unique products, have a relatively easier time. The nature of the brand itself also greatly affects brand linkage. New names, or existing names in new categories, do better on average, probably because they succeed in arousing greater interest. Difficult and abstract names (like combinations of letters) do not score well on brand linkage. Names which viewers can associate spontaneously and easily with a product category, like descriptive names, do better.

10.3   Established brand associations help

The final factor which influences brand linkage is the use of brand associations which people have built up in their memories – a certain advertising property (consistent use of a 'permanent' (well-known) personality, for instance) proves to be a tremendous help in achieving the right brand linkage.

However, that probably applies equally for other consistently used brand signals, such as a specific jingle or piece of music, a specific set colour, set design principles or tone of voice. Clearly these must be distinctive from what other advertisers use, especially when they belong to the same product category.

Klein (MSW) established that, measured over all product categories, an average of 22% of people who can remember a commercial, mention unique signals which help them to identify (and remember!) the right brand.

In view of the failure rate in achieving the correct brand linkage, this problem should certainly not be underestimated. Strong, unambiguous brand signals are always needed, and should be properly integrated in the advertisement or commercial. An effort should always be made to feature the brand as early on in the commercial as possible. If possible, repeat it several times, and support it auditively. Obviously, this is not an absolute condition for correct brand linkage, but it certainly helps.

This is particularly important with new campaigns. The longer a campaign has been running, the easier it becomes for the 'receiver' to identify the brand quickly; that is one of the main reasons to aim for continuity in advertising.

When a concept is used which builds up to a dénouement and a climax, care must be taken to give the brand a central place in the dénouement and to feature it for long enough. Brown (1986) also concludes that the crux of the matter is how well the brand is integrated in what happens in the commercial. Boring commercials result in low brand recall. But the same happens with interesting commercials, in which the interesting content does not relate to the brand. So, basically, a good connection must be made between the brand and the message, by way of the creative idea. If the brand is not part of the idea, brand linkage is in danger.

10.4   Brands in advertisements

With advertisements the brand should, if at all possible, be located in the photography and/or in the headline. If that is not possible or difficult to do, it should at least have another good location which is hard to avoid, even for cursory readers, with their scanning glances. Readers must know immediately who the advertiser is, without having to look around or think about it. If it is not immediately apparent from the illustration or the headline, the brand logo must have a prominent location. An analysis by Gallup & Robinson (Waring, 1986) shows that, if, under those circumstances, too small a brand logo is used, or if it is inconspicuous, brand linkage is 55% lower.

Brand linkage
(if brand not obvious from illustration or headline)

Big/prominent logo	112
Medium-sized logo	90
Small/inconspicuous logo	45
Average (index)	**100**

Source: Waring, 1986.

10.5   Cohesion

With press advertising it is true to say that the better the visual, headline and brand form a cohesive whole, the greater the chance of correct brand linkage. The use of double spread often entails specific problems. Art directors tend to treat them as twice one page: the fold is treated as a division between the left-and the right-hand page. Gallup & Robinson's analyses demonstrate that this usually results in a considerable loss of effectiveness. The effect of double spread is heightened by treating the entire space as a 'whole'. In other words:

- the main illustration encompasses the fold;
- the headline goes across the fold;
- the product or idea is depicted on both pages;
- the brand can also be identified on both pages.

10.6   From medium reach to advertising reach

We can take the *average* scores with a 30-second television commercial, as measured in particular by ASI in the United States, to get an idea of the extent to which medium reach is converted into effective persuasion in favour of the advertised brand. This is illustrated in the diagram 'Medium reach and effective persuasion' on the following page.

The starting point is the viewers who say they watch television (or whose viewing has been objectively ascertained with the 'peoplemeter', as it is called). As we saw in Chapter 3, of these viewers an estimated 35% are lost because they do something else during the commercial breaks, or zap over to another channel. So, in this case, our 'advertising reach' is about 65% of the medium reach. ASI ascertained that 41% of the viewers can remember having seen a certain commercial shortly after its transmission. So with 24% (65% – 41%) some sensory perception probably took place, without having left any traces in the memory, or of which the traces had 'evaporated' before the interview. This is probably pre-attentive perception.

Of the 41% of viewers who remember having seen the commercial, 18.5% (45% x 41%) can no longer remember the right brand. Again, this may be a matter of incorrect perception, but also of loss of memory. That leaves, on average, 22.5% of television viewers who can remember having seen the 30-second commercial and who are also able to name the correct brand. However, the commercial has not had a positive effect, in the sense of persuasion in favour of the advertised brand, with all these viewers. This is a sensitive area (what effect are we aiming for, and how can we measure it reliably?) and so it is not possible to provide soundly-based averages. We shall suffice with an unknown 'x' for effective communication.

Medium reach and effective persuasion

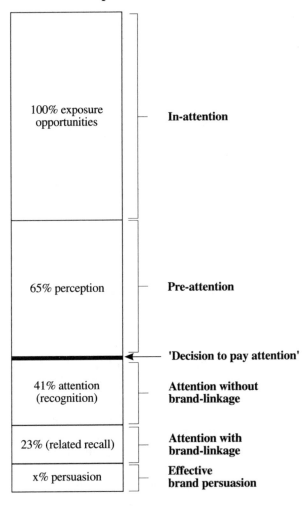

100% exposure opportunities — **In-attention**

65% perception — **Pre-attention**

'Decision to pay attention'

41% attention (recognition) — **Attention without brand-linkage**

23% (related recall) — **Attention with brand-linkage**

x% persuasion — **Effective brand persuasion**

Source: Giep Franzen based on ASI scores.

It is also possible to draw up a diagram, for example, for full-page full-colour ads in women's magazines, based on average scores known for advertisements in 'Margriet' and 'Libelle', as researched by the Dutch NIPO and Admedia (RRO-survey).

From medium exposure to ad-effectiveness:
Average performance 1/1 page full colour ads in women's magazines

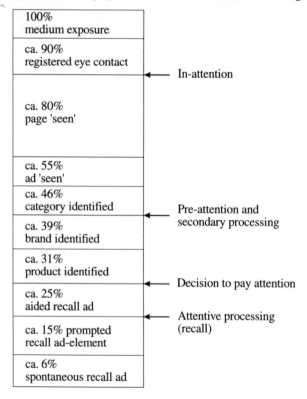

Source: RRO recognition and NIPO recognition and recall research scores in the Netherlands.

Eye-tracking research has taught us that eye contact with an advertising page averages about 90%. In one test situation readers themselves said they had 'opened' on average 80% of the pages. However, they only recognized 55% of the full page full-colour advertisements. So with 25% of the physical page contacts, nothing remained in the memory; exposure probably lasted less than 0.75 seconds. With 46% the product category was identified correctly, with 39% the brand and with 31% the article involved was recognised. All these scores are based on *recognition*.

Aided recall averaged 25%. So here the processing level was such that the respondent could still recall the advertisement, with some prompting. This probably entailed primary processing (level 4 in our arrangement). With 15% of the contacts, readers still remembered elements of the advertisement. And with 6% of the full page full-colour ads spontaneous recall was involved – i.e. processing at the 'deepest' level. These figures illustrate that 'advertising reach' is a tricky term. What does it relate to in our arrangement? The 90% eye contacts? The 55% recognised ads? Or the 39% in which the brand was registered? It is impossible to disconnect advertising reach from the level of advertising processing.

Part 3

Liking advertising

11 Advertising that is liked

For decades the prevailing view was that it was not important what consumers thought about advertising. The only important consideration was what they thought about the product or the brand, based on the information (claims) which that advertising succeeded in conveying to them about the product. Ad recall and brand attitude shifts were considered important. In those days ad likeability barely counted. In the sixties, Rosser Reeves (who devised the Unique Selling Proposition theory) even suggested that the liking of advertising would detract from sales.

"Liking be damned," he said. *"Effectiveness goes hand in hand with irritation."*

Influenced by the prevailing, purely rational 'multi-attribute-models' of consumer choice processes, prior to the eighties, scientific literature took hardly any notice of the influence consumer attitudes to advertising might have on their attitudes towards brands.

11.1   Likeability and market effects

Recent, wide-ranging research by ARF, aimed at validating various copy testing techniques, established the response to various questions in various research situations. Each time 5 pairs of two different commercials were used for one brand. The response was then compared with the known effect of the commercials in question. Performance in the market-place had established which commercial was effective in increasing sales, and which was not, or was less so. The question which correlated best with that effect proved to relate to liking of the advertising.

The respondents could indicate their appreciation by way of a 5-point scale:
- I like the ad very much;
- I like the ad;
- I neither like nor dislike the ad;
- I dislike the ad;
- I dislike the ad very much.

In 87% of the cases, these likeability scores could be used to predict the 'winning' commercial correctly. Correlations of other scores with the winning commercials were as follows:

1. 87%   likeability (overall reaction);
2. 87%   told me something new about the product;
3. 87%   spontaneous ad-recall;
4. 84%   overall brand rating;
5. 80%   this ad is enjoyable;
6. 73%   top-of-mind awareness;
7. 73%   tells me a lot about how the product works;
8. 73%   I learned a lot from this ad;
9. 60%   I find this advertising artistic;
10. 60%   main point communication.

Some correlation also existed between certain scores and the losing commercials:

73%   this advertising is boring;
60%   this ad doesn't give any facts, it just creates an image;
60%   this ad insults the intelligence.

One conclusion was that advertising that is appreciated (i.e. likeable) is more effective than advertising that is not very likeable. These tests received a great deal of criticism, especially due to the fact that far-reaching conclusions were drawn from only 5 cases. In view of the variety of advertising attributes which prove to influence likeability (more about this later), and the differences in the contribution these attributes make to the likeability of advertising for different product groups, some caution is indeed called for.

In a similar analysis by Kuse (1991) conducted with seven different pairs of effective and less effective commercials, no correlation whatsoever was found between likeability and effectiveness in the marketplace! Yet the analysis did establish a 100% correlation between persuasion scores and empirically-ascertained effectiveness. However, a third study, carried out in 1992 by Gallup & Robinson (Miller, 1992), based on 8 commercials, including 2 pairs, for which recall and persuasion scores were available, again confirmed the ARF's original findings. In particular, strong correlation was found between likeability and persuasion.

11.2   Likeability no guarantee for effectiveness

Back in 1985 the, meanwhile discontinued, 'Ogilvy Center for Research & Development', tested the effect of likeability of 73 commercials for 57 brands in 11 product categories. There proved to be a connection between likeability scores and brand attitude measurements (using the Mapes & Ross method) before and after exposure to the commercials. The results were as follows:

Brand preference:	I like the commercial			
	Total *100%*	A lot *100%*	Somewhat *100%*	Neutral *100%*
More	14.6%	20.1%	14.3%	9.8%
Less	3.3%	3.9%	4.8%	1.6%
Net difference	**+11.3%**	**+16.2%**	**+9.5%**	**+8.2%**

67% of the respondents who liked the advertising a lot proved to have no increase in brand preference, compared with 77% of those who liked it somewhat and 83% of the 'neutrals'.

The conclusion was that likeability is not a guarantee for persuasion, nor is it absolutely necessary or sufficient to achieve it, but that likeability certainly can reinforce the effect of advertising.

Biel (1990) suggests, in view of this research, that likeability does have a persuasive effect, because it directly affects our feeling about a brand.

"When we like the advertising, we are more inclined to like the brand as well. It is just a form of traditional emotional conditioning."

11.3   Ad likeability and reach

When people see a commercial they like, they are less inclined to 'zap' it away, or switch their attention to other stimuli in their surroundings. So likeability also influences the actual reach of advertising, and can help to 'deepen' the level of information processing.

MacKenzie and Lutz (1986) discovered in laboratory tests that attitude towards the ad (Aad) has a greater influence on brand attitude than brand perceptions. They claim that likeability probably also affects our attention. It would seem, at a very early stage in the chain of effects, to influence the duration and intensity of attention. They advise advertisers to ensure that they maximise the 'Aad', by allocating bigger production budgets, producing more commercials, and replacing them faster.

11.4   Likeability and recall

Since likeability has become such a focal point, many advertising research companies have extended their standard tests to include a question on likeability. They have also tried to expose the connection between likeability scores and other effectiveness criteria. That does not mean they reveal correlation with actual market effects, but with measurements of recall and shifts in attitude, amongst other things.

For example, the Dutch NIPO include in their standard recall test a question on the likeability and irritability of advertising. With 218 tested print ads, the following connection with spontaneous recall was found (Van Doorn, 1991):

Assessment of advertisement	Spontaneous recall
Likeable	20.3%
Iirritating	9.5%
Not likeable/not irritating	8.2%

GfK in Germany (Munzinger, 1992) found only a slight connection between likeability and recall with television commercials. ASI (Walker, 1991) also found a correlation between the two, which was admittedly significant, but not substantial. But if strong liking is involved, a strong correlation does, indeed, prove to exist. An analysis by McCollum Spielman Worldwide (MSW) (Klein, 1991) also led to the conclusion that liking is not a reliable predictor of recall scores. Though they did find a correlation with the recall of arguments.

11.5   Likeability and persuasion

On the whole, GfK discovered a very weak connection between likeability and persuasion scores. The connection did, however, prove to be relatively strong for foods and household products. Similarly, ASI did not find a strong correlation between liking and persuasion. McCollum Spielman (MSW) found a stronger correlation with persuasion than with recall, especially when emotional appeals were involved. But no significant connection was found for rational (hard-sell) approaches. However, a strong connection was apparent between 'disliking' and persuasion. If consumers really dislike a commercial, their brand attitude is adversely affected.

ASI discovered that when liking and recall coincide, there will be a stronger correlation with persuasion. GfK encountered higher likeability with commercials which score well for both recall and persuasion, and lower likeability if recall and persuasion are also low.

11.6   Likeability: attitude toward the ad

The questions used in these tests are, in fact, attitude measurements: do you find the advertising nice, pleasant, likeable, or not? It is an operationalisation of 'attitude towards the ad', a term which came on the scene in 1981 in more scientifically-oriented advertising literature (Mitchell and Olson). The term represented a correction to the prevailing multi-attribute choice models, supplying insight into consumers as largely holistic, emotionally-operating beings, rather than purely rational, analytical and algebraic.

In a review of advertising processing models, Ester Thorsen says on the subject ('Consumer Processing of Advertising', in 'Current Issues and Research in Advertising'):

> *"Those who accept the concept of the 'reason-driven consumer' may object to the idea that people's feelings about ads could influence their attitudes toward brands. Unless one assumes that a brand's attributes include its advertising, Aad models are inconsistent with multi-attribute models. MacKenzie, Lutz & Belch (1986) introduced the notion that Aad may affect Ab (Attitude toward the brand) directly or through brand-cognition."*

> She continues: *"These studies leave little doubt that the individual's response to the ad itself is a powerful predictor of ad-influence on brand-attitude."*

In the models of advertising effect a dichotomy now arose: instrumental (utilitarian) choice factors were joined by image factors. Scientific models of how advertising works translated the latter into the notion of Aad. They took the following form (Moore and Hutchinson, 1983):

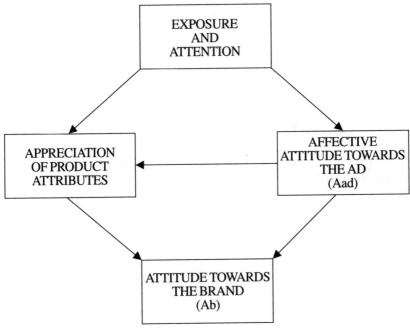

Source: Moore and Hutchinson, 1983.

In this way all non-rational factors in the notion of Aad were, in fact, combined. Clearly all manner of arguments were found against it, for instance that no distinction is made between the emotional associations with the brand which are generated by the advertisement, and the emotional reactions aroused by the attributes of the advertisement itself. It is (almost) impossible to separate reactions to the content, and to the form and execution of advertising. Both play a part in determining Aad.

In 1989 MacKenzie and Lutz carried out a laboratory test into the relative influence of Aad on Ab (Attitude towards the brand). Although the test only related to the effect of one advertisement (for a watch) and no generalisations can be made, they concluded that Aad in this case had a considerable and direct influence on Ab and, far less, on cognitive brand associations. Moreover, this slight effect on brand associations proved to have no effect on brand attitude. They concluded that, in that case, persuasion is more likely to result from advertising execution variables than from specific information on the product or the brand.

Mittal (1990) also used laboratory tests into the connections between Aad and the instrumental and emotional stimuli of a series of advertisements for shampoo and for wine. His conclusion was that Aad is probably the result of what is communicated in the advertisements (content) and how it is done (form and execution). He divides the relevant factors into three groups: utilitarian attributes, image attributes (including user associations) and Aad. His model now looks like this:

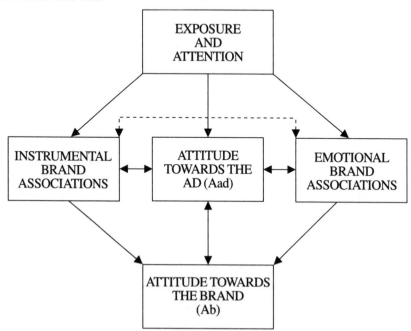

Source: Mittal, 1990 (the terms have been adjusted to those used in this publication).

One might, however, object to the fact that Aad in Mittal's case is once more a combination of reactions to the 'advertising as advertising', and of reactions to the specific (rational and emotional) brand stimuli which the advertising represents. It is a combination of appreciation for a certain aspect of the advertising (particularly the concept and the execution) and of the overall liking for the advertising in its entirety (content, and concept/execution).

11.7   Advertising attributes

If these are to be separated, a new term will be needed to designate the attributes of the advertising as such which contribute to the effect. However, in both advertising literature and scientific research, the attributes of advertising and the response to them are constantly intertwined. So they, too, will have to be separated in a model. We shall be using the terms 'advertising attributes' and 'viewer response' from here on. The various connections can be represented in the diagram 'Advertising attributes' on the next page.

Let us now review its various elements and their correlations.

11.8   Three kinds of stimuli

A reader or viewer whose attention has been activated by a piece of advertising, encounters three different kinds of stimuli:

1.   Instrumental stimuli;
2.   Symbolic stimuli;
3.   Advertising attributes: form and execution stimuli.

11.8.1   Instrumental stimuli

These include all information – verbal, visual or auditive – which relate to the concrete attributes, the effect and the effectiveness of the product or service. They are also termed 'functional' or 'utilitarian' stimuli.

11.8.2   Symbolic stimuli

The symbolic stimuli combine all stimuli representing psycho-sociological factors. There are several categories in this group.

Social factors

Stimuli representing certain types of users, their characteristics, characters and competencies – such as, their age, sex, social class, vitality, attractiveness, etc. We usually refer to them as stimuli with which we wish to establish or influence a 'consumer image'.

Advertising attributes

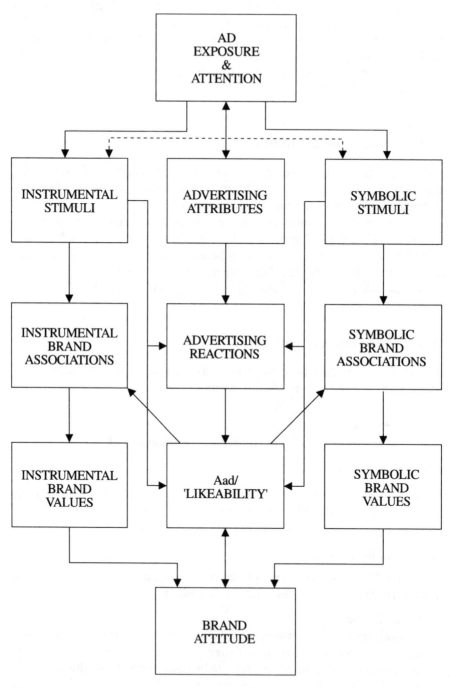

Source: Giep Franzen.

Emotional factors

Stimuli which enable use of the product or brand to be associated with certain specific feelings, like cheerfulness, companionship, warmth, intimacy, adventurousness, security, safety, etc.

Situational factors

Stimuli which enable use of the product to be associated with certain (social) situations or circumstances. For example, with various moments in a day, such as 'something for breakfast' or 'something to follow the main meal'. Or with special days. With situations within the home, or outside it. With situations involving a lot of people, or else with intimate moments when a person wants to enjoy something privately.

11.8.3 Advertising attributes as stimuli

All attributes relating to the form and execution of advertising 'as advertising' should be distinguished as a separate group. They include the use of music, jingles, and the many forms of humour. As well as the use of certain forms of conception, like presenters, slice-of-life, vignettes, demonstrations. Plus all kind of entertainment, like song, dance, slapstick and show.

Every advertising communication is a combination of these three groups of stimuli. Clearly they do not work in isolation. Advertising attributes, in particular, strongly influence the processing of the 'factual' instrumental and symbolic stimuli.

11.9   The formation of brand associations

Stimuli which are perceived and processed can result in the formation of associations with the brand. That is nearly always the advertiser's intention. But whether it does, in fact, occur depends on a number of conditions. Learning processes are involved. The level of advertising processing, repetition and the way in which the stimuli and the brand are juxtaposed (contiguity) determine whether and to what extent associations are formed.

11.10   Reactions to advertising

In our model the advertising attributes especially generate reactions to advertising. These reactions include: 'lively', 'boring', 'interesting', 'attractive', 'clear', 'original' and so on. This is a topic to which we shall return later. However, research shows that these reactions are also determined by the 'factual' stimuli presented in the advertising. A reader or 'receiver' reacts to the advertising as a total constellation of stimuli, so to the form and the content alike. Ultimately it leads to an overall appreciation for the ad (termed Aad by scientists and likeability by researchers). As we shall discover, that, too, is an evaluation based on the content of the advertising and of the advertising attributes. It is definitely not an evaluation based solely, for instance, on the entertainment character as advertising practitioners tend to imagine.

11.11 Values

When the instrumental or symbolic factors which are associated with a product or brand coincide with the consumers' views on what is personally or socially desirable, we refer to 'values'. A value represents a preferred way of 'being'. Values can relate to the product's or to the receiver's 'being'. In the former case we refer to instrumental (or functional) values. They are preferred entities, attributes and achievements of the product itself. In everyday advertising practice we usually call them 'product benefits'. In the latter case we usually refer to symbolic values, which comprise four different categories: expressive, impressive, central and social values.

11.11.1 Expressive values

These symbolic values may primarily relate to our relations with others, and how we should like others to see us. Expressive values cover being accepted, 'being somebody', being appreciated, giving and receiving affection, real friendship, togetherness and acquiring status and power.

11.11.2 Impressive values

Symbolic values can also focus on our self-perception; they are then called 'impressive values'. They cover things like feeling good about ourselves, a feeling of self-respect, self-realisation, relaxation, inner harmony, competence, the experience of pleasant things or sensations, hedonism and the enjoyment of life.

11.11.3 Central values

Symbolic values can also consist of ideal conceptions of life, those we should ultimately prefer for ourselves. They are, as it were, the highest ideals to which we aspire. And so they are termed 'central values'. Think, for instance, of freedom and independence, being spared misfortune, health, wisdom, an adventurous life, self-fulfilment and close ties with our nearest and dearest.

11.11.4 Social values

The last group are the 'social values', which are our ideals with respect to our personal surroundings and to society as a whole. They include world peace, national liberty, a clean environment, an 'honest' society.

Brand associations which coincide with the values of groups of consumers can be termed value associations.

11.12 Attitude to the brand

The attitude to the brand or brand likeability is primarily determined by the values which the brand represents in consumers' perception. Although, as we have already seen, the results of empirical research are not unanimous as regards the direct influence of ad-likeability on attitude to the brand, there are enough indications that it may well be the case.

11.13 Long-term effect

Brown (1991) developed an interesting theory to explain the differing results and the limited effects found, in particular, in American and German likeability studies. Almost all these studies measure reactions shortly (20 minutes or 24 hours) after exposure. So they measure what respondents have stored in their 'short-term memory', and how that immediately affects brand attitude. Consumers are asked to take decisions, on the spot. For that they need an argument, or at least something with which to rationalise their decision. And that is why 'new information' scores so well.

However, in everyday life, people often base their decisions on what is stored in the long-term memory – especially things that are experienced intensely and repeatedly. Pleasant things, in particular, are retained. If, at some stage, someone grows tired of the brand he uses, or has had a negative experience with it and would like to try a different brand, he will be more inclined to select one which is connected in his long-term memory with pleasant 'advertising experience'. What Brown implies is that the influence of advertising likeability on brand attitude is a long-term effect. It no doubt only comes about when a brand has been advertising for years in a way which the person concerned appreciates. It probably cannot be adequately measured with attitude-shift questions, immediately after exposure. You are not likely to switch brands after you have seen one nice commercial. Our own research methods would seem to be getting in our way.

11.14 No generalisations

We should always be aware that it is impossible to generalise for all product categories on issues of this type. And that is exactly what happens all too often. We try to establish whether likeability or Aad has a direct effect on the attitude to the brand (Ab), on the basis of one case only (McKenzie and Lutz, in 1989, based on a watch advertisement), or of only four cases (ARF copy research validity project) or of a larger number of purely fast-moving consumer goods (many analyses by large advertising research companies). A distinction is sometimes made between product categories (for instance between foods and non-foods), but these are not satisfactory a priori classifications in that area either.

After all, completely different configurations of consumer values are the focal point of choice processes for different product categories. Sometimes choice is based primarily on instrumental values. With another product they are not involved at all, and symbolic values will be what count. In our analyses we should always make that primary distinction between products. In addition, the degree of 'enduring product involvement' should be added as a criterion for classification. If we adopt a high and a low variant for each of these three product dimensions, we obtain a classification matrix as reproduced in the figure on the following page.

It contains six different squares which are determined by these dimensions. (The seventh and eighth would seem to be improbable options: i.e. the one standing for products which are neither instrumentally nor symbolically important, but are high involvement, and the one standing for instrumentally and symbolically important, but low involvement products.) Each square contains examples of products which are typical for the nature of that particular selection process. So, as far as each of these groups is concerned, we must now discover whether (or to what extent) ad likeability makes a direct contribution to generating or reinforcing a positive attitude to the brand (brand likeability).

11.15 'Approach' products

We cannot as yet find a definite answer from the available empirical research. But there are strong indications, to say the least, that likeability does indeed directly affect the attitude to the brand, especially with products with which symbolic values are an important factor in the selection process. Most products of this type are also called 'approach products'. They represent something enjoyable and include many foods, beverages and all kinds of products which we choose partly because of their aesthetic function. Advertising will almost always attempt to emphasise the pleasurable aspects of these approach products. We usually try to make it entertaining, aesthetic and appetising. The more successful we are, the more the advertising is appreciated, and the more effectively the choice of such product will be influenced.

11.16 'Avoidance' products

Products whose instrumental values are central in the selection process can largely be classed as 'avoidance products'. They usually help us to 'avoid' a problem, or help us solve it. Advertising will almost always try to emphasise the problem-solving attributes of these products. Consumers have to be reminded of things they prefer not to think about. The more effectively we do that, the less 'pleasant' the concomitant advertising is felt to be.

An analysis by MSW (1991) of 251 tested 30-second commercials revealed a clear influence of likeability on attitude to the brand with an emotional approach. It was particularly apparent with confectionery, desserts and cars. Yet no effect of likeability on attitude to the brand was noted with the hard-sell approach. We can assume that likeability also plays an important part with all products which do not perform either an instrumentally or a symbolically important function. For goods like raisins, peanuts, potato crisps, batteries, toilet paper, light bulbs and so on ad likeability may well be the main 'highway' towards influencing brand choice.

INSTRUMENTAL VALUES	–	+	–	+
SYMBOLIC VALUES	–	–	+	+
	1	2	3	4
HIGH PRODUCT INVOLVEMENT		Insurances, otc-drugs, investment funds, washing machines, computers, electric razors, 35mm cameras, economy cars, stereos, hair-colouring, etc.	Jewellery, watches, china, compact discs, perfume, wine, etc.	Luxury cars, outer apparel, furniture, running shoes, holidays, jeans, spectacles, etc.
	5	6	7	
LOW PRODUCT INVOLVEMENT	Glue, paper tissues, batteries, toilet-paper, motor-oil, peanuts, potato chips, lamps, garbage bags, raisins, chewing gum, etc.	Detergents, toothpastes, cleansers, denture adhesives, disinfectants, deodorants, shampoo, suntan-lotion, etc.	Popsicles, coffee, beer, cola, cigarettes, desserts, greeting cards, etc.	

12 Advertising reactions

Wells, in particular, was the one who developed, in the early sixties, the first standardised scale technique for measuring consumer reactions to advertising 'as advertising'. He used factor analysis of a large number of comments as the basis for twelve pairs of words in order to establish these reactions. This first 'EQ-scale' (EQ standing for emotional quotient), with a later version termed 'son of EQ scale', was used to measure three basic factors:

- attractiveness;
- meaningfulness; and
- vitality.

In a later version (1967) of this technique by the Heinrich Bauer Foundation in Germany, a scale technique was devised with 18 advertising attributes, which could be condensed into 5 factors.

Factor 1:   Vitality
- fresh;
- lively;
- beautiful;
- attractive;
- moves.

Factor 2:   Serenity – 'stationariness'
- quiet;
- serious.

Factor 3:   Age/boredom (negative appeal)
- old;
- boring;
- ordinary;
- not beautiful.

Factor 4:   Meaningfulness
- meaningful;
- convincing;
- interesting.

Factor 5:   Implausibility (negative appeal)
- not credible;
- not serious;
- not significant;
- not clear.

These factors could be depicted in diagram form as follows:

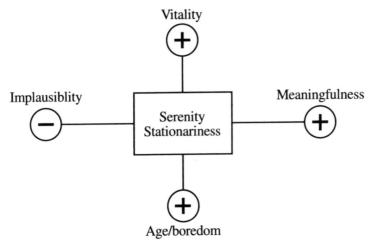

Source: Heinrich Bauer Stiftung, 1967.

Experience with measuring instruments of this type, both in the United States, by Wells, and in Germany, by Bauer, showed that there was a significant correlation between recall scores on the one hand (proved impact) and EQ scores on the other. The 'meaningfulness' factor, in particular, proved to have a great effect on recall.

In 1971 Wells developed a measuring instrument for ascertaining reactions to television commercials. He started from a pool of 1,000 words or comments, and using a series of factor analyses, ultimately reached a set of questions with which 6 basic factors could be measured:

- humour;
- dynamism;
- sentimentality
- uniqueness;
- irritation; and
- personal relevance.

In 1984 Der Stern (Argus test) readjusted the Bauer scale somewhat, to produce seven factors: the 'MMA-items' as they are called (R. Danke, 1986):

Factor 1:   Personal relevance
- meaningful;
- demanding;
- convincing.

Factor 2:   Dull, boring
- dull;
- boring.

Factor 3:   Cheerful, lively
- cheerful;
- lively.

Factor 4:   Harmony, emotion
- harmonious;
- emotional.

Factor 5:   Implausibility
- not serious;
- not credible;
- not clear.

Factor 6:   Inappropriateness
- irrelevant;
- incomprehensible;
- unrelated.

Factor 7:   Originality, conspicuousness
- something different;
- striking.

Meanwhile Schlinger (1979) had also developed a Viewer Response Profile with which to evaluate television commercials. In 1984 it was adjusted by the University of Leiden for Admedia, for research into reactions to print advertising. Since then it has been part of the Dutch RRO (Reclame Reactie Onderzoek – Advertising Reaction Research), operated by Admedia. It resulted in 24 statements. Factor analysis of the scores of 33 Dutch magazine ads tested with this set of questions (sample 4,533 persons) produced four factors:

Factor 1:   Motivation
- I shall certainly buy it sometime.
- This ad ties in well with what I need.
- This ad was about a product that I should like to try sometime.
- This ad gave me an idea.
- I fancy it.
- It is a brand I'd certainly recommend to others.
- I picked up some new information from the ad.
- This ad appealed to me.

Factor 2:   Likeability
- I found this ad amusing.
- I enjoyed looking at this ad.
- This ad gives you a pleasant feeling.

- This ad appealed to me.
- It is an ad that sticks in your mind.

Factor 3:   Irritation
- I found this ad confusing.
- I found this ad hard to understand.
- I found this ad far-fetched.
- This ad irritated me.
- I found this ad boring.
- I have seen this so often that I'm starting to find it boring.

Factor 4:   Attitude to the brand
- It is a reliable brand.
- This brand gives value for money.
- Other products with this brand are of good quality.
- It is a brand I would certainly recommend to others.

The four factors account for almost 60% of the total variance in response patterns to the statements. The most important factor, accounting for 36% of variance, is that of motivation. It reflects the reader's interest in the product and the advertisement. The person concerned wants to buy the product, it ties in with what he/she needs, or else the advertisement gives him/her an idea. The next factor is likeability, accounting for 10%. It comprises entertainment, enjoyment, amusement. Irritation as a factor explains 8% of the variance, covering alienation, confusion and over familiarity. The last on the list is attitude to the brand. The statements relate to the brand's reliability, value and quality. Almost 5% of the variance is accounted for by this factor. Upon closer analysis, irritation can be divided into two components, one accounting for 'alienation' and 'confusion', the other for 'boredom/over familiarity'. Comparison with a factor analysis carried out in 1984 produces the following hypotheses:

- Reactions to information or relevant news in advertisements would especially seem to be prompted by subjective considerations. "Ties in with what I need", "I should like to try it", but also "gave me an idea".
- Irritation consists to some extent of lack of credibility, but also to some extent of a lack of clarity, and thirdly of boredom, because the ad in question has been seen so often.
- The factor of 'likeability' seems to have lost importance to that of 'motivation', which has actually increased in importance. Evidently people pay less attention to the appearance of an ad, looking for elements which tie in with subjective needs. A nice picture on its own is no longer sufficient, it must tell something that connects up with the consumer himself (or herself).

12.1 Five basic factors

Since Schlinger's Viewer Response Profile came about in 1979, a whole series of tests have again been carried out in the United States with a view to cataloguing viewer response to television commercials, and to tracing these back, to essential basic factors, by means of factor analysis. The two most recent and comprehensive analyses were carried out by O&M (Biel and Bridgewater, 1990) and Aaker and Stayman (1990).

The O&M analysis comprised 80 commercials, a total sample of 1277 respondents and 133 respondents to each commercial. Aaker and Stayman's test covered 80 commercials and a sample of 300 respondents per commercial. Both used the same Viewer Response Profile stimuli, which Schlinger had developed earlier. Both not only measured ad-likeability, but also its connection with advertising attributes and response to the advertising. When reduced to five basic factors, the two tests came up with practically identical findings. Admittedly they are 'labelled' differently, but the make-up is largely the same. The factors are:

O&M	Aaker & Stayman
Meaningful	Informative/believable
Rubs the wrong way	Irritating/silly/worn out
Ingenuity	Amusing/clever
Energy	(Lively)
Warm	Warm

The five basic factors in each of the two foregoing analyses represent the following viewer responses:

12.1.1 Viewer response – O&M study 1990: 5-factor solution

Meaningful	Worth remembering
	Effective
	Easy-to-forget
	Pointless
	True-to-life
	Believable
	Convincing
	Informative
Rubs the wrong way	Seen-a-lot
	Worn out
	Irritating
	Familiar
	Phoney

Ingenuity	Clever
	Imaginative
	Amusing
	Original
	Silly
	Dull
Energy	Lively
	Fast-moving
	Appealing
	Well-done
Warm	Gentle
	Warm
	Sensitive

12.1.2 Viewer response – Aaker and Stayman, 1990: 5-factor solution

Informative/believable	Informative
	Believable
	True-to-life
	Worth remembering
	Convincing
Irritating/silly	Irritating
	Silly
	Pointless
	Phoney
	Dull
	Forgettable
Worn-out	Seen-a-lot
	Familiar
	Worn-out
Amusing/clever	Imagination
	Clever
	Original
	Lively
	Amusing
Warm	Gentle
	Sensitive
	Warm

The results of all the efforts over the last decades to chart readers' and viewers' responses to advertisements and television commercials actually have a great deal in common. Whether five, or six, or possibly seven basic factors are ultimately opted for, mainly depends on what demands correlation is expected to meet. But the burning question continues to be: to what extent does each of the factors influence attitude towards the advertising?

13 What determines likeability?

Biel and Bridgewater (1990) were the first to research the connection between viewer responses and ad likeability. Their conclusion was that the overall contribution each of the basic factors makes towards explaining ad-likeability differs from one product category to another. Consequently, no hard and fast conclusions can be drawn. Nevertheless, without completely ignoring these differences, we can say something about the importance of each basic factor. Biel and Bridgewater's analysis revealed that the most important factor for ad-likeability is *meaningfulness*. And that tallies with the correlation with aided recall, which had been established years before by both Wells and Bauer.

The second factor is whether or not something possesses negative characteristics - so *'rubs the wrong way'*. The third is *liveliness*. Ingenuity did not apparently contribute much towards ad-likeability in these tests, and nor did *warmth*. The slight influence of ingenuity, which would seem to coincide with what advertising circles call 'entertainment' is an unexpected finding, to say the least.

Each of the five factors made the following relative contribution to the ad likeability of the specific product groups (expressed as standardised betas).

Relative contributions of the basic factors to ad likeability

	Foods and beverages (n = 34)	Non-foods (n = 42)
Meaningful	.71	.54
Energy	.50	.36
Ingenuity	.28	.23
(Doesn't) rub the wrong way	(.24)	(.52)
Warmth	.18	.22
(standardised betas)		

Source: Attributes of likeable television commercials; A Biel and C.A. Bridgewater, Journal of Advertising Research, June/July, 1990.

Altogether, with foods, 73% of the variance in ad-likeability was explained, with non-foods 81%. Let us now analyse each of the factors in turn.

13.1   Factor 1: Meaningfulness

By far the most important factor explaining likeability is the extent to which the commercial is *meaningful* for the viewer. This applies to both commercials for foods and for non-foods (household goods, pharmaceuticals and toiletries).

Meaningfulness is primarily determined by the informative content, probably not only the factual product information, but also 'newness'. It is also important whether the commercial is *true-to-life*.

Credibility is also an important component, which, in turn, is tied in with information presented in a true-to-life way. Commercials which score well for meaningfulness are also felt to be believable. People find commercials which meet these requirements worth remembering. The commercials are not pointless, and so are judged to be *effective*.

These results largely coincide with an earlier factor analysis of pre-test results of hundreds of television commercials, tested over a period of 10 years by SSC&B (Moldovan, 1985). There, 'credibility' proved to be by far the most important factor in explaining the persuasive effect of the commercials: 72% of the variance in persuasion scores. The credibility factor in that survey was a combination of realism, reasonableness, openness, credibility and 'convincingness' of the commercials. *What it, in fact, amounts to is the extent to which an advertisement or commercial is felt to be a realistic and plausible reflection of real life, to be 'true', reliable and believable.* This factor proved to have almost identical importance for all tested product categories, and throughout the entire 10-year period which the survey covered. Laboratory tests (MacKenzie and Lutz, 1989) show that the credibility of advertising is partly determined by the advertiser's reputation. So not only does likeability affect brand attitude, but brand attitude also affects likeability.

A second factor which emerges from the SSC&B analysis is what Moldovan calls 'clarity'. It relates just as much to the informative content as to the unambiguous processing of that content. It consists of the following aspects: information, good presentation of the product, conveys the message well, and is clear. However, clarity in this sense is much less important than credibility.

13.1.1 Personal relevance

The factor of 'meaningfulness', which emerges in the O&M and Aaker and Stayman analyses, also contains a component which can be termed 'personal relevance': the commercials to which this applies are considered to be 'effective', 'worth remembering', 'not easy to forget'.

The same component occurred as an independent principal factor in a Leo Burnett (Olson, 1985) analysis of the trial-generating effect of 65 launch commercials. Once more the same Viewer Response Profile scales were used on which O&M's and Aaker and Stayman's measurements were based. We shall return to this in the chapter on trial-generating advertising.

We also know from other research that commercials for new products score higher on 'personally-relevant information' than advertising for existing products. The fact that something new is being announced is apparently appreciated as such. Products which have been around for a time obtain higher scores in this respect when product or packaging improvements are introduced or a new use is demonstrated. An analysis of 400 cases in the IRI data bank, examining the effect of an increase in advertising expenditure with established brands, revealed the use of 'new messages' as the main factor for success. We shall return to this later. The new information need not be anything crucial, but must be something interesting, information which is of use to viewers and which can give them a fresh idea.

The 'personal relevance' factor also emerged in the SSC&B analysis as one of the factors explaining the persuasion of commercials. It was represented by the following comments:

- got a kick out of seeing it;
- would enjoy seeing it again;
- it was personal and intimate;
- feel I have experienced the same thing;
- catches my attention;
- appeals to people like myself.

This factor expresses the extent to which viewers 'feel along with' the commercial, put themselves into that situation, play a kind of imaginary part in the commercial. Commercials score well for personal relevance if they portray personalities, situations and events with which viewers can identify. Commercials can also get very low scores in this area – something which often happens if a viewer resists what he sees.

In short, the 'meaningfulness' factor can be said to consist of relevant information which is communicated in a credible, and, in particular, a human way. Meaningful commercials talk to people about other (special and nice) people. They show how they go through life, how they experience products, and how they solve minor problems. They do this in a way with which viewers can empathise, and so is credible. And they do it in a way which is interesting visually and appeals to the imagination.

13.2   Factor 2: Underestimating viewers

The second factor which influences ad-likeability is *underestimation of viewers*. It is practically the opposite to 'meaningfulness'. It has a very negative effect on likeability. The commercials in question are ones people dislike. In fact, 'dislikeability' would be an appropriate term here.

There are various possible causes. In the Aaker and Stayman survey, this factor is divided into two components: 1) dull and 2) irritating, silly. The dull commercials are the ones which people have 'seen before'. That need not really be so, but may be due to the use of a *worn-out cliché solution*. It has something of 'oh, not that again!'

A test with 529 television commercials (Aaker and Bruzzone, 1985), amongst other sources, pinpointed the following factors which caused irritation:

- *The product itself*, together with the way in which it is advertised. There are still subjects which can be sensitive and with which people do not wish to be confronted too specifically: sanitary towels, ointment for haemorrhoids, contraceptives, and funeral insurance. Strong emphasis on the packaging or the effect of the product can cause irritation.

- *The personalities in the commercial:* people who are not likeable, or people who are not acceptable in the context of the product.

- *The situation* in which a product is used or demonstrated is unnatural, unlikely or exaggerated.

- *Something unpleasant happens to the people in the commercial:* a relationship (mother-daughter, man-wife) is threatened, someone is insulted because of his/her appearance, or someone has an ailment.

- *The message* is worn out (a detergent that washes whiter), implausible, 'over promising' (one drop of Dreft is enough to wash up all the dishes of a big restaurant) or makes people feel uncomfortable (insurance to meet funeral expenses).

- *The reasoning* is illogical or the arguments are exaggerated. The commercials are felt to be unreal or exaggerated.

In commercials subtle moments of irritation sometimes also exist which could easily be avoided or removed if one is aware of them. They may relate to the choice of actors, in relation to the product, or to the way they interact. Irritation can also be avoided by:

- creating a cheerful mood, for example with music. In the Aaker & Bruzzone study commercials with music proved to have a lower than average score for irritation;

- creating a warm feeling, for example using children or animals;

- choosing a believable presenter;

- using a mild form of humour. There are indications that exaggerated humour causes irritation;

- useful information, realistically presented.

So, underestimation has the opposite effect to a true-to-life approach and credibility. With underestimation, viewers feel they are not taken seriously or are even being tricked. In the O&M study this factor was given the label 'rubs the wrong way'. It is a factor which has a very negative influence on advertising effectiveness. Not only because it may produce a negative brand-attitude, but also because it affects the advertising reach (due to mechanical zipping and zapping, or psychological zapping).

13.3   Factor 3: Liveliness

One of the attributes which distinguishes television commercials from print ads, is their movement. The experience of the intensity of this movement, together with the pace of the sound, forms the foundations for the third basic factor making a substantial contribution to ad-likeability: the liveliness or energy of the commercials. It is less important than meaningfulness. Viewers feel stimulated by the advertising. It also emerged as an independent factor in the SSC&B and Leo Burnett analyses. In the former it stands for the reactions: fast, short, interesting, holds my attention. In the Leo Burnett analysis: people in the commercial get my attention, the commercial is enthusiastic, amusing and fun to watch and listen to.

13.4   Factor 4: Originality

This is the factor which many advertising people rate highest, though the O&M study shows that it does not influence ad-likeability substantially.

This was also established in the extensive survey by ARF into the validity of copy testing methods: the influence of 'cleverness' – often the main component of originality – also turned out to be of less importance. As far as viewer response is concerned, the characteristics which scored well on this factor, apart from *originality*, were especially *imagination, ingenuity and amusement*. However, in an analysis by GfK (Saupe 1991) originality does prove to have some effect on likeability.

It is dangerous to use the word 'entertainment' in this context, because it has all kinds of meanings of its own in advertising circles. Earlier research (Schlinger, 1979) revealed that 'entertainment' had a far wider meaning for television viewers than mere amusement. Some commercials were felt to be 'entertaining' because they used popular personalities, or because the situations portrayed were rated positively. For consumers entertainment equals a pleasant experience occasioned by the commercials, an opportunity to smile for a moment or to be pleasantly diverted. It is an evaluative term, with a broad content.

These, and other findings from the studies in question, suggest that commercials in which meaningful information is less important than, or even sacrificed for 'originality', cannot count on much liking from consumers. Originality can help, if added to meaningful information, and if it succeeds in 'wrapping' the information in an original and relevant way. Originality at the expense of content is counterproductive.

13.5   Factor 5:   Warmth

The fifth factor is human warmth. Aaker, Stayman and Hagerty (1986) defined these emotions as the direct or indirect experience of a romantic, family or friendly relationship. Warmth is a positive feeling of limited intensity (compared, for example, with anger or disgust) and is measured with words like 'gentle', 'sensitive' and 'warm'. Most commercials which evoke this feeling depict friendship or family ties, or a relationship between humans and animals, or among animals.

'Warmth' is closely connected to a feeling of happiness and pride. When students were asked to recall happy moments, they especially referred to pleasant times spent with other people, such as reunions with people they were fond of and had not seen for some time (Smith and Elsworth, 1985). Commercials in this category do, in fact, tend to be those featuring people who feel good about themselves.

Commercials with animals make the greatest contribution to ad-likeability (so even greater than meaningful commercials). But once they had been taken out of the O&M sample, warmth actually proved to have little influence on ad-likeability. This might be because they contain insufficient relevant product information (something which tends to characterise these commercials). But Aaker and Stayman also found that, with repeated exposure, the level of response does seem to increase with commercials of this type. Which suggests the effect might be greater in the longer-term than when measured immediately after exposure in the test situation.

13.6   Other factors

13.6.1 Product category

We have already seen from O&M's study that ad-likeability is connected with the product category which is being advertised. This is stronger for foods and beverages than for household goods, pharmaceuticals and toiletries.

13.6.2 Advertiser/brand

MacKenzie and Lutz' (1989) laboratory tests revealed that ad-likeability and liking for the advertiser (or advertised brand) are also closely interconnected. The author is also aware of that, from the large amount of qualitative research carried out in the Netherlands: advertising for the supermarket chain, Albert Heijn, and the coffee, tea and tobacco company, Douwe Egberts, is generally greatly appreciated in the Netherlands, just because it relates to Albert Heijn and Douwe Egberts. This would seem to be connected with the use of brands: people start to like what they use, and probably also the advertising concerned. In our diagram 'Advertising attributes' (as shown on page 130), this means that brand attitude (Ab) has an effect (positive or negative) on the attitude to the advertisement (Aad).

13.6.3 Interestingness

Numerous surveys pinpoint 'interestingness' as an important factor in ad-likeability. NIPO, in particular, used this term in its standard recall test, noting that it correlates strongly with recall scores. Berlijne established a strong connection between the two even in 1960. 'Interestingness' would seem to be an overarching factor of appreciation, which does not coincide with ad-likeability, but is related to it. It is not clear with which of the O&M and Aaker and Stayman subfactors it corresponds.

13.6.4 Uniqueness

An attribute of advertising which is not explicitly included in the lists of questions in the studies we have referred to, and has not emerged as a background factor either, is uniqueness. Schlinger's first version of the 'Viewer Response Profile' questionnaire did include the factor 'distinctiveness'. It stood for 'unusual, different from the competitors' advertising, unique, distinctive'. This factor was left out of later versions of VRP.

However, in a survey among advertising experts into the question why so much award-winning advertising also proves to be successful in the market-place (Green, for Leo Burnett, 1990), uniqueness did emerge as the most important factor. These experts defined it as: 'A new look at a product, a new angle. The presentation of the product or its attributes in a way which has not been used before. The discovery of a new relationship between the product and its environment. An idea which shows the product as if this were the first time.'

In this sense it is the opposite to 'rubs the wrong way', which is, after all, a combination of the aspects 'familiar', 'seen-a-lot' and 'worn out', amongst others. It probably largely coincides with the factor of originality, which combines the aspects 'clever, amusing, imaginative and original'. As we have seen, this factor plays a relatively minor part on viewers' liking of commercials.

13.6.5 Music

In an analysis of the test results of 965 German commercials tested by GfK (Saupe, 1992) music emerged as the factor which most influences likeability. This often relates to the use of popular melodies which make people feel good. The more the music is enjoyed, the more effective the commercial, both as regards recall and persuasion.

13.7   Summary

The enormous value of the studies we have quoted is not primarily the fact that they might add new dimensions to what we already knew. Many experienced advertising people may be feeling they have encountered nothing completely new. However, the great merit of the analyses is that, yet again, they underline what it is all about, and put an end to all kinds of highly personal views. They show that viewer appreciation of the advertising itself can be an important factor for advertising effectiveness. And they once more confirm the prime importance of personally-relevant information, which is communicated in a human, relevant way and not subordinated to forced originality.

14 How important is likeability?

As we have already seen, the results of analyses relating to the influence of likeability are not unanimous. Perhaps because a 'universal truth' was looked for, and too little attention paid to the connection between the factors which determine likeability and the influence of various likeability factors on advertising effectiveness for various types of products.

14.1 Meta analysis

Brown and Stayman (1992) conducted a meta analysis with 60 articles describing laboratory tests into the effects of 'Aad'. They ascertained that Aad did indeed have a direct effect on the attitude towards the brand ('Ab'), but that this effect should not be overestimated. In fact, they reached the same conclusion as most advertising research companies based on their empirical findings. But Brown and Stayman did discover that Aad had a distinct effect on brand cognition and so a pronounced positive effect on Ab. So likeability does indeed affect advertising processing in a very positive way. They also observed that the product category, existing brand attitudes and the medium influence Aad.

At all events, likeability is important in the very first stage of advertising processing. If consumers do not like an advertisement or commercial they will immediately switch their attention to something else, at least with print advertising. And with television advertising they will be inclined to zap or else also switch their attention ('psychological zapping'). That risk is especially pronounced if 'dislikeability' comes into it. If advertising is boring, childish or irritating, and a viewer feels he is being underestimated, he will turn his back on the advertising and switch off mental reception to an increasing extent (MSW). However, if positive likeability is involved it can lead to 'deeper' processing. MSW, in an analysis of 251 commercials, noted that the more consumers like a commercial, the more they remember of it. Saupe (1992) further analysed the likeability effects of 965 commercials tested in Germany by GfK. He, like MSW, reached the conclusion that likeability did not have a pronounced effect on awareness and persuasion scores, in measurements of all commercials. MSW noted that likeability was responsible for 11% of the variance in these scores, with influence on persuasion being greater than on awareness. Saupe discovered that awareness scores with commercials with high likeability were 15% higher, on average, than those of commercials with low likeability.

However, when specific product groups are considered, the differences become greater. Saupe's analysis in particular reveals that it is less a matter of whether a commercial is likeable than what is likeable about it. That is what determines whether likeability affects the advertising effect in the specific category.

14.2   Two kinds of likeability

It is in fact a good idea to split likeability, as Baldinger suggested, into two sub-variables, which relate to the main basic factors:

1.   message likeability;
2.   execution likeability

14.2.1 Message likeability

This especially covers the component of 'meaningfulness' which Wells encountered back in 1960. It also emerged in almost all later tests and analyses as one of the most important likeability factors. It relates to the information content, the 'newness' of the information, its relevance for the readers or viewers, and its credibility and convincingness. In short: "what does this product have to say, and what's in it for me?"

14.2.2 Execution likeability

This relates to likeability of the way in which the advertising is made, its liveliness and inventiveness, and the good feelings it arouses. As well as likeability of specific advertising attributes: the music, actors, presenters, situations and actions. These two sub-variables of likeability differ in the influence they have on the effectiveness of campaigns for various product categories.

14.3   When instrumental values are important

With products which perform an essentially instrumental function the likeability of the message is mainly important. If we present likeable new information and succeed in doing so in a credible and convincing way, consumers appreciate it. If, however, we use non-functional originality, it can increase likeability – but without achieving better persuasion. The advertising attributes for which the commercial is liked do not have much connection with the product or product benefits in that case. Higher likeability will not contribute to persuasion either. When instrumentally high-involvement products were involved, like trucks, capital goods, financial services and audio/video products , Saupe (1992) encountered practically no correlation between likeability and advertising processing. He also noted that with campaigns with low likeability scores, the vast majority entailed rational approaches. If viewers reject a message, it also has an adverse effect on likeability.

14.4   When symbolic values are important

For products with which symbolic values play an important part, execution likeability is important, if not essential. With typically symbolic low-involvement products, like toiletries, beverages and foods, Saupe (1992) ascertained a clear correlation between likeability and advertising effect, particularly on awareness scores. MSW also noted a stronger connection between likeability and awareness and persuasion scores when emotional appeals were used than with rational approaches. They also observed that if 'dislikeability' is involved at the same time as emotional approaches, it has a distinctly negative effect on persuasion. Saupe ascertained that emotional approaches were very much in the majority with commercials with high likeability scores.

14.5   When neither instrumental nor symbolic values are important

When products are involved for which neither instrumental nor symbolic values are very important in the choice process, execution likeability is probably of great importance for advertising effectiveness.

The main thing is to get attention for a product for which people's involvement is very low. Moreover, persuasion cannot really be based on product attributes or symbolic associations. The only remaining option is to create liking for the brand by means of attractive advertising, through the process of 'classical' conditioning.

Part 4

Persuasion

15 Brand awareness

The ultimate goal of all advertising is to influence people's behaviour. When advertising for branded articles is involved this relates to influencing *choice* behaviour. When a choice actually has to be made in the shop, a consumer is faced with the task of combining the knowledge he has stored in his memory with the current information stimuli (price, the salesman's recommendations, etc.) which are reaching him from his environment. He will base his choice and the actual purchase on this.

Advertising has the task of pre-programming that choice as much as possible, ensuring that the brand is present in the consumer's memory in such a way that it exercises the maximum positive effect at the moment that the decision to buy is reached.

Three aspects are decisive in this process:

1. the salience of the brand in the memory, thereby presenting itself as a 'candidate': i.e. *brand awareness*;

2. the *linkage of the brand* to the product category;

3. the perceived differences compared with alternative brands: i.e. *positioning*.

Questions as to how the selection process eventually turns out and which strategies consumers pursue do not fall within the scope of this book. But it is worth examining what is known about how these three basic aspects work.

15.1   Connection with behaviour

Over the years, research has shown that a strong correlation exists between brand awareness and buying behaviour. The Strategic Planning Institute (Burke and Schoeffler, 1980) suggests that higher brand awareness leads to a higher market share, and the Profit Impact of Market Strategy (PIMS) data bank also repeatedly notes a strong correlation between brand awareness and market share.

Clearly it is not a one-sided causal connection: the two influence each other. The degree of influence depends, amongst other things, on the type of product, what stage the brand has reached in its life-cycle, and its market share. That decides whether many or few people have the product in their homes and whether they use the brand every day or once a year.

Stapel and Van Doorn (1991) illustrate this connection using the following diagram, which was compiled from tracking research in the product categories of vacuum cleaners, colour televisions and electric coffee makers.

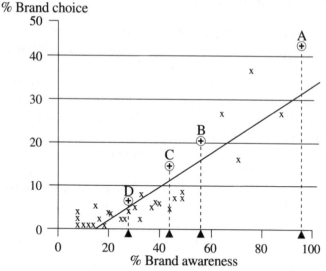

Source: NIPO Brand Monitor, Stapel and Van Doorn, 1991.

In 24 out of 28 product categories which NIPO followed in brand monitor research, there proved to be a correlation between brand awareness and buying behaviour of over 0.90. In the other four categories the lowest was still 0.83, and the average over all categories was 0.94.

Obviously, it continues to be a moot point – which came first, brand awareness or buying behaviour. Cause and effect can only be separated if we are able to follow the development of both elements for the same person over a longer period. The author knows of little research on the subject. A longitudinal study in Spain (Léon and Olàbarri, 1992) revealed that, when respondents were asked about the brands they knew in a particular product category, in 51.6% of the cases the brand first mentioned proved to be the brand that was subsequently purchased. The percentage decreases somewhat in time, but not much. When measured for a number of product categories during a six-month period, 'top mention' correctly predicted 40% of the subsequent brand purchases.

In the same survey, the advertising salience share (the share a brand has in a person's ability to remember, unaided, an important element of any previous campaign for a brand in a given product category) proved to have a very strong correlation with the brand's share in subsequent purchases of people concerned. In 4 out of 5 product categories the correlation varies between 0.77 and 0.99! Not surprisingly, the researchers recommend measurement of the mental share of the brand advertising.

In the NIPO analysis in the Netherlands quoted above, brand awareness is very closely linked with the factor 'good advertising' (a consumer's general assessment of advertising for a brand). The connection between brand awareness and brand loyalty runs through the (necessary) intermediary stages of 'availability', 'top quality' and 'value for money'.

The structure of the connection and the scope of the causal effects are apparent from the following diagram.

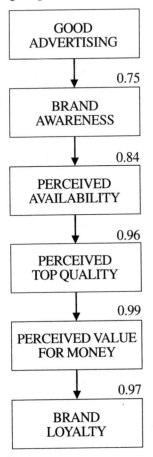

Source: NIPO Brand Monitor.

15.2 Brand mind-position

Woodside and Wilson (1985) introduced the term 'brand mind-position', meaning the specific spontaneous awareness of a brand. In an open-ended question into which brands a person knows in a category, is the brand named as the first, second or third? Or is it not named spontaneously at all? In a test (of modest scope) they established with seven brands the connection between the brand mind-position and propensity to purchase measured by means of the 'constant-sum' method (division of 10 points among the brands).

Brand mind-position and probability to buy

Brand mind-position	Burger King	McDonald's	Wendy's	Coca-Cola	Pepsi Cola	Banker's Trust	C&S Bank
				Propensity to purchase			
First	7.1	7.1	6.8	8.2	8.8	8.0	7.1
Second	5.4	5.1	6.0	6.0	5.5	5.4	5.2
Third	4.3	2.6	5.4	5.0	5.0	3.8	3.5
Total	**5.6**	**5.3**	**6.2**	**6.9**	**5.6**	**5.1**	**4.9**

Source: Woodside and Wilson,
Effects of consumer awareness of brand advertising on preference, 1985.

The connection between the top-of-mind advertising awareness (brand in question first to be named in reply to the question: have you recently seen advertising for product...?) and the brand mind-position was also examined.

Top-of-mind advertising awareness and brand mind-position

Top-of-mind advertising awareness	Brand mind-position	Burger King	McDonald's	Wendy's	Coca-Cola	Pepsi Cola	Banker's Trust	C&S Bank
					Brand			
Yes	First	80	71	44	74	43	67	50
	Second	13	14	24	16	29	0	33
	Third	7	14	32	10	14	33	0
No	First	10	44	6	40	4	24	24
	Second	38	26	22	24	38	19	23
	Third	52	34	72	36	58	57	53

Source: Woodside and Wilson, 1985.

As a result of this test Wilson and Woodside were able to draw up the diagram ('Advertising exposure and the propensity to purchase') for the correlations.

Of course, we still have not answered the question: which aspects of advertising contribute to top-of-mind advertising awareness and to brand mind-position, and by how much.

The connection between advertising and resulting brand awareness is best measured from a zero base. Indeed, many tests have confirmed this connection for new products. Market simulation models like Assessor, BASES (developed by Burke) and NEWS (developed by BBDO) are based on it too.

The connections are more difficult or impossible to follow for established brands with high spontaneous awareness. However, there is no reason to assume that they do not exist.

Advertising exposure and the propensity to purchase

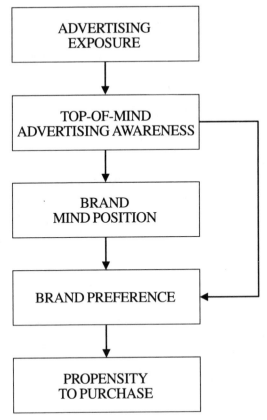

Source: Woodside and Wilson, 1985.

Brand awareness, which is termed 'salience' in psychology, and described by Moran (1990) as 'mental presence', is the result of the sum of received and registered communicative stimuli relating to a brand, both quantitatively and qualitatively. In that sense, brand stimuli in the pre-attentive stage also make a contribution, but presumably only a marginal one.

Some advertising does little more than ensure brand exposure at a low level of attention. In practice, it does prove to be effective in generating and maintaining brand awareness. Much outdoor advertising (in particular neon and name signs) and sponsorship programmes are solely aimed at, and achieve, just that. The main question with respect to television and print advertising is to what extent they manage to get attention, what level of attention they bring about, how long they hold on to it and whether they succeed in *focusing the attention on the brand and on the message*.

15.3   Measuring advertising recall

Recall (spontaneous, aided or related) can help us to get an impression of the extent to which an advertisement/commercial has been given attention. However, over the years, the measurement of advertising recall has become a highly controversial topic. Partly for reasons of principle:

> *"Advertising is not meant to be remembered, but to have a useful effect"* (Knecht, 1990),

and partly because the results were not thought to be particularly reliable.

Lawrence D. Gibson (1983) listed a great many studies which had been conducted on recall and persuasion research. He concluded that recall scores not only depended on the advertising and on the product, but also on a great many 'environment' variables. The main one probably being the surrounding programme. Commercials which are broadcast during programmes which viewers rate highly obtain considerably higher recall scores than those broadcast during less popular programmes (average of 25% compared with 15%). Lloyd and Clancy (1991) also reach the conclusion, on the basis of an extensive test, that involvement in the programme has relatively strong influence on recall scores. The place within the programme also proves to be important. As we saw in Chapter 4, the place of the commercial in the break also greatly influences recall scores. So the test-retest reliability of recall measurements based on on-air viewing is limited. (Although Burke analyses do demonstrate that 87% of the test-retest discrepancies are not significant, and ARS also reports an 89% correlation with an analysis of 74 test- retest cases.)

Research companies have established empirical standards which take the product category and the length of the commercial into account, amongst other things. But the influence of the surrounding programme has not yet been included.

15.4   Recall and emotion

David Ogilvy once said:

> *"It is open to question whether recall tests even measure recall. I believe they measure the viewer's ability to articulate what he/she recalls, which is a very different thing."*

Mapes and Ross analysed 800 commercials in their data bank, including 64 'feeling commercials'. They ascertained that the recall scores of the latter were on average 24% below the average of all commercials. Yet persuasion scores were only 4% lower. At one time Foote Cone and Belding (1981) determined recall of 'feeling commercials' by showing consumers a series of commercials which had also been on a cable network the day before. The brand names were masked for the test. The DAR (Day-After Recall) scores were also determined. Recognition scores proved, on average, to be 41% higher than recall scores. With the factual commercials the difference was 19%, with the 'feeling' commercials 68%! These tests suggest that recall, which was only determined verbally 24 hours after exposure, may not be such a good measure of communication which is primarily non-verbal, emotional and symbolic.

15.5   Recall and attention

The principle and the structure of the correlation between attention and recall have never been adequately established either: what level of attention is measured? What does recall signify after 20 minutes? After 1 hour? After 24 hours? After 72 hours? What is the significance of spontaneous recall compared with the various kinds of aided recall? And lastly, the connection between recall and advertising effectiveness is not thought to be concrete enough: to what extent is recall a precondition for persuasion?

There would seem to be three different views on the subject:

1. An advertisement/commercial needs a minimum level of attention in order to communicate: after that, its effectiveness in the persuasion process depends on its content.

2. The level of attention is important, but an insufficient condition for effectiveness. What matters is attention plus persuasive communication.

3. The main function of advertising is to bring a brand to consumers' notice, the more successful it is in doing so, the more effective it is. So recall as such certainly is important.

There is, in fact, little point in laying down a generally-applicable theory on the importance of recall. After all, the relative importance of attention and persuasive communication depends on the nature and course of the process of consumer choice for the advertised product, and on the brand's position in the memory of the target group. In addition, we should also bear in mind the different methods of measuring recall, and how they affect acquired attention. A great many variables in the measuring method influence the scores – just think of forced exposure, the nature of the questions, the length of time since the exposure, the composition of the sample and even the interviewers.

15.6　Recall and brand awareness

A survey by RSC' reveals a relatively strong correlation between measured recall of commercials and the development of brand awareness with new brands. With a given number of gross rating points (GRPs), higher recall scores result in considerably higher brand awareness than is the case with lower scores. The following graph, based on recall measurements by RSC, depicts this (Henderson Blair, 1988).

Development of brand awareness in relation to recall and GRPs

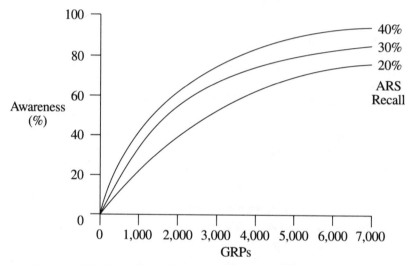

Source:　Henderson Blair, Journal of Advertising Research, December 1987.

15.7　Recall important for persuasion

Bagozzi and Silk (1983), Leigh and Manon (1986) and Zinkham, Locander and Leigh (1986) demonstrated in laboratory tests that, in general, recall and recognition are reasonable indicators of the (level of) processing of advertising.

Klein (1989) comes to the conclusion, based on the method used by MSW (recall measurement 20 minutes after forced exposure), that communication of the message is dramatically lower with low recall than with high recall.

After Stewart and Furse (1984) had analysed the test results of 1,059 television commercials they commented:

> *"We have noted that when recall of a commercial is low, the persuasive effect of a brand message is nearly always half of that with high recall".*

Mapes and Ross, also following their analysis of test results of a great many commercials, observed:

"Almost all the persuasion we measured was done so with people who remembered the commercial. So recall is a prerequisite for persuasion. But obviously a high recall score is not yet a guarantee for that persuasion".

Having analysed the scores of 5,000 commercials tested by RSC, Kuse (1991) reached the conclusion that 21% of the commercials with related recall scores of over 23% had better persuasion scores, compared with 8% of those with recall scores of below 23%.

Mapes and Ross conclude, from various validation tests, that 'day-after' recall particularly affects the purchasing behaviour of people who prefer the brand, but scarcely affects the behaviour of non-buyers.

Finally, in ARF's comprehensive experiment, establishing which measuring method best predicts which of two commercials will be most successful in the market-place (a result which was confirmed empirically beforehand), a question using only the product category as a recall stimulus proved to predict the 'winning' commercial in 87% of the cases.

So there is good reason to take a closer look at the connections which have been found between recall scores and the underlying variables. We should bear in mind however that measured recall not only depends on the attention which advertisements or commercials have received. Whether or not they contain elements which are easy to remember or whether their contents quickly fade from people's memories is also an important factor. Brand-related advertising recall also depends on whether proper brand linkage has taken place during processing of the advertising. In other words: measured recall stands for a great many more factors than just attention during processing.

15.8   Advertising awareness.

Advertising awareness is also being tested to an increasing extent. Advertising awareness being the answer to a question like: "Have you recently seen advertising for brand X?" So not the recall of a specific advertisement or commercial which was in the paper or on television the day before, but more general recall of advertising for a brand. If this question is asked at fairly regular intervals, the development of advertising awareness can be followed in time (tracking research). It is used a great deal in England and Germany. The scores are related to advertising expenditure for the brand, and with developments in purchases (penetration, buying frequency, total sales volume, etc.).

This type of research also has its supporters and opponents. Feldwick (1991) maintains that there are no clear correlations between intermediate advertising effects, like advertising awareness and the ultimate developments in sales. He claims that advertising awareness (in which context he is referring to the 'Awareness Index' – a specific method used to express advertising awareness which is used by Millward Brown in England) is no guarantee for persuasion.

> *"We (BMP/DDB Needham) know of a number of campaigns with high scores for advertising awareness which have not achieved their objectives, and campaigns with low awareness scores which have proved very effective in the market-place."* In addition: *"a high awareness score is neither essential nor sufficient for effective campaigns."*

Brown refutes this with a number of cases confirming a strong correlation between advertising awareness and developments in sales. In particular, he tracked advertising awareness of the brands in the English chocolate market for a longer period, which explained sales developments to a large extent (Colman and Brown, 1983). Here again, there is little point in generalising. As we saw earlier (Wilson and Woodside, 1985) there is a correlation between top-of-mind advertising awareness and brand awareness, as well as between brand awareness and propensity to purchase.

It would seem very likely that in markets in which impulse purchases play an important part and in which choice processes are simple – such as the markets for chocolate and petrol – sales are indeed closely related to advertising awareness. When important instrumental and/or expressive values play a primary role in the choice process, the correlation is probably less, or not apparent, certainly over shorter periods.

It is also likely that a correlation will come about between recall scores and advertising awareness. RSC (Kuse) in fact ascertained a 78% correlation between related recall scores which had been adjusted based on advertising pressure (number of GRPs) and the development of advertising awareness.

Brown (1992) confirms that there are indeed no attractive validation studies relating to the influence of advertising awareness on buying behaviour, but that Millward Brown is tracking the advertising awareness of about 1,250 brands (some for 13 years already), and that, on the whole, a lasting correlation with sales developments has been found for established brands. By comparing campaigns that had won English EFFIEs (for which advertising awareness scores were also available), Brown discovered that 79% had awareness scores that were above the average.

15.9 Persuasion measurements

Research into the extent to which advertisements and commercials influence brand choice is nearly always based on measurements of persuasion before and after exposure to advertising. Comparison of the scores is thought to help explain the persuasion power of the advertising: the 'pre-post attitude shift', as it is called. Sometimes attitude is measured only after exposure and the scores are compared with those of a control sample which had not been exposed to the advertising.

Various types of questions are used to measure attitude, for instance:

- brand choice question;
- overall brand appraisal (usually on a 5-point scale);
- constant sum (division of a set number of points over the various brands); and
- propensity to purchase (usually on a 5-point scale).

The burning question, of course, is whether the attitude shift measured after one or two exposures to the advertising is in fact a reliable gauge of the persuasion power which a campaign will have in the market-place.

Opinions tend to differ – as they do on recall scores as well. Many tests have been carried out into the validity and reliability of these measurements in general, and of certain measuring methods in particular.

Trial purchases compared with persuasion scores and GRPs

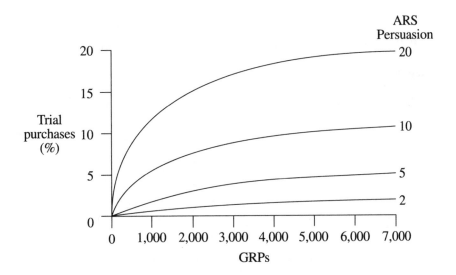

Source: Henderson Blair, Journal of Advertising Research, December 1987.

With product launches, there proves to be a strong correlation between persuasion scores of commercials and the number of households that have made a trial purchase. Advertising pressure obviously plays an important part as well. The relationship between these three factors is depicted in the graph 'Trial purchases compared with persuasion scores and GRPs' on the previous page. It is based on research by RSC (Henderson Blair, 1988).

In an extensive copy research validity project by ARF in 1991, a high correlation was noted, in particular between the measured propensity to purchase (with the pre-post method), overall brand appreciation (with post-measurements) and the empirically established effect of the tested commercials in the market-place.

MSW also conducted comprehensive validity research (Klein, 1990), comparing the test results of 1,165 commercials – from 412 campaigns for 16 product categories – with their market results, as assessed by the relevant advertisers. Substantial correlation was noted, especially between persuasion scores and assessment of the market results. 86% of the commercials with high persuasion scores (commercials with low recall scores) and 91% (those with high recall scores) also proved to be successful in the market-place. Of commercials with low persuasion scores the figures were only 30% (with commercials with low recall scores) and 40% (with those with high recall scores). So persuasion measurements reveal a considerably higher correlation with market results than recall measurements.

	III	I
High	a) 24% b) 40%	a) 71% b) 91%
Related recall after 20 minutes	**IV**	**II**
Low	a) 13% b) 30%	a) 79% b) 86%

Low	High

Attitude change

where,	**a)**	= commercials which exceed objectives;
	b)	= commercials which meet objectives

Source: MSW; Klein, 1990.

But we may not forget that quite a considerable part (40%) of the commercials with low persuasion scores and high recall scores do fulfil the market objectives.

RSC (Kuse, 1990, 1991; Rosenberg et al., 1991) also examined the validity of recall and attitude measurements. In 1964 they had already noted, in an analysis of the market share developments of 23 brands in the United States, that 31% of the changes in shares could be explained by persuasion scores. In a later analysis in West Germany 24% could be explained in this way.

In an analysis of 24 split-cable tests (RSC, 1991) persuasion scores proved, in all cases, to forecast the most successful commercial correctly – but no correlation was found with recall scores. An analysis of the persuasion scores of 5,000 commercials showed that these measurements do not favour factual/rational approaches. Almost the same percentage (17% of the rational and 16% of the emotional approaches) were well above average. RSC's conclusion: 'selling the feeling can sell'.

Walker (1990) reports on a validity test based on 30 cases, using a split-cable test. In 7 out of 10 cases recall scores correctly predicted the market success of the commercials; in 6 out of 10 cases persuasion measurements did. Recall and persuasion measurements combined resulted in 10 out 10 correct predictions!

This test and other research into the validity of persuasion measurements shows that, in general, there is indeed a great correlation between the results of these measurements and results in the market-place. And, in addition, that reliability does depend on the way in which the measurements are carried out.

Time and again it is apparent that it is not enough to measure only one aspect of advertising effectiveness. It will depend on the campaign objectives and strategy, but it is preferable to have a combination of ad recall measurement, communication of the central message, emotional response, likeability, overall ad awareness *and* persuasion. Measurement of these effects should be supplemented with diagnostic questions to indicate how a campaign might be adjusted. However, considerations of time and money will usually mean that partial measurement of advertising effects will have to suffice. Consequently, it is essential to choose the right effect to be measured. The wrong choice can result in the wrong conclusions, and be counterproductive.

After a very far-reaching analysis of the relevant literature and of studies including those quoted in this chapter, Stewart et al. (1985) reached the conclusion that much of the controversy concerning research methods in fact arises from a lack of vision as to the desired advertising effects, and from the fact that the various methods are not really suited to measuring those specific effects. As these authors ascertain, recall is not a good gauge for persuasion, but does increase or decrease it. So there is a point in measuring recall, even when persuasion is the main objective. And if name and brand awareness are the prime objective, recall is indeed the foremost criterion for effectiveness.

In view of the influence that 'environmental' variables have (for example, the type of programmes surrounding television commercials), laboratory tests, in which the variables can be monitored, have advantages compared with measurement in real-life conditions. Laboratory tests also make it possible to attune the samples properly to the selected target group(s).

16 Factors which influence advertising recall

The following overview of the factors which affect recall of television commercials is mainly based on the analysis by Stewart and Furse, which was repeated by Koslow and Stewart. Whenever results from other analyses are included (Mapes and Ross, ASI), they have been named specifically.

These factors can be grouped according to several aspects. What follows below is a 'face-value' arrangement.

16.1 Factors with a positive influence on recall

We differentiate between three groups of elements:
  a. those which *activate attention*;
  b. those which *facilitate storage in the memory*;
  c. those which *jog the memory*.

16.1.1 Elements which activate attention:

A *humorous or amusing tone* proves to have the greatest influence on recall scores. That has been confirmed by other studies (Sternthal and Craig, 1973). ASI analyses (Walker, 1990) show that the measured attention for humorous 30-second commercials averaged 45%, for non-humorous 38%.

A *relevant product message:* something in the commercial relating to the product and/or brand which is worth paying attention to. A message which differentiates the brand, something about convenience, a demonstration of the product in use, or usage results.

A *relevant situation*, relating to the purchase or use of the product in an understandable way. So not cars on top of mountains. But a little *fantasy and exaggeration* as dominant elements can also attract our attention.

Commercials which start with a good key idea are better remembered (Mapes & Ross, 1982). If it takes too long for viewers to discover what the commercial is getting at, they will lose interest prematurely.

An analysis by Mapes and Ross (Ogilvy an Raphaelson, 1982) revealed that *well-known people* contribute towards recall. The same was apparent from ASI analyses, provided the people were mentioned by name. If the name is not used, some of the viewers have their doubts and that has an adverse effect on recall.

The use of a *presenter* who addresses the viewers has a limited positive influence, especially when the person is plausible in the context of the product (ASI).

Dialogues between people are rather more effective than monologues held by presenters (ASI).

A *cheerful tone* (ASI) aids attention. And, lastly, the use of *babies, small children and cute animals* also promotes attention (ASI).

16.1.2 Elements which facilitate storage in the memory

They include *mnemonic devices:* a distinctive element in the visual and/or sound which quickly becomes embedded in the memory. For example, a jingle, a well-known tune, a characteristic visual, a good slogan, a rhyme.

The use of *'permanent' people over a period of time* also dramatically increases recall (ASI). The *length* of the commercial is also an important factor in this context: it would seem that the faster something is over, the sooner it is forgotten.

16.1.3 Elements which jog the memory

The ease with which advertising can be traced in the memory depends mainly on the brand name and other brand signals. Advertisements with *a good brand name which is easy to remember* are easier to recall.

Visual brand recognition, especially at the end of the commercial, can also help us to dig the advertising up out of the memory at a later stage.

The number of times that a brand is named or shown, as well as the total time the product is on the screen, have a very important effect on measured recall.

16.2   Factors with a negative influence on recall

Again three groups of elements are relevant:
   a.   factors which require *too much cognitive effort*;
   b.   a *lack of relevant information*;
   c.   *elements which impede memory-jogging.*

Recall is adversely influenced in particular by:

16.2.1 Factors requiring too much cognitive effort.

To start with, *too much information:* on ingredients, composition, too many explanations which affect recall adversely. (However, Stewart and Koslow's study, 1979, did not confirm this conclusion.) *Too many words on the screen* – two or more times, or more than 10 words at a time require too much effort (ASI). *Commercials that are hard to follow* result in lower recall scores. Too many cuts, too many short scenes, too many situation shifts (Mapes & Ross), moving camera shots or the camera too close to movement (ASI) are all elements which make it hard to follow what is happening on the screen, and to remember it later on.

Distracting elements also have an adverse effect. If, for instance, there are too many people on the screen a lack of focus soon tends to occur.

Disturbing loud music (ASI) which is dominant or lasts throughout the whole commercial can also be a negative influence on recall. However, that does not include simple jingles, musical logos and soft background music, or the use of popular sons, which can in fact work positively.

Sounds which compete with words (ASI) are also negative in their effect. They make it difficult to understand what is being said. So auditive simplicity is important.

Distance and abstractness detract from recall. It may be due to a lack of a central character. In general, *voice-over commercials*, in which no central character appears on the screen obtain lower scores (ASI). Similarly, the use of *animation, stills, storyboard techniques* and of *graphics* and *graphic illustrations* can result in an 'aloof' commercial. The same applies to the use of *cartoons* for adults. However, for children, cartoons and animation actually aid recall (Mapes & Ross).

16.2.2 A lack of relevant information

A lack of relevant information can result in lower scores. This may be the outcome of evoking *too much emotion, and only emotion.* Commercials with no cognitive content whatsoever are not remembered well (this is confirmed in the ASI analyses)

In addition, (too much) *emphasis on user satisfaction* without linkage to relevant information, has an adverse effect on recall. This is especially the case with established brands. That also includes oversimplified testimonials, without further informative content.

16.2.3 Factors which impede memory-jogging

Factors which impede memory-jogging, like the use of a *difficult, unknown brand* or *(too) late identification* of the product and/or of the brand. If it takes too long before it is clear what the commercial is about (thanks to the pack, product, brand name and other brand signals) recall scores drop.

The effectiveness of commercials, which may otherwise be successful, can be adversely affected if the brand is not properly linked with the creative idea.

Another factor which may be relevant, although it did not emerge in the analyses, is the use of stereotyped, worn-out elements. 'Uniqueness' of advertising is rarely explicitly measured, and so is not singled out as an explanatory factor.

17 Topicality and agenda-setting

Besides all the variables we have been discussing, there is another independent quality of advertising which influences brand awareness: *the ability to give the brand a topical context*. This factor has not been dealt with specifically, nor has it emerged explicitly from the comprehensive advertising studies on which the present publication is based. Nevertheless it probably does do a great deal to establish a brand in our memory. Topicality in the sense of something which is happening at *this very minute*, demanding our attention *now*, about which we are talking *now*. In communication science it is called 'agenda-setting'.

Advertising in this sense puts the brand at the centre of our interest for a moment. It does not entail communicating instrumental advantages (unless they are so new and important that they represent a topical dimension). Nor does it entail developing expressive associations or all kinds of dimensions which can contribute to ad-likeability. Rather, it is an independent effect. As such, it can contribute to ad-likeability. But we should try to dissociate it from ad-likeability in our strategic thinking and treat as an independent issue.

Sutherland and Gallowan (1981) tested the effects of salience with 267 housewives. They reached the conclusion that brand salience (awareness) especially influences choice when consumers have to choose from a limited number of alternatives, but found no significant differences between these alternatives. The brands which are evaluated are those which are most salient.

17.1   Agenda-setting

The mechanism of agenda-setting also has an indirect effect on choice. Salience influences what people think other people think, making selection easier for themselves. They choose the brand they think others (would) also choose, the popular brand. "It should be OK." That, in turn, is deduced from the extent to which it is featured in the media, or is a topic of conversation, compared with other brands. The frequency with which respondents say "a brand is advertised a lot" and "is popular" correlates with their choice. So, in that sense too, it is a good idea to measure 'advertising awareness'.

Advertising which has as one of its objectives to make a brand topical, and so obtain interest for it, has two possible options:

1.   It can link the brand with a topical issue in its surroundings (like beer in a heat wave). The product and the issue must have a logical connection.

2. It can also seek topicality in the brand itself, or in its 'world'. The brand creates its own topicality, as it were, by presenting itself in a new, unexpected way, which gets attention. There are endless ways of doing that.

On the whole, it is better to create topicality for the brand rather than 'borrow' it.

17.2   Lack of topicality

When brands are made 'topical', this puts them up front in consumers' experience. They acquire a more prominent place within the perceived set of alternatives. So the brand in question is 'stage-managed', as it were. But the opposite can also take place. We have become so accustomed to the existence of a brand, and it has had so little to say that is new over the years, that it has gradually 'merged with the wallpaper'. It has become 'part of the scenery' of life: it is there, but we no longer notice it. Apart from a drop in perceived product quality, this *lack of topicality* is probably the foremost reason why brands decline.

Lack of topicality is a danger which can also affect advertising. If the same message is expounded year in year out, often in much the same way, the same negative effect comes about that we encountered when we dealt with ad-likeability: a reaction of "we've seen it all before".

An advertising campaign can be based on the creation of brand topicality, for which readers or viewers are prepared to work up fresh interest. In this way it can create or boost brand awareness.

18 Brand-to-product association & differentiation

If a brand is to be an alternative in a choice, it is not sufficient for it to be well-known. Well-known as what? The brand Chum is very well-known. But it is unlikely to be considered when a consumer is selecting a brand of lemonade. Chum is closely linked in our memories with dog food, not with soft drinks.

That sounds obvious, but invariably something goes fundamentally wrong in the communication process, because the brand is linked in consumers' memories with products other than the one which is being advertised.

People do not think primarily of a brand when they make a purchase: first they think what they need – a product (beer) and then the brands (shall I buy Grolsch, Heineken, Amstel or Bavaria?). The degree to which a brand is seen as an alternative depends on the degree to which it is associated in people's memories with the product or product variant, *compared with other brands*.

Products are fixed in our memories as associative networks. Brands are part of these networks, but the extent to which they are varies tremendously. When we think of light bulbs we probably think immediately of Philips. When we think of computers, we think of IBM, Digital and Apple, and possibly, after quite some time, also of Philips.

A product (category) is a collection of alternatives, all of which serve the same purpose in the perception of consumers. What a category is, and which alternatives belong to it, is not determined by either the manufacturer or the retailer, but by the consumer him- or herself (Pieters, 1990).

The intensity of the association between a brand and a product category greatly influences whether or not a brand in that category will be seen as an alternative in the selection process. That can be a problem, in particular for brands which a manufacturer links with entirely different categories, like umbrella and company brands. The association of the brand with the different products will then tend to vary greatly. It will be perceived as an alternative in one category far more than in another. A very close association with a certain product category can also considerably hamper the development of associations with other categories.

Wright (1977) once suggested that what people remember best about advertising is a 'problem framework', a way of reflecting on a product. The problem framework comprises the product attributes, which are thought to play a part in selection, and the brands from which a choice should be made. Advertising ensures that a consumer's world is conveniently arranged: "this is what I should look out for, and that is what I can choose from". In that sense, too, agenda-setting is one of the main functions of advertising (Ghorpade, 1986).

18.1 Differentiation

In theory, there are only two reasons why a consumer chooses a certain brand from the set of alternatives which present themselves as prime candidates to him in his own memory and in the store:

- the alternative is cheaper; or
- in his perception, it has more to offer in some respects than the alternatives.

The concept of 'more' can, in turn, consist of two dimensions. In the consumer's perception it can offer more, as regards central (generic) instrumental or emotional product attributes. The brand is positioned as the norm, 'mid-market'. It can also differentiate itself from the alternatives because it represents for the consumer certain important instrumental or emotional attributes, which differ from the norm. The consumer perceives these attributes less, or not at all, in the alternatives (segmentation and niche marketing).

The second function of advertising, after 'providing a candidate', is to create perceived differences, compared with competing brands, in dimensions which are relevant for specific groups of consumers (target groups).

When consumers are confronted with products which start to resemble other products in a physical or instrumental sense, they will go in search of other dimensions on which to base their choice. They feel uncomfortable when they have nothing with which they can justify their choice for themselves.

In this way, fairly trivial product attributes can prove to be decisive in the choice process. That means that, with many products for which fundamental improvements are not possible, the dimensions relating to the emotional experience of brands also start to play a growing part in the choice process.

Differences which are experienced as meaningful are always difficult to create on the basis of central (generic) product attributes or generic emotional product perceptions. In fact, the pioneers and the market leaders are always the ones to claim that position and, in consumers' perception, nearly always occupy it. Other brands are nearly always second best in that respect – and it takes a great deal for them to depose the pioneers (market leaders, also in consumers' minds).

Military manuals state that for a successful frontal attack you need to outnumber your opponent in troops/material by 3:1. It is a moot point whether that might also apply in marketing. However, it is certainly true that anyone other than the market leader needs considerably greater deployment of means of communication, if they are to acquire a perceived lead in generic attributes. The consequence is that the basis for brand preference will nearly always be sought in secondary instrumental attributes and in differences in emotional response.

18.2   Brand-differentiating message

Two analyses of the test results of television commercials (Stewart and Furse, 1986; and Stewart and Koslow, 1979), both relating to over 1,000 cases, reveal that *the existence of a brand-differentiating message is the most important factor for persuasion*. That finding was new, although the idea behind it, of course, was not.

Back in 1942 Borden had already concluded that effective advertising was the basis for product differentiation. Later practitioners embellished the idea (Reeves' USP philosophy) and elaborated on it (Ogilvy's image differentiation). Later still, the development of theories on choice processes, often supported by laboratory research, only served to confirm it.

A brand-differentiating message can be the result of the product strategy or the advertising concept. It may be something distinctive about the actual product, or the advertising may communicate a characteristic which the alternatives do have, but which consumers do not yet associate with the product.

The analyses of 1,059 tested commercials (Stewart and Furse) show that the effect of a brand-differentiating message is influenced negatively by the fact that the commercial is not easy to understand, and positively by its impact (expressed in the recall score). The effect on choice is twice as great with a high as opposed to a low recall score.

In an analysis of the test scores of 5,000 commercials for 1,300 brands in 200 product categories, RSC (Rosenberg et al., 1991) ascertained that 25% of the commercials with a brand-differentiating message had better persuasion scores, compared with only 10% of those with no brand-differentiating message. Commercials with a differentiating emotional benefit proved, on average, to do better than those with a rational product benefit.

It illustrates yet again the fact that the inevitable argument that advertising is not meant to be remembered but to create brand preference is erroneous, to say the least. Persuasive advertising which is recalled well proves to work better than advertising which achieves less spontaneous recall.

18.3   Other factors

According to the analyses we have been discussing, there are three other factors, alongside the product-differentiating message, which can contribute toward or detract from persuasion. (Stewart and Furse, 1986; and Stewart and Koslow, 1979) They can be summarised as product focus, quantity of information, and abstractness.

18.3.1 Focus on the product

Clear focus on the product has a positive persuasive effect. It can consist of:
- information on convenient use;
- information on new products and new attributes;
- indirect comparison with competitors;
- demonstration of product use or of its results.

The total time devoted to the product also proves to be very important.

18.3.2 Too much information

The negative effects on persuasion mainly originate from an excess of information. It can be due to:
- the number of propositions and psychological appeals;
- information on components and ingredients;
- information on nutritive values and health; and
- explanatory graphs.

Not that consumers are not interested in this information. They just do not want it when they are relaxing in front of the television.

18.3.3 Abstractness

An *unclear, abstract structure* of commercials affects persuasion in a negative way. It may result from:
- no central character;
- more than four people on the screen; and
- the time which elapses before product and brand are named.

The main conclusion is that commercials must have a clear product focus. They must emphasise as much as possible the advantages of using the brand in question, compared with the alternatives, and so do simply. When consumers watch television, they are not interested in all kinds of factual product information. And they are certainly not interested in technical features and product ingredients, if they are not translated into usage benefits.

"The essence of an alternative is not what it is made from, but what that results in" (Pieters, 1990).

18.4   News

The results of the analyses differ somewhat for established brands and for new products. With the latter, the fact that something new is involved (if it is communicated explicitly) is, as such, a way of differentiating the brand from its competitors. It is a reason for many people to try the brand. But once the newness has worn off, the advertiser is once more faced with the job of differentiating his brand somehow.

A large single-source survey in 1991, based on 400 cases in the IRI data bank (to be discussed in more detail later on) showed that in order to achieve a short-term effect with established brands it is essential to break through the status quo. As a rule it is not enough to increase the advertising budget. It is important to *do* something new.

With established brands, shorter-term growth (1-3 years) is primarily achieved by addressing new target groups. Or by communicating new messages to existing users. That usually requires a new copy strategy. The ideal thing is to be able to announce a product innovation. But relevant news about an existing product can also activate consumers.

When products are involved which fit in with consumers' natural inclinations to switch brands, the effect of something new is greater than with products which command considerable brand loyalty.

18.5   Persuasion power finite

Since split-cable tests have been possible, it has proved easier to track the effectiveness of advertising for established brands over a longer period. RSC (Henderson Blair, 1988) analysed 20 cases for which recall and persuasion scores, advertising pressure reflected in gross-rating points, and sales trends were available. The conclusions were that there is a strong correlation between higher persuasion scores and sales trends. However, with low or not-so-high persuasion scores, increased advertising pressure did not increase sales. Around 40% of the commercials which RSC tested obtained persuasion scores which can generate sales.

Later experiments (Henderson Blair, 1991 and 1992) led to the conclusion that a commercial's persuasion power drops fast when the consumer has 'processed' it. That was already the case after a few exposures in lab. tests. In the market-place it is accompanied by an increase in effectuated GRPs. On average, a commercial is said to lose 60% of its persuasion power after 1,250 GRPs. When the number of GRPs increases, recall and ad awareness do continue to increase. The learning process continues, but persuasive power drops exponentially.

Wear-out curve

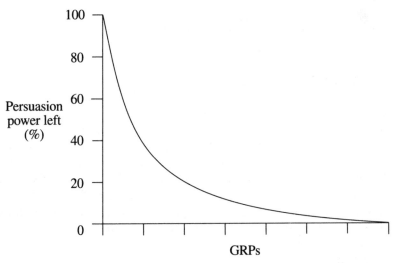

Source: Henderson and Blair, 1991 and 1992.

This reflects the principle of 'effective reach', as formulated early in the nineteen-eighties by Michael Naples. A minimum number of contacts are needed to have an effect ('wear-in'), after which the additional effect per contact drops ('wear-out'). If the target group has been 'reached effectively', the commercial has done its job. In order to ensure high campaign effectiveness, commercials must, therefore, be replaced in time. Endless repetition detracts from advertising effectiveness.

19 The effect of basic forms

19.1 Classification of basic forms

In advertising a number of basic forms are used, with constant variations. A whole gamut of execution variables is used, ensuring that every new commercial is slightly different from all its predecessors. But, in essence, it is always a repetition of something that has been used time and again.

A number of large-scale analyses, on which much of this book is based, have also examined the correlation between certain basic forms and facets of how advertising works. Before this is discussed, it is useful to have a summary of the most-used basic forms. There are 8 different groups:

1. Announcements;
2. Displays;
3. Association transfers
4. Lessons;
5. Drama;
6. Pure forms of entertainment;
7. Imagination;
8. Special effects.

19.1.1 Announcements

This entails direct presentation of facts, with no use of people. The facts are assumed to speak for themselves. The great majority of retail advertising is based on this form. Announcements are factual and logical. There are three subforms:

a. pure presentation of facts;
b. factual explanation;
c. product messages.

19.1.2 Displays

This includes all forms which are primarily based on a product's appearance. The visual product is supposed to speak for itself, and readers or viewers are supposed to be able to interpret the product without intervention from anyone else – and draw their own conclusions. There is no fundamental difference with the display of products in shop windows, stores and showrooms. This basic form is nearly always used if a product is primarily selected on account of its appearance, as is the case with fashion, furnishings and jewellery. But also if 'appetite appeal' is important, as with foods, beverages, etc. Subforms are the product-as-hero, extreme close-ups and 'a camera in love with a product'.

19.1.3 Association transfers

Here the brand and/or the product are combined with another object, person or situation, with the intention of having consumers transfer their associations with the latter to the advertised brand or product. This works along the lines of 'classical conditioning', as discussed earlier. After repeated exposure to both elements, the brand eventually starts to evoke the same value associations as the (unconditioned) stimulus. This form is used especially when expressive and central values are to be linked to a brand. Almost all advertising for perfumes and for personal care products make use of it. A specific variation is the 'life-style' concept.

a. Life-style

A succession of scenes which depict the life-style of a person or group of persons, with no plot or dialogue, often using music which evokes a feeling which matches the style. Sometimes life-style is used to mean a distinctly modern, young, affluent and dynamic style, although that is but one of the many different life-styles we encounter is society.

b. Metaphor

A parallel is drawn between the product/brand and something else. For example, a panther which is used as a metaphor for a fast car.

c. Metonymy

The meaning of the original object is transferred to the product/brand, like a flower turning into a perfume.

19.1.4 Lessons

Lessons are direct presentations of facts and arguments, intended to teach readers or viewers something, or convince them of something. Lessons relate explicitly to what readers or viewers are supposed to believe, and why. Their effect is primarily rational and their construction logical. They state, explain, elucidate, reason, compare and try to convince. They always focus on a product's attributes, effect, effectiveness and other rational benefits. They use visual and verbal resources. There are various subforms which basically amount to the use of different stylistic devices.

a. Presenters

The use of a person with a dominant presence, speaking into the camera and conveying the main message. He or she may carry out a demonstration, or supply a commentary about what is happening on the screen, actually acting as a newscaster. The presenter may interview someone else, as a newscaster also sometimes does.

b. Testimonials

These also make use of a person with a dominant presence, suggesting or claiming that he or she is a user of the product. They speak into the camera or to someone else, and convey the main message in a convincing way. Interviews are a much-used device.

c. Demonstrations

The advertising shows how (well) the product works. It displays the product attributes and benefits in use, or by way of a situation before and after use. Demonstrations usually involve the use of presenters or testimonials.

d. Comparison

The product and its effect are compared directly with a competing brand, which may or may not be specifically named.

e. Analogy

Use is made of a similarity or resemblance with other items or events in order to make the attributes or effect of a product clear or plausible. It often involves an unexpected connection between two phenomena which are seldom compared.

f. 'How to...'

Here the use of the product and the results which can be achieved with it are explained and/or demonstrated. All recipe advertisements are covered by this device.

19.1.5 Drama

Drama entails the interplay between two or more people in a 'true-to-life' situation. There is a continuity of action: a beginning, a middle and a 'happy ending'. Small stories are involved, with a plot showing how the world works, what people can experience, how they react in certain situation and how they get on together. Unlike in the lessons, viewers are not addressed directly, they are the observers. They learn by watching others, and draw their own conclusions on the product. Dramas primarily appeal to the emotions. Again, there are various subforms:

a. Slice-of-life

Literally: a brief encounter with everyday life. Basically, these are dramatised dialogues, dealing with everyday events, which everyone encounters on occasions, or which we imagine we might encounter some day. The product is the climax of the story (if it is any good!). The story usually shows how the product provides an emotional reward.

b.   Problem...solution

Generally a variation on 'slice-of-life' advertising, in which the story develops around a problem to which the product offers a fitting solution. The case-history form is sometimes used.

c.   Vignettes

A small series of independent sketches or visual situations, with no continuity of action. The product plays a part in each vignette. This device works according to the principle of repetition.

19.1.6 Pure entertainment

The use of all kinds of entertainment which are also encountered in television programmes, in the cinema and the theatre. For example: musicals, shows, comedies, slapstick, horror and satire. All forms have in common the fact that the form outshines the content of the advertising. The product and the message tend to disappear rapidly from view.

19.1.7 Imagination

The use of cartoons or other film and video techniques, in which a certain event or effect is portrayed, without it being experienced as realistic. This is often done to avoid literal interpretation and in order to avoid disbelief. It facilitates a degree of exaggeration, without jeopardising credibility. Viewers are aware of the exaggeration, but accept it because it is only 'make-believe'.

19.1.8 Special effects

There is a long list of execution variables which can be elevated to a basic concept from time to time. They are always artistic resources, which differ greatly on account of their visual or auditive character. This group comprises animated films, cartoons, certain camera and recording techniques and all kinds of different video techniques. It also covers the use of specific music and tunes as vehicles for commercials.

These foregoing basic forms are not mutually exclusive. Advertisements and commercials are often combinations of two forms.

McCollum Spielman Worldwide (MSW) compared the test results of commercials with the basic forms used, and with a series of other execution characteristics. In 1976 the results of an analysis of 4,564 commercials, tested in the early seventies, were made available. In 1990 another 7,729 commercials were analysed which had been tested in the nineteen-eighties. In both cases, the characteristics of the commercials were related to the scores for the three basic criteria which MSW had applied:

Awareness:	unaided brand recall, measured 20 minutes after a single forced exposure in a controlled programme and commercial environment;
Communication:	recall of the central message;
Persuasion:	pre/post attitude change after repeated exposure.

The testing methods of GfK in Germany are partly based on those of MSW in the United States. Unlike MSW, who use larger groups of respondents who are invited into a theatre, GfK carry out their tests on an individual basis. GfK have meanwhile compiled a data bank of over 4,000 commercials, which have been tested in Europe according to these methods. A great many analyses have been carried out, based on this data bank, into the effect of certain basic forms. The results of the American and German analyses are summarised below.

19.2   Influence of characteristics on scores

The selected basic form and the specific execution characteristics explained 48% of the variance in measured awareness and 19% of the variance in persuasion scores in the MSW analysis of commercials in the eighties.

Message-related characteristics explained 7% of the variance in awareness scores, but 66% in persuasion scores (attitude shift). In the 1990 analysis a change was observed compared with that of commercials in the seventies. The influence of execution characteristics on awareness had increased, that on persuasion had decreased. The influence of message-related characteristics on persuasion had increased.

Explanation of variance in test scores

	Execution characteristics		Message characteristics	
	1970s	1980s	1970s	1980s
All products:				
Awareness	**41%**	**48%**	**7%**	**7%**
Persuasion	**22%**	**19%**	**57%**	**66%**
Healthcare and personal-care products:				
Awareness	44%	47%	12%	12%
Persuasion	27%	27%	16%	17%
Foods:				
Awareness	50%	57%	19%	21%
Persuasion	42%	44%	69%	73%
Snacks:				
Awareness	73%	71%	23%	21%
Persuasion	45%	32%	31%	39%

Source: McCollum Spielman Worldwide Ad*Vantage/Act executional analysis II, April 1990.

This suggests that the basic form and the execution together determine the extent to which a commercial is given attention, and that the message in particular determines the degree of persuasion. However, marked differences are apparent from one product category to another, as the following overview shows. The execution characteristics affect awareness scores very strongly with snacks. The message characteristics largely explain the variance in persuasion scores with foods.

Only a few basic form and execution variables accounted for the majority of variance in the test scores. They are summarised in the following table:

Form and execution characteristics which greatly influence test scores

Awareness	Communication	Persuasion
1. Unique visuals	–	–
2. Mood	–	–
3. Music	–	–
4. Brand in first 5secs.	–	–
	1. Slice-of-life	–
	2. Comparative demonstration	1. Comparative demonstration
	3. Monadic demonstration	2. Monadic demonstration
	4. Factual/logical	3. Factual/logical
	5. Problem-solving	4. Problem-solving
		5. Presenter

Source: McCollum Spielman Worldwide Ad*Vantage/Act executional analysis II, April 1990.

19.3   Characteristics which ensure awareness

It is interesting to see that the characteristics which explain awareness are very different from those which account for communication of the central message and persuasion. The MSW analysis revealed 4 factors which explain most of the variance in awareness scores:

19.3.1 Unique visual concept

These are commercials in which the brand and the central message are well integrated in a strong visual concept. Television is primarily a visual medium (after all, it is tele-vision) – and so it is not surprising that strong visuals have the greatest influence on viewers' attention.

19.3.2 Mood

Meaning commercials which are primarily based on sensory and emotional appeals, and which do not communicate factual, rational product benefits. In the seventies commercials of this type did not much influence awareness scores. Consumers would seem to be increasingly attracted to emotional rewards in an ever-harder world.

19.3.3 Music

The use of well-known melodies and performers proves especially to influence awareness scores strongly. We have already seen from GfK analyses that music contributes substantially to commercial likeability.

19.3.4 Brand in first five seconds

In the seventies a good brand pay-off in the last 5 seconds had even greater influence on awareness scores, but in the eighties it proved important to feature the brand in the first five seconds. This illustrates the viewers' shorter attention span, in a world of communication overkill.

So awareness is especially influenced by artistic and aesthetic variables, which appeal to our eyes and ears. They ensure attention, but not communication of the main message, or persuasion.

19.4 Characteristics which communicate the main message and 'persuade'

Practically the same set of characteristics proves to be responsible for most variance in communication scores as in persuasion scores. These are characteristics which principally relate to the content of the commercials, i.e.:

19.4.1 Slice-of-life commercials

These commercials are best at communicating the main message. An important part is probably played by the fact that the 'slice-of-life', more than any other basic form, enables viewers to identify with the people and events in the commercial. However, having analysed 5,000 tested commercials, RSC (Kuse, 1992) established that slice-of-life commercials had somewhat lower persuasion scores than average.

19.4.2 Demonstrations

Often as part of slice-of-life commercials, or combined with presenters or testimonials, are an important factor in explaining variance in both communication of the main message and in persuasion. Kuse (1991) also observed that demonstrations get above-average persuasion scores. MSW

(1991) analysed 348 commercials involving demonstrations in a separate study. Comparative demonstrations obtained slightly better average scores than monadic, especially with household products. Monadic, on the other hand, did better for foods.

Implicit comparisons, in which the competitor is not named or depicted, proved to be slightly more effective than explicit, especially as regards persuasion. Traditional hard-sell comparisons work better than those with an approach which involves humour or emotion. Explicit comparisons do not entail any special problem for correct brand linkage; it is neither better nor worse than with the average commercial. However, it is important not to have the competitor longer on the screen than strictly necessary, and to keep the spotlight well focused on the advertised brand.

19.4.3 Factual/logical commercials

The product attributes and advantages are presented directly, with or without the use of presenters or other basic forms.

Consumers prove to continue to expect convincing arguments why they should prefer one product to another. The more risks a choice represents and the more expensive the product is, the more important information will be.

19.4.4 Problem-solving

This is one of the most powerful basic forms for both communication and persuasion, especially when problems are involved which viewers themselves feel to be important and which occur frequently. But when commercials of this type are made, care must be taken not to pay the problem more attention than the solution. If the problem is dramatised too exuberantly, there is a danger that it will stick in the memory, whilst the solution is forgotten.

Presenters, if they are well selected, can contribute to a commercial's persuasiveness.

19.4.5 Testimonials

A number of basic forms did not emerge from the analysis as factors with much influence on the variance in test scores. That includes testimonials. GfK analysed the test scores of 185 German testimonial commercials and compared them with the average scores of 988 different commercials which were not based on testimonials. Testimonials proved to score worse than slice-of-life across the board. On average, they were remembered worse and liked less. They did prove to be more credible. When testimonials were combined with a visual demonstration, persuasiveness and credibility increased.

The ideal testimonial used ordinary people, showing the product in use. However, interviews in the street with ordinary people have a negative effect: all their scores were below the norm (Munzinger and Musiol, 1986). Actors are less convincing than ordinary people. Testimonials with experts are also weak, on average. Credibility scores are mediocre and awareness and persuasion poor. Comical types are definitely not liked – all concomitant scores are low on average. Testimonials should be limited to one person, if at all possible. And they must make a natural impression, so definitely not too professional or else they will be seen as paid actors who have learned their texts by heart. But they should not be to 'primitive' either, because that would focus too much attention on the person, with the risk of the product playing second fiddle.

19.4.6 Stars

The use of stars from sports, theatre, music or television for testimonials obtains higher awareness scores, but, of all types of testimonials, results in the lowest scores, on average, for persuasion. Stars often make for extreme scores, both in a positive and in a negative sense. If stars are used, their image should match that of the brand, and they should be plausible as users of the product.

19.5   No pure entertainment

If we summarise briefly the findings of the MSW and GfK analyses, we can conclude that the persuasive effect of commercials is still largely determined by the relevant information and arguments which are conveyed in a 'human' and warm way, and by the use of appeals which represent an emotional reward for use of the product and the brand. All basic forms and stylistic devices which do not primarily aid communication of the central message, or activate relevant feelings, would seem to be counterproductive.

Consumers want advertising to take them seriously, and at the same time to be made in such a way that it appeals to them. Their attitude does not change for the better if a brand treats them to pure entertainment or uses inappropriate devices. So no musicals, shows, comedies or slapstick. No extravaganzas and video gimmicks. No celebrities who are not relevant to the product. All these devices attract attention to themselves and only distract it from the product, message and brand. Yet advertising should be special in its execution, especially in that it makes proper use of powerful visuals and music which are its own. At the same time, it must stick close to the product and the brand, and, in fact, to the everyday lives of ordinary people.

20 How humour works

20.1 What is humour?

Although everyone knows, intuitively, what humour is, it proves to be very difficult to define. Unlike 'laughter', which is a reaction to humour and is easy to perceive and describe, the phenomenon of humour is harder to describe, because it is abstract. Descriptions of humour usually refer to an antithesis between reality and intention; a playing with meanings by which an antithesis or incongruity apparently comes about. The elements of a joke or humorous occurrence clash, are in conflict with one another or contradict one another. When the 'receiver' processes the unexpected and, consequently, surprising incongruity, he will try to solve it. If he succeeds, he has understood the humour. He will laugh at the contradiction between what he thought he could expect and what actually confronted him.

So the essence of humour is incongruity. However, some other phenomena are based on antitheses too, without humour being involved. Humour differentiates itself by:

1. The degree of incongruity and so the intensity of the feelings of pleasure and excitement in solving it. Humour is characterised by moderate incongruity. Minimal or extremely high levels of incongruity are not humorous.

2. The ease with which the incongruity can be solved, and so the short duration of the feelings of pleasure and excitement.

3. Its triviality, which is apparent when the antithesis has been resolved.

Rothhart and Pien (1977) distinguished between two types of incongruity: impossible and possible. Impossible incongruity is based on elements which are impossible, given the receiver's knowledge of reality. A talking monkey, for example. Possible incongruities are based on elements which are unexpected or inappropriate, but are possible: a monkey operating a copier.

Raskin gives the following causes for the occurrence of incongruities or antitheses:

"Incongruity is caused by errors of judgement, resemblances, disguise, confusion of gestures, ignorance, the creation of a mistaken interpretation or expectation, distraction or focus of attention on an odd point in the middle of a question, incorrect reasoning, mistakes caused by linguistic automatism, automatism of perception and interpretation, confusion of words, and wit."

And lastly, Van Duin and Papousek define humour as:

"The ability to see the ridiculous in unexpected situations involving two or more concepts which are each other's opposite in at least one dimension, or are open to two or more interpretations."

20.2 Functions of humour

People appreciate humour as an intellectual challenge they are set when they have to resolve the contradiction between the expected and the unexpected.

Humour can also have an aggressive function – Plato said that laughter is largely at the expense of others. And humour can also perform a psycho-social function: it can emphasise the differences between people, but it can unite them too. Laughter which humour generates brings people together. If we can laugh together, differences disappear for a moment.

20.3 Processing humour

The obvious effect of humour is that people laugh. The phenomenon of laughter is explained by the arousal theory. The term 'arousal' indicates the level of general activation, from deep sleep to great excitement. The discovery of the contradiction with humour first causes an increase in arousal, its solution causes a decrease. The fast, moderate rise, followed immediately by a moderate drop in arousal generates feelings of excitement and pleasure.

The processing of humour is characterised to start with by cognitive effort: the stimuli are pinpointed and interpreted, and the incongruity between the two is resolved. That results in an emotional reaction: feelings of excitement and pleasure. During processing, the level of general arousal first increases, then abates.

20.4 Advertising effects

These attributes of humour are also decisive for how it works in advertising.

1. As a result of the perceived contradictions, humour can attract considerable attention and raise the level at which the advertising is processed. And that results in greater recall and advertising awareness.

2. Humour generates feelings of excitement and pleasure, and can therefore, contribute to likeability of the advertising.

3. Likeability, in turn, means less zapping, either of a psychological or a mechanical nature. Attention is retained for longer.

4. The feelings of excitement and pleasure can coincide with the feelings which are associated with the product or usage situation. That can strengthen the attitude toward the brand. But if incongruity is involved, the opposite effect may occur: humour can impair the positive brand associations.

5. The higher level of attention and advertising processing can mean that the central message is processed and remembered better. But if the humorous antithesis is detached from the product and the message, it can also deflect attention from them. *"Attention is deflected from learning to laughing"* (Cantor and Venus, 1980).

6. The humorous content of the advertising can also completely absorb attention, meaning that not even brand-linkage is achieved.

7. Humour can reduce the tendency to look for counter-arguments. It can make up for the 'pedantic' side of an advertisement, facilitating acceptance of the message.

20.5 Selective appreciation

If the desired effects are to be achieved, the incongruity in the humour must be recognised and resolved, in order for the comical element to be discovered. The 'seeing of the joke' depends on its complexity, and on the receiver's intellectual skills and prior knowledge.

Appreciation of a certain type of humour depends on a person's age and sex. Men enjoy sexual and disparaging humour, women would seem to prefer innocent and nonsense jokes. Appreciation of humour is also linked with culture. The Spanish often laugh at different things from Germans, Glaswegians find different things funny from Cornishmen, advertising people are amused by different things from construction workers. So it is no mean task to appeal to the taste of 'the masses' with humour.

20.6 Higher recall

MSW (1982) analysed the effect of 500 humorous television commercials. Compared with other basic forms, humorous commercials more often have above-average scores for recall, but less often for persuasion. ASI's analysis (Walker, 1990) confirmed that humorous commercials obtain higher recall scores on average. However, compared with commercials with celebrities and 'ordinary people' fewer commercials obtained above-average scores for persuasion. This is particularly valid with commercials for new products.

Laboratory tests have already shown that attention for the humour often detracts from attention for the product and the message. This was confirmed by analysis of the test scores. Proper portrayal of the humorous contradiction sometimes proves to take so long that little time is left to formulate the message properly. That is especially difficult with new products, for which receivers have not yet accumulated any knowledge, and for which a great deal has to be communicated as a result.

Chattopadhyay and Balsu (1990) also conclude, after a laboratory test, that humour for established brands works better than for new brands. They suggest that humour is most appropriate for reinforcing existing positive brand attitudes. For new brands it is less effective, because it often deflects attention from the product claims.

In the MSW analysis 41% of the humorous commercials for established brands scored below the norms for recall and/or persuasion.

Test scores humorous commercials

	Established products	New products
Recall after 20 minutes:		
Above the norm	45%	33%
Same as norm	39%	30%
Below the norm	21%	37%
Attitude shift:		
Above the norm	34%	23%
Same as norm	37%	24%
Below the norm	29%	53%
Overall performance:		
Same as norm or above		
the norm for both criteria	59%	33%

Source: McCollum Spielman Worldwide – 'Focus on Funny' in Topline, July 1982.

Analysis of the results of 70 humorous commercials tested by GfK (Merz, 1989) did not reveal a significant correlation with persuasion scores, not even for commercials with good recall scores.

20.7   Incongruity with 'product feelings'

The low scores in the MSW analysis often indicated incongruity between the feelings of pleasure aroused by humour and the feelings associated with which the product or usage situation. Humour is often counterproductive with coffee and tea, for which it is important to evoke taste sensations and enjoyment. Nor does it work very well for serious matters, like financial services, for which complicated messages often have to be conveyed, or for over-the-counter drugs. And, most especially, when expensive status-linked products and brands are involved (for example, clothing, jewellery, travel, cosmetics, audio equipment), those receiving the message prefer to be approached seriously. So, on the whole, the higher the enduring product involvement, the less suitable the product is for the use of humour.

Humour can be particularly effective with products which are associated with fun – like many snacks, confectionery, chewing gum, cat food.

20.8 Dominating humour

The commercials which would seem to run the most risk are those using highly exaggerated or caricatural situations, absolute absurdity, peculiar people, idiocy, blunders and horseplay. Most so-called slapstick commercials score badly for all criteria. The use of funny characters is a risky business too. They are inclined to absorb attention and distract from the product and the message. The same goes for lisping children and funny animals: admittedly, they arouse attention, but the message is rarely conveyed. In all these examples humour soon dominates the entire commercial-processing operation.

20.9 Effective humour

However, humour can be very effective, as the MSW analysis also demonstrates. The commercials concerned are mainly ones in which the basic form is not determined by humour, but in which humour is an element which is added to another basic form, like slice-of-life, vignette and problem/solution concepts. In such cases, the humour is not occasioned by strange characters, but by funny experiences of ordinary people in which the product plays a central role. The secret of the effective use of humour lies to some extent in the part the product plays in the situations and occurrences.

20.10 Does humour work in advertising?

That depends. Primarily on the product for which it is used, and on the position of the brand. Also on the target group and the communication objectives, and obviously on the way in which it is used. Provided it is done well, humour can be very effective, especially when advertising and brand awareness are the prime objectives.

It can also reduce the inclination to zap, and so have a favourable influence on effective advertising reach. Humour can contribute to ad likeability and so, indirectly, to attitude to the brand. If the product category is associated with feelings of relaxation and enjoyment, it can directly contribute to a positive attitude to the brand. If it is used functionally in the 'packaging' of the central message, it can also make a substantial contribution to the processing and understanding of that message, and so to the persuasiveness of the advertising.

Part 5

From trial to brand loyalty

21 The ATR process

Could it be that, as a result of the advertising for a brand, a positive attitude gradually develops, which causes loyal consumers to switch eventually from brand X to brand Y, and then remain loyal to that brand for many years? No, that is seldom, if ever, the way it happens. Brand choice is not such a simple process. Usually people do not swap one brand for another at some specific moment. Nor does a new customer in a market usually have such a strong preference for one specific brand and buy it regularly, deliberately excluding other brands. The development of a pronounced brand preference and buying behaviour which reflects brand loyalty is far more likely to be a process which gradually evolves with time.

The ATR process

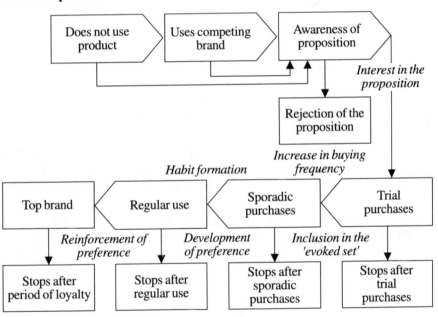

Source: Giep Franzen, 1982.

21.1 First trial purchases

The process starts with a consumer getting to know a brand and developing some interest in it. That may result in him purchasing it once, experimenting and getting experience with it. That might be the end of the process. The first experience with use of the brand might not have been positive enough. Or else the consumer's awareness of the brand was still so fragile that it just did not come to mind the next time he bought the product in question. Maybe the consumer did not encounter the brand again in the shop, or maybe he did not 'see' any more advertising for it. The first purchase was merely a slight deviation from his normal buying behaviour, and the consumer returned to his old buying habits.

But sometimes the first trial use of a new brand leads to a second or third purchase. Even then an end can come to these repeat purchases, more or less unconsciously. The brand is just 'forgotten'. Sometimes a buyer may consciously decide not to buy the brand, possibly because of unsatisfactory brand experience. But, more often than not, he has developed no clear preference for the new brand. Or else he no longer comes across it in the store. Some preference must first be developed and the consumer must encounter the brand on the shop shelf before regular or continued brand use occurs.

21.2   Repeat purchases

However, trial does sometimes lead to a series of repeat purchases. The consumer becomes more and more aware of the brand. He develops 'readiness-to-buy', when it suits him. Gradually the consumer develops a growing inclination to buy the brand again when he is confronted with it. It is included in the 'consideration set'. But this does not necessarily result in continuous brand use. External circumstances can still easily prevent that. The brand may, for instance, be out of stock or hard to locate on the shelf. Other brands may also constantly obstruct its development, with price reductions or promotions.

However, the new brand may start to operate as the second or third alternative alongside his top brand. It can also get stuck at that stage, and later lose ground as a candidate. but it may also be purchased more frequently, alongside the old brand.

21.3   Developing preference

A consumer gradually develops an emotional relationship with the new brand and starts to buy his old favourite brand less frequently. Finally the situation may be reached in which the 'new' brand has his main preference. Only when a strong preference exists does the brand become the top brand. By then it has obtained a permanent place in the purchasing pattern. And that, in turn, is expressed as brand loyalty in the consumer's buying behaviour.

The character of this process, which Ehrenberg termed ATR (Awareness-Trial-Reinforcement), depends greatly on two key questions. Does the consumer use the product or not? Or does he already use the product, but a competing brand? In advertising terms this means: do we have to make users out of non-users? Or do we have to convert a user of a competing brand into a user of 'our' brand? In both cases awareness for the brand must be developed. The difference lies in whether or not the consumer involved has product experience and whether he has a preference for a competing brand.

If a consumer is not yet a user, the advertising will especially have to concentrate on the generic product functions. If the ties with a competing brand have to be cut through, advertising will have to concentrate on developing differentiated brand associations.

21.4   A fragile start

Once interest has been aroused for a new brand proposition, trial purchases may follow. Willingness to do this varies greatly from one product category to another. In one case, there can be such a strong preference for an existing brand that it prevents experimentation with other brands. In another, there are consumers who have a spontaneous need for variation in product use. There one exposure to a new brand proposition will be enough to induce him to make a trial purchase.

Products which are purchased frequently and are low priced usually encounter reasonably spontaneous willingness for trial purchases. New product propositions certainly are. Little persuasion is needed to get a consumer of savoury snacks to try a new variety. Trial purchases are not by any means always the result of the advertising process.

A special display in a shop may also be inviting. A temporary price reduction may have a stimulating effect. And if the much-purchased brand is out of stock, that alone can be a reason for a trial purchase of a new alternative brand.

However, a decision which is reached with such ease, does not make a great impression either. Even after one or more trial purchases little of great importance has taken place as regards affinity with the brand. Deeper feelings about the brand still have to be developed. With the same ease with which the trial purchase came about, the brand can again be dropped. That is often what happens when there has been a large-scale promotion, for example the door-to-door distribution of samples. Admittedly, substantial trial use is achieved, but when the action has finished, the vast majority of purchasers will return to their old buying habits. As if nothing had happened.

21.5 'Singular' brand use

In most markets people often use more than one brand. They buy two, three or more brands fairly regularly. In other markets consumers focus on one brand, which accounts for a very large share of their individual purchases. That is, for example, the case with cigarettes, coffee, razor blades and sanitary towels.

In both types of market a brand's position can be expressed in its share in the individual purchases. In theory, the ATR process does not differ in the two types of markets. Although the second type does reflect more of a 'brand-switching' character. After all, a new brand has to break through a strong preferential relationship between a consumer and a competing brand. And then it is far more difficult to achieve trial use. If that does succeed, the results will be greater at the end of the process. If the process is successful, a new preferential relationship may come about. The brand may well account for almost all a person's purchases in the relevant product group.

This is a common situation in the cigarettes market. Brand ties are so strong that new brands have a very hard time penetrating. The percentage of people saying they have occasionally smoked the brand in question grows extremely slowly. A new brand will have a very hard job to come between a smoker and his favourite brand. If it does manage to do so, the majority of trial users will still return to their old brand. However, some will develop a preference for the new brand, slowly but surely. At some stage those smokers will buy only the new brand. That is why brand shares in the cigarette market only grow extremely slowly. Only a fraction of the new brands manage to penetrate the market, and of them only a few achieve real brand preference. And of all the new cigarette brands, only a few have lasting success. However, once they are successful, their smokers will often be loyal to that brand for decades. So market shares are extremely stable. They do change, but often only by tenths of a percent per year. Cigarette brands only 'pass away' when the last of their smokers do.

21.6 'Plural' brand use

In complete contrast to the situation on the cigarette market, we have brand use in the snacks market – there plural brand use is prevalent. Purchasers are, by definition, geared to trying out new options. Penetration is not usually hard to achieve. New products which catch on can soon acquire a large share of the market. Obviously they are always vulnerable. They never achieve undivided brand preference. They always have to settle for the purchaser's shared preference. And they live under the constant threat of being ousted by yet another recently-launched variety.

Simmons recently demonstrated that, in a sample of 50 product categories in the U.S., 72% of consumers were using several brands at the same time.

The following table gives the loyalty classes for a number of brands in six product categories in the Netherlands:

Percentage of purchasers per loyalty class		Loyalty measured in value/year	
Product	0%-40%	40%-90%	over 90%
Coffee	2%	38%	60%
Soup in packets	4%	60%	36%
Crisps	15%	69%	16%
Family washing-up liquid	14%	50%	36%
Washing-up liquid	3%	39%	58%
Shampoo	8%	52%	40%
Toothpaste	3%	48%	49%

Source: AGB-Attwood Nederland, 1989 period.

22 Six brand behaviour typologies

McQueen (1991) analysed for Leo Burnett the buying behaviour of thousands of families over a two-year period. As a result he was able to formulate five brand behaviour typologies.

22.1 Group 1: One-off buyers

Consumers make a trial purchase once only, and then stop. Clearly that cannot be the brander's intention, but it is often the outcome of his advertising or promotional approach ('try me once'). A short, sharp introductory campaign, followed by a long, profound silence will often have this result. Negative brand experience can also result in a one-off purchase ('this once, and never again').

22.2 Group 2: Repeated trial buyers

Consumers buy the brand a number of times after the first purchase, and then stop. This is prolonged trial use. It cannot be the brander's intention either. But not everyone can become a loyal customer, and this behaviour does at least suggest a successful strategy in promoting trial purchases. Prolonged trial use is quite common when a consumer has not been able to assess the product properly after one trial purchase. This may be due to uncertainty: the product tastes different, but you have to get used to it. Or else it may be due to advantages which are hard to confirm, as is the case with most toiletries. Tartar will not be perceptibly less after one tube of toothpaste. However, untimely conclusion of the introductory campaign may again be the reason for consumers to lose interest. As yet they do not have a real tie with the brand, but the brander has spent his budget. That is quite a frequent occurrence.

22.3 Group 3: Sporadic users

The third type are people who use the brand now and then. A brand like that does not usually account for more than 20% of a consumer's purchases in the product category, about half the share which a repertoire brand generally represents.

Sporadic use has several causes. It may result from the product's attributes. The product may be a variant, which is especially suitable for special situations and moments, as is currently the case with espresso coffee in the Netherlands. The products concerned have attributes which do not fit particularly well into everyday consumption patterns. So they owe their existence to the very fact that people want to break out of the daily routine now and then. Maybe we eat Cheddar cheese every day, and buy Gorgonzola a couple of times a year.

A second reason for sporadic use may be the fact that a consumer has such strong emotional ties with this top brand that he only occasionally buys another, second or third brand. He has nothing against Amstel lager, he considers it a decent beer, but he is a real Heineken drinker. He is only prepared to buy Amstel as an exception, if one day the shop is out of Heineken.

A third possible cause is the fact that the brand is not yet strong enough. It does have the status of an 'accepted brand', but has not yet succeeded in building up a real preferential position. That applies for many 'young' brands. They are still very vulnerable.

A fourth reason is connected with some purchasers' responsiveness to prices. They do have brand preferences, but react primarily to special offers. If a brand has an active promotions policy it can attract these purchasers from time to time, but when the offer has finished, they will switch just as easily to another brand in their repertoire which is on offer. They just are not prepared to spend more money for an acceptable brand than necessary. They often have no profound emotional ties with a brand. They change around so much that no one brand is permanent enough to constitute a larger share of their purchases.

22.4   Group 4:   Repertoire-buyers

This group buys the brand in question with the same regularity as several other brands. We refer to repertoire-buyers when the brand represents between 20 and 40% of all of their purchases in the relevant product category. This buying behaviour occurs particularly in categories in which variation plays an important part (snacks and desserts). The brands involved are often fairly unique, but their attributes are not linked to the basic motivations for the product group. The uniqueness also entails limitations (people quickly tire of the product, for instance). Repertoire brand behaviour may also be connected with needs which differ according to situations and circumstances. For example, we drink Indian tea at breakfast-time, Ceylon tea at tea-time and a herbal infusion at bed-time. Or we drink a special premium brand of beer when we have visitors, our 'everyday' beer on everyday occasions, and a low alcohol beer when we have to drive. Many cosmetics also belong in this group: we use different creams at different times.

A repertoire brand may also signify an intermediate stage, in the process of becoming a top brand. Consumers gradually include it in their customary behaviour. That may be the result of the brander's deliberate policy. He first tries, with a product variant with differentiated attributes, to acquire a place beside the consumer's top brand. Once he has managed on that score, he introduces a more generic variant which could take over from the top brand. Consumers have become acquainted with the brand, by way of the first variant, and have developed a degree of acceptance or even preference for it. So it is easier for them to switch to that brand for the generic product.

22.5   Group 5: Top brand buyers

Many consumers have one top brand in a certain product category for which they have a pronounced preference. A top brand buyer is someone for whom that brand accounts for over 40% of his purchases in the category concerned, even when a great many other brands are available. Top brand buyers buy the brand at least 50% more often than one of the other brands they also buy. The products involved are those which generate considerable (taste) habituation and constant satisfaction, and in which one variant meets the basic need. As a result, it accounts for most consumption – take coffee, tea, beer, cigarettes and sanitary towels, for example. In specific situations or specific moments people do use other variants (brands), but these never represent a large share of total individual consumption. Consumers associate their top brand in product categories like these more and more with the central values with which the product is linked. If all goes well, advertising will constantly reinforce those associations. Crucial in all this are the feelings aroused by product use, which a top brand gradually 'hijacks' for itself as it were.

The phenomenon of 'top brand behaviour' occurs in all categories, although the share of the top brand does vary from one category to another. It is a gradual process. It is never the result of a few trial purchases, but of a process of gradual reinforcement of behavioural tendencies, of habit-forming, which in turn produces a strengthening of brand attitude. Attitude and behaviour influence each other, and are constantly confirmed and reinforced by the advertising stimuli. With some brands, strong identification can occur with symbolic brand meanings: a consumer recognises his own values in the brand. "I'm a real Camel smoker."

We can add a sixth group to McQueen's classification:

22.6   Group 6: 100% brand-loyal buyers

These are the real members of the brand's fan club. They actually only want that brand and no other. If it is out of stock, they prefer to postpone their purchase rather than accept what they feel is a poor alternative. They rarely form a large group, but they are extremely important for a brand: they can account for a substantial share of its turnover.

Uncles (1985) drew up the following figures for 100% loyal brand users of instant coffee in the United States.

	Percentage of purchasers 100% brand-loyal in one year
Maxwell House	20%
Sanka	20%
Tasters Choice	24%
High Point	18%
Folgers	13%
Nescafé	15%
Brim	17%
Maxim	11%

Source: Uncles, 1985.

The Simmons analysis quoted earlier revealed that, in measurements covering 50 categories, on average 28% of users use only one brand.

A further subdivision can be made, into short-term and long-term 'loyals'. Short-term loyals are only loyal to a brand for a limited period. They then switch to another brand, to which they are again loyal for some time. They would seem to be constantly searching for the 'ideal' brand. They discover a new brand, but get tired of it after a while. Possibly because another candidate has come along with something new.

Long-term loyals use their brands loyally for years. This group is usually far larger than that of short-term loyals. 'Their' brand has a high emotional value for them. They trust it blindly and consider it to be far superior to all other brands. So they are not open to advertising for other brands either. Long-term loyals are usually found most with the major brands in a market.

This means that in many markets a connection can be perceived between a brand's penetration and relative buying frequency of that brand. Leading brands not only have more users, but those users buy them more often than people who buy 'smaller' brands.

The situation for brands of instant coffee in the United States was as follows (Uncles 1985):

Brand	Penetration in one year	Buying frequency
Maxwell House	25%	3.6x
Sanka	21%	3.3x
Tasters Choice	22%	2.8x
High Point	22%	2.6x
Folgers	18%	2.7x
Nescafé	13%	2.9x
Brim	9%	2.0x
Maxim	6%	2.6x
Average	**17%**	**2.8x**

Source: Uncles, 1985.

Penetration is the most important factor for the market share. But purchasing frequency would also appear to increase in line with penetration. A brand which grows stronger and stronger, gains in two respects: it attracts more users, and they purchase it more often. Clearly, the position of brands in most markets is mainly determined by top brand buyers and real brand loyals. In markets in which variation is important or in which there are varying moment- or situation-linked needs, repertoire buyers play a part.

23 Advertising which stimulates trial purchases

In Ehrenberg's ATR model, 'trial' results from accrued 'awareness'. 'Reinforcement' generally stands for the strengthening of brand attitude, which can come about thanks to continued trial use.

23.1 Awareness

What does awareness mean in this context? Is it mere 'consciousness' of the brand? Or is more involved – proposition awareness, knowledge of what a brand signifies, its attributes and its benefits? If so, can that be classified as awareness, or should we insert other steps between awareness and trial?

Ehrenberg himself indicates that 'interest' can be involved. In this way he is getting back to the first stages of the old AIDA model (attention-interest-desire-action). It might be more appropriate to call his model AITAR: awareness-interest-trial-attitude-reinforcement. The pure awareness-trial sequence may occur when trial results from promotional activities, such as sampling and in-store demonstrations. The awareness-interest-trial sequence will mainly occur when advertising causes curiosity, or arouses an expectation from the product which has not yet been confirmed (or refuted!) by product use.

23.2 Arousing curiosity

We have already referred to research carried out by Leo Burnett (Olson, 1985), in which the well-known trial-generating effect in the market-place of 65 launch commercials was compared with scores on VRP scales. (O&M's and Aaker and Stayman's likeability measurements were based on the same scales.) The commercials which were effective in generating trial use proved to score well on the following statements:

1. The commercial showed me the product has certain advantages.
2. The product is important to me.
3. The commercial reminded me that I'm dissatisfied with what I'm using now and I'm looking for something better.
4. During the commercial I thought how that product might be useful to me.
5. The commercial made me feel the product is right for me.

Commercials with a low trial effect had low scores. This confirms that a degree of 'curious expectation' can precede trial.

The second factor in Leo Burnett's analysis which proved to influence the trial-generating effect was labelled 'stimulation'. It expresses the extent to which respondents assess the commercials as obtaining and maintaining attention. It is the most important factor for the development of awareness.

23.3   The human factor

Experts analysed the quality of the commercials which did well for the trial factor in Leo Burnett's study. They came up with the following characteristics:

- The commercials generally feature a clear and significant benefit (point-of-difference) of the product. They succeed in dramatising this in some way, by:
  - dramatising the consumer's problem;
  - emphasising the end-benefit of the product for the consumer, more than the 'unadorned' attributes of the product;
  - by demonstrating the benefit in a relevant and accessible way, by supplying more than 'lab. proof' – for example, a demonstration which could have taken place in the consumer's own home;
  - placing it in a situation that is interesting, but also realistic for the product.

- They mainly use visual means, instead of relying on auditive (verbal) information.

- They make sure that viewers can empathise with the situation and identify with the actors.

- They often tackle the viewers' scepticism head on, in a direct attempt to support credibility.

23.4   Arousing expectations

We have seen that it is not only a matter of pure awareness of a new brand, but also of arousing curiosity, expectations, interest in the proposition: "what might the brand mean for *me*?"

Effective, trial-oriented advertising must appeal to the target group's self-interest. Is that an attitude? Rossiter calls it an, 'attitudinal inference about the brand's likely quality, prior to purchase'. He also suggests that consumers must have a:

*"tentatively held though sufficiently favourable belief or attitude toward the brand prior to trial, which is sufficient to instigate a trial purchase. The belief or attitude may then become more confidently held **after** trial".*

In other words, consumers who do not use the brand yet, and consumers who have experimented with it but do not yet include it in their 'brand repertoire' perceive the advertising arguments as just that: advertising arguments. Some will reject these claims: "this argument doesn't mean anything to me". Or "I don't believe the brand is really as good as it claims". But others will give the brand the "benefit of the doubt", as it were: "I want to see if the brand really is as good all that". Only when the product has been a used a few times will the attribute be linked, in direct association, to the brand. It then becomes a 'brand-belief'. Gradually that person will include the brand in his own routine behaviour. And he will form a positive attitude to the brand which, in turn, will ensure that he is satisfied with his choice.

24 Brand associations among users and non-users

For consumers product use itself is definitely the most important source of information on the attributes and benefits of the product. That is certainly the case for all products in which the instrumental or sensory characteristics can be perceived directly. If something works well or tastes good, you can discover that best by trying the product yourself, rather than reading about it. Advertising can confirm your own initial experience, but cannot change it essentially.

So there is always a strong correlation between product use and brand associations. Even usage frequency also effects brand associations considerably. Castleberry and Ehrenberg (1990) analysed the average 'belief-score' for four products:

Average percentage of persons with a belief vis-à-vis a brand

	Frequency of use			
	Regularly	Occasionally	Infrequently	Never
Breakfast cereals	38	30	21	14
Detergents	58	33	25	17
Fast food restaurants	55	47	36	30
TV news-programmes	56	47	35	28
Average	**47**	**39**	**29**	**22**

Source: Castleberry and Ehrenberg – Brand Usage, a Factor in Consumer Beliefs, 1990.

With products whose main attributes are not patently obvious during use, like foods low in polyunsaturated fatty acids, low-calorie beverages and most OTC pharmaceuticals, advertising will, amongst other things, have to ensure that consumers know about these attributes.

But, in theory, advertising always has an affirmative function vis-à-vis existing users of a brand. It ensures that they do not forget the brand, by constantly bringing it to their attention. And always reminding them what it means to them. What it does, in the instrumental sense, and what it tells about them, in the impressive and expressive sense.

24.1 Five attitude groups

After (repeated) trial use of a new brand, a positive, a neutral or a negative attitude comes about. These attitudes can vary greatly in intensity. Negative trial experience can result in immediate rejection of the brand. A more positive experience can result in the brand being included in the selection of acceptable alternatives.

By this stage there are five groups in the market:

1. people who do not know the brand yet;
2. people who know it but have not yet tried it;
3. people who have tried and rejected the brand;
4. people who have tried it but are neutral about it; and
5. people who accept the brand as an alternative and prefer it to a degree.

In the latter three cases selective perception will play a part. Numerous tests show that those who reject a brand, also display advertising-avoidance, and that users of the brand become increasingly open to advertising stimuli for it. The size of the five groups is often represented as a graph – a 'market map' as it is called. At a glance you can see the situation at a given moment, the longitudinal axis represents development in time. Clearly more details can be added to the market map.

Evergood coffee: the market map

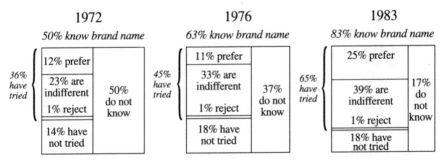

Sources: Norwegian Magazine Publishers Association;
H. and F. Hansen, 'Patterns of Brand Loyalty', European Journal of Marketing, 1986.

Recall scores are always considerably higher among users of the advertised brand than among non-users. And users of a brand always react more positively to advertising for 'their' brand than non-users (Schlinger, 1979).

Brand awareness and the role of advertising

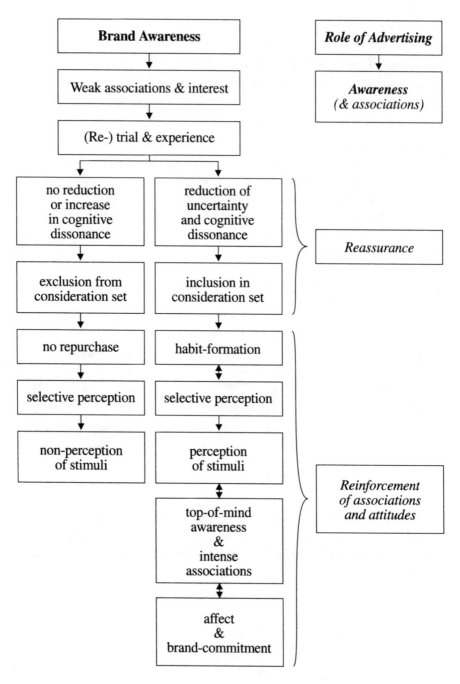

Source: Based on Hugh Murray 'So you know how Advertising Works', Management Decision.

214

24.2 Interaction of brand use and advertising

The constant interaction between use of the brand and the processed advertising stimuli relating to it, brings about an ever-richer and more intense associative network. Consumers start to connect certain product attributes more and more with their own brand; non-users do that less, if at all.

Ehrenberg gives an example of the situation in relation to cereals in Britain. The scores for 'popular with all the family' vary as follows for users and non-users.

Cereals 1973	Corn Flakes	Weetabix	Rice Krispies	Shredded Wheat	Sugar Puffs	Frosties	Special K	All Bran	**Average brand**
Buy Regularly ('Use'), %	48	29	13	12	10	9	7	7	**17**
Percentage saying 'popular' among:									
Users of brand	83	70	65	67	51	54	43	34	**55**
Non users	40	14	13	6	11	7	4	3	**8**
All respondents	**61**	**31**	**20**	**13**	**15**	**12**	**6**	**5**	**15**

Source: BMRB, 1964 and 1984; Field Control, 1973 and 1974.

Of all cereal-consumers, 15% claim that Sugar Puffs are popular with all the family. Of Sugar Puffs users, 51% claim that it is popular, while only 11% of non-users claim that the product is popular.

So positive attitudes are generated by usage experience. Consumers always believe that the brands they use are superior in most respects to those they do not use. They adjust their attitudes to their behaviour.

24.3 Evaluative associations

This phenomenon means that a brand's associations with positive attributes correlate greatly with the percentage of people who use the brand, and so with market shares. Ehrenberg's example with cereals only serves to confirm this:

Percent associating brand with attribute

Cereals 1973	Corn Flakes	Weetabix	Rice Krispies	Shredded Wheat	Sugar Puffs	Frosties	Special K	All Bran	**Average brand**
Buy Regularly ('Use'), %	48	29	13	12	10	9	7	7	**17**
Tastes nice	64	41	34	23	29	22	18	10	**30**
Easy to digest	60	40	25	19	21	20	23	19	**28**
Dad with the family	61	31	20	13	15	12	6	5	**20**
Come back to	65	32	11	11	6	7	6	4	**18**
Reasonably priced	59	26	8	13	5	5	5	5	**16**
Average	**62**	**34**	**20**	**16**	**15**	**13**	**12**	**9**	**22**

Source: BMRB, 1964 and 1984; Field Control, 1973 and 1974.

This connection is very pronounced for more or less 'generic' attributes in a product category. 'Nice taste' applies, for instance, for all kinds of foods, beverages and snacks. In a sense these are 'evaluative associations'.

24.4   Differentiating associations

If a brand has a physical attribute or effect which clearly differs from competing brands, this is reflected by the associations. Again this is apparent in the cereal example:

Percent associating brand with attribute   *(Greatly divergent scores in brackets)*

Cereals 1973	Corn Flakes	Weetabix	Rice Krispies	Shredded Wheat	Sugar Puffs	Frosties	Special K	All Bran	Average brand
Buy Regularly ('Use'), %	48	29	13	12	10	9	7	7	**17**
Stays crispy in milk	42	(6)	26	18	14	11	9	5	**16**
Nourishing	45	(52)	18	(32)	19	14	(19)	(19)	**27**
Lots of food value	27	(36)	9	(26)	9	8	(18)	(15)	**19**
Helps keep you fit	21	(25)	8	(17)	8	8	(27)	(36)	**11**
Has natural flavour	49	39	(11)	28	(5)	(5)	14	18	**21**
Fun for children to eat	16	12	(56)	5	(50)	(42)	5	1	**23**
Average	**33**	**25**	**15**	**17**	**12**	**10**	**12**	**8**	**17**

Source: BMRB, 1964 and 1984; Field Control, 1973 and 1974.

These could be termed 'differentiating associations'. They can also result from advertising, if it communicates a distinctive claim consistently for many years. Differentiating associations can occur among users and non-users alike, as the following table shows:

(Greatly divergent scores in brackets)

Cereals 1973	Corn Flakes	Weetabix	Rice Krispies	Shredded Wheat	Sugar Puffs	Frosties	Special K	All Bran	Average brand
Stays crispy in milk:									
Users	49	(9)	58	51	36	27	40	7	**36**
Non users	38	(5)	21	13	11	10	7	4	**14**
Nourishing:									
Users	56	(50)	40	(71)	44	32	(50)	(59)	**54**
Non users	35	(40)	15	(27)	17	13	17	16	**22**
Helps keep you fit:									
Users	28	(46)	21	(50)	15	24	(77)	(72)	**42**
Non users	14	16	6	13	8	7	(23)	(33)	**15**
Fun for children to eat:									
Users	20	19	(69)	15	(62)	(76)	13	0	**34**
Non users	13	9	(54)	3	(49)	(39)	4	1	**21**

Source: BMRB, 1964 and 1984; Field Control, 1973 and 1974.

Although the scores among users are again considerably higher, non-users also achieve high scores in some respects ('Cornflakes stay crisp in milk').

24.5   Associations and market share

The *average* attribute score is considerably higher with users than with non-users.

Average attribute scores

Cereals 1973	Corn Flakes	Weetabix	Rice Krispies	Shredded Wheat	Sugar Puffs	Frosties	Special K	All Bran	**Average brand**
Users of brand	59	55	45	53	39	38	50	41	**46**
Non users	35	21	17	14	14	12	11	10	**14**

Source: BMRB, 1964 and 1984; Field Control, 1973 and 1974.

So the more users a brand has, the more people will say it has certain (positive) attributes. Some associations ('tastes nice') are in fact a way of saying, in different words, 'I like this brand' and 'I use this brand'.

Other associations result from really distinctive product attributes, or from claims which advertising has consistently linked with the brand over the years. With brands which differ little from one another at the product level, the associations among users do not differ much either. In other words, the associations of Heineken for a Heineken drinker, Amstel for an Amstel drinker and Grolsch for a Grolsch drinker are very similar. But, for each brand, there is a great difference between the associations made by users of the brand in question and by users of competing brands.

24.6   Associations are persistent

Associative networks of longer-established brands prove to be persistent.
Ehrenberg's example with cereals again confirms this:

(Greatly divergent scores in brackets)

RTE Cereals	Year	Corn Flakes	Weetabix	Rice Krispies	Shredded Wheat	Frosties	Special K	All Bran	**Average brand**
Buy Regularly ('Use'), %	1964	50	28	17	18	8	6	7	**19**
	1974	56	33	18	17	9	7	8	**21**
	1984	46	38	26	13	17	6	11	**22**
Mainly evaluative									
Tastes nice	1964	54	24	20	17	12	7	4	**20**
	1974	67	41	34	30	27	19	12	**33**
	1984	58	39	40	25	38	21	13	**33**
Reasonably priced	1964	62	23	(12)	19	9	7	9	**22**
	1974	54	20	(8)	14	6	3	5	**17**
	1984	55	37	(16)	17	9	7	8	**22**
Partly descriptive									
Stays crispy in milk	1964	43	(5)	23	14	10	5	3	**16**
	1974	49	(14)	28	21	17	14	8	**23**
	1984	43	(7)	32	21	29	11	7	**27**
Fun for children to eat	1964	11	3	(51)	2	(8)	0	0	**3**
	1974	17	16	(60)	7	(41)	8	1	**10**
	1984	9	9	(67)	3	(44)	2	1	**5**

Sources: BMRB, 1964 and 1984; Field Control, 1973 and 1974.

Something does change, but in fact not very much, considering that the
figures cover 20 years. If nothing fundamental happens in the market-place,
like the development of a preference for other types of products (for example,
detergents without phosphates or beer without alcohol), or if no real
innovations occur in the brand or product itself, or if manufacturers do not
make any big marketing mistakes, associative networks are very much
inclined to remain unchanged over the years. Advertising can confirm them,
but it is very difficult to change them fundamentally, and it takes a lot of time
and money. Associations, once established, are very persistent.

25 Advertising for established brands

In 1991 IRI in the United States conducted analyses of a database of 400 cases which might well prove to be a milestone in advertising history. All cases related to fast-moving consumer goods. The database contains Behaviourscan purchasing data, market shares, copy-test results, media expenditure and media plans, competitors' expenditure, and advertising attributes. It was used to examine the correlations between developments in sales and market shares on the one hand, and advertising spending, advertising attributes and copy-test results on the other. In particular the shorter-term effects of increased advertising spending and of changes in copy strategy were ascertained.

The analysis produced a number of striking findings, which we shall now summarise (Lodish 1991, Lubetkin 1991, Sylvester 1992):

1. An increase in advertising budget alone is not always enough to achieve an increase in sales volume. With established brands higher advertising spending caused larger sales in 46% of the cases. Yet with new products higher sales were noted in 58% of the cases.

2. Short-term (within 1 to 3 years) effects are the result of change. By maintaining the status quo you will not raise sales. Change may consist of autonomous developments in the market, like growth in the number of users. Or it may be as a result of alterations in policy, like a different brand strategy, advertising strategy or media strategy. New target groups can be addressed in this way, or new messages communicated to existing users. An increase in advertising spending on its own will not usually have the effect of increasing sales.

3. Combined with the previous point, prime-time exposure of television commercials (i.e. between 8 and 11 pm) proved to be more effective than exposure during the day. This would seem to be because during the day mainly 'heavy' viewers are reached, whereas in the evening 'light' viewers are reached as well. So, in the evening a greater variety of people are reached than during the day.

4. Concentration of spending in certain periods is more effective in raising sales than an even distribution of budgets. That is probably partly due to the greater effort required to break through the ever-increasing communication clutter. A quick succession of exposures would seem to be more effective than exposures with long intervals.

5. Synergy exists between consumer promotions and theme advertising, but not between trade promotions and theme advertising. Frequent trade promotions have a modest effect on sales. It is difficult to achieve an additional effect at the same time by increasing the advertising budget.

6. Of the more than 20% higher sales achieved for the average successful brand by increasing the budget, 6% was the result of increased penetration, and 14% was due to increased buying frequency among existing users.

   Lodish's (1991) explanation for this is that higher frequency may well occur among occasional purchasers of the brand who develop greater brand loyalty. In his view, this is also a form of extending the number of loyal users. McQueen (1991) also believes that existing users are receptive to strategies focused on new users and which are based on a new claim or a new use.

7. It is easier for smaller or medium-sized brands to obtain long-term effects than for large, long-established brands. Smaller brands are more likely to achieve large (in percentage terms) sales increases; with large brands the relative effects are smaller, but the absolute increases are more spectacular. That is a typical 'big-brand effect'.

8. If an increase in the advertising budget succeeds in the first year in increasing buying frequency among groups of users, its effect will still be visible in the second and third years. With an average increase in sales of over 20% (with successful brands!) in the first year, 14% will be retained in the second year and by the third year it will still be 7%. So the effects of successful television advertising continue to be felt for three years. But if television advertising has no visible effects in the first year, they will not occur in the next two years either.

25.1 No convincing correlation with copy-test results!

The analysis had another startling result. Copy-test scores were available for 103 of the 389. The 103 cases represent both new and established brands, and recall and persuasion scores alike. However, on the whole no convincing correlation was found between recall and persuasion scores on the one hand, and higher sales or higher market share with a higher budget on the other. With established brands a .69 correlation was found with recall scores, but that was greatly influenced by a few extreme scores. A significant, but limited correlation was also noted between persuasion scores and sales trends. The general impression was that there certainly is a correlation, but it is not very convincing. There was a consensus among experts in an ARF forum on this research that too few cases are available for definite conclusions to be drawn. These results are bound to fire the doubts as to the validity of recall and persuasion scores. In attitude measurements which belong to standard copy-test methods, it is implicitly assumed that advertising will generate a change in brand attitude right after one or two exposures. The burning question is whether that is a realistic assumption. Is the reaction in a test situation a sufficiently valid indication for the same effect which occurs later in the market-place? Does it not favour rational, instrumental product claims compared with more emotional, expressive approaches? Might it not be that the affirmative effect on existing, regular users of the brand who already have a positive attitude to it cannot, by definition, be expressed in the scores? And do these measurements work with large, well-established brands?

Let us summarise once more how advertising works for established brands.

25.2   New users

The sale of every brand is the result of two components: the number of users (i.e. brand penetration) and the average buying frequency. Every brand loses users. That is, to some extent, the natural consequence of their mortality. And, to some extent, it is the consequence of their changing consumption habits: older people do not generally drink coke any more, and few senior citizens are users of beer. Every brand also loses users to competing brands. Perhaps because consumers have to economise and are obliged to switch to cheaper alternatives. Perhaps, too, because a competing brand has come along with a proposition which proves to be problem-solving for some users in a changing situation. For example, it contains no caffeine, or no sugar, or no alcohol, or very little tar or nicotine.

The main task, therefore, of brands wishing to stay healthy for a longer period of time and certainly those wishing to grow, is to attract new users. They must, at all events, get their 'fair share' of new generations entering the market. And if they wish to increase their market shares, that will not usually succeed unless they recruit new users. So a brand has the job of contriving to be included in the repertoire of existing users, alongside competing brands.

25.3   Increasing buying frequency

Average buying frequency is the second component which determines sales, and changes in them. We have seen that, measured over a great many product categories, on average 72% of users use more than one brand. They often ring the changes with three or more brands. A brand can grow by acquiring a larger share in that 'repertoire'. That is, by raising the degree of loyalty of its existing users.

In the long-term, penetration is the main contributing factor to growth (or decline!) in turnover. But, as the IRI's analyses show, in the shorter term (1 to 3 years) higher buying frequency is the main cause for higher turnover.

So advertising for established brands always has four objectives:

1. Ensure the brand is chosen by new generations of product users, generally as one of the brands in their repertoire of acceptable brands.
2. Ensure the brand finds its way into the repertoires of users of competing brands, as one of the acceptable alternatives.
3. Increase buying frequency of existing repertoire users of the brand itself. So to promote greater brand loyalty.
4. Protect brand preference of buyers displaying absolute brand loyalty: the core of the consumer franchise (short- and long-term loyals).

The relative importance of these four tasks may vary from one case to another. It will depend on purchasing habits in the product category, and on the market position of the brand in question. We shall not discuss it further in the present book. But it is appropriate to raise the question of how advertising can contribute to achieving these four objectives.

25.4   Attracting new generations

A brand which does not manage to recruit new users is faced with certain decline. Established brands with sizeable market positions (numbers 1, 2 or 3 in their markets) will primarily have to seek out new users among new generations entering the market. Some brands succeed in building up a slow, but sure growth in market share over the years, because they are able to acquire a greater percentage of 'novices' than their market shares might suggest. Other brands crumble away slowly as the years go by, because they are no longer able to appeal to younger generations.

25.5   Trial purchases

New users may also be 'poached away' from other brands. Usually that is the hardest task. It is almost impossible to turn an inveterate Coca-Cola drinker into a true Pepsi drinker. Advertising which tries to go against long-established attitudes and buying habits, is fighting human nature. But there are also many product categories in which several brands are generally alternated. And there are users with brand attitudes which are not so much of a 'religion'. Repertoire buyers and short-term brand loyals are the groups in which we have a chance.

25.6 Marginal marketing

Research will have to show with which groups a trial strategy might succeed. And the tactical resources will have to be considered carefully. Can advertising indeed help to stimulate trial purchases. Or are promotional means more appropriate, after which advertising will again have a primarily endorsing and reinforcing job?

Holloway (1991) calls this strategy 'marginal marketing'. He argues that there is no point in wasting money on people who will not budge. Long-term brand loyals of competing brands are usually impossible to turn around. So look at the attitude of users to the brand or brands they currently use.

Divide them into three groups: (1) the immovables, (2) the more or less loyal users of competing brands who nevertheless are susceptible to a different (new) proposition, and (3) the regular switchers, who might be equated with 'ships that pass in the night'. They will never be of lasting interest.

The important thing is to find out whether competing brands have more or less loyal users who can be lured into trying 'our' brand for once. Advertising with a trial function should meet the criteria which emerged from the cited tests. It is not enough for it to confirm to loyal users of the brand what they have known for a long time. To start with, it will have to succeed in arousing curiosity about the product. To that end, it can tell something new about it. That will preferably be related to a special attribute which is of value for prospective users. It need not always be immediately convincing, as long as it is intriguing or possibly even provocative. It must bring about a reaction like: "perhaps I should try that brand sometime".

Advertising which focuses on eliciting trial purchases must have high attention value. It must give people the feeling that "this is a brand everyone is talking about and that everyone seems to be buying". Brown (1991) suggests basing this on an interest spectrum.

Have heard a lot about it			Haven't heard anything about it
Curiosity	*Interest*	*No interest*	*Suspicion*

In fact, his arguments are based on the principle of agenda-setting: make sure people are properly aware of the brand, so that they cannot ignore it. That they have the feeling that the brand in question is evidently receiving a great deal of interest. That this is the brand that evidently is currently setting the tone.

The IRI analysis of 400 cases (1991) confirmed that advertising which succeeds in increasing sales in the shorter term (1 to 3 years) by attracting new users, and by increasing buying frequency, especially ensures that the brand stays 'fresh'. This advertising is characterised by a copy strategy containing new information and new arguments. It succeeds in breaking through existing attitudes, by means of product innovations or new information on the existing product.

25.7   Promoting adoption

As we have already seen, brand loyalty is by no means achieved by an initial trial purchase. It takes (a great deal of) time to develop. Deep, positive feelings, as encountered among loyal users of major brands, only come about in the course of many years. By no means all products and brands are able to build up close emotional associations and strong brand preference.

In some markets it seems as if every user has to be 'won over' again for every purchase. So the reinforcing task of advertising for existing brand users should be seen as a re-trial function. In other words: in such cases, in order to encourage repeat purchases and increase a brand's share in one consumer's purchases, the same kind of stimuli are needed as for first trial purchases. This occurs with products which are not purchased regularly and with which there are no emotional ties, such as many household goods and over-the-counter medicines. It also occurs with products for which the need for variation is great, which have a great many sporadic and repertoire buyers. For instance, biscuits, savoury snacks and desserts.

But the more often a brand is purchased and used, the more a consumer starts to associate the generic attributes of the category with that brand. Original, expectant curiosity, the "let's see if the brand really is as good as it claims" gradually develops into a positive assessment. What initially was only felt to be an advertising claim is gradually accepted as a good brand attribute. Advertising confirms and reinforces the consumer's own perception of usage experience. Gradually a greater difference is perceived compared with the alternatives: "yes, this brand really is better."

With some brands deep emotional ties develop as the years go by. The brand becomes integrated in the user's self-image. "I am a real Grolsch drinker" or "I am a real Saab-driver". The user has become brand loyal. In some markets and with some people that even results in absolute rejection of alternatives. Selective perception starts to play a part. These people avoid exposure to advertising for competing brands in the relevant product group. And look-out for advertising for their own 'beloved' brand. They start to believe that they are impervious to advertising. "I always use brand X, I'm not interested in the advertising for other brands". Forgetting how it all came about!

25.8   Revitalising brand experience

At this stage advertising encounters more or less loyal users of the brand. Its principal task is to give them a regular pat on the back, as it were: "There, you see, you really are using the right brand". "Everyone uses it. Keep up the good work."

Advertising which addresses a brand's existing users, always meets existing awareness and associations. They may be latent to some degree – people get used to the 'permanent' things in their lives. They are no longer constantly aware of them. That is why advertising has the job of demanding attention for the brand, again and again, and activating users' awareness and perception of it. Not always with a view to changing brand associations, but just to evoke them again, have them felt again, and then return them, refreshed, to the person's memory.

Research (Schlinger, 1979) has shown that commercials score well with existing users if they show the product and the brand in a way that ties in with their own experiences. Commercials do not reinforce existing associations and attitudes if they locate the product in a context which is far removed from actual usage situations, or if they use unimportant or exaggerated arguments. Advertising which consumers feel does not 'match' the brand is immediately rejected. This is especially true of major, widely-liked brands, like Douwe Egberts coffee in Holland. Brands like these cannot afford to do anything rash. Yet they must make a constant effort to stay interesting. They not only have to keep on confirming existing usage experience and emotions, but they must ensure that, in their users' eyes, they are always up to date and innovative.

It is hard to pin-point how advertising works with these major brands. Their associative networks have become so ingrained, and consumer attitudes have become so set that attitude (persuasion) measurements intended to ascertain the response to individual commercials do not in fact work any more. That is a great limitation of most surveys which form the foundations for this book. Only measurements of attention (awareness), Viewer Response Profile, communication response and likeability are still of any use. We can only attempt to discover how advertisements and commercials influence the images of, and attitudes to, big brands in the longer term by tracking research. So, in practice, the extent to which campaigns for brands of this type are really 'efficient' and 'effective' is largely a matter of personal assessment and trust.

25.9   Likeability important

There are in fact only two reasons to change brands. The first is a new, attractive proposition from another brand. For instance, a consumer is confronted with a commercial or advertisement introducing a product improvement or focusing attention on an unknown attribute or application. The consumer's reaction is: "Perhaps I should try it sometime". In persuasion measurements that will be expressed as an attitude shift. It is a short-term reaction (within 20 minutes or 24 hours) to a fresh stimulus from outside. The consumer is prepared to take a mental decision to buy, as it were, because there is a concrete reason to do so.

The other reason to change brands is an 'internal' one. A consumer becomes rather tired of a brand he has been using for some time. Perhaps he has even had a bad experience with it. Be that as it may, there comes a day when he is ready to try something else. He need not abandon his old brand for ever, but he decides to try another brand for a change. In that situation, a consumer reacts primarily to the impressions (images, associative networks) of other brands acquired over the years. The 'values' these associations represent for him will often play the main role in his new choice.

But very probably a generally positive feeling he has acquired about the brand, partly thanks to ad-likeability, will also have a positive effect on his choice.

A likeable advertisement or commercial which a person encounters in a test situation is not likely to be sufficient reason for him to be far more positive about a brand right away. So we observe neither an attitude shift nor a correlation with likeability. But a brand which advertises over the years in a way that the 'receivers' appreciate (positive Aad) gradually acquires a positive attitude (Ab), which can, at some stage, result in a decision to buy in favour of the brand

26 Objectives and principles of communication

In this book an attempt has been made to review what has been learnt from large-scale empirical research into how individual advertisements work. We have pointed to the limitations of the standardised methods which are currently in use: it is impossible to test and measure everything. These methods fail, in particular, to provide proper insight into the specific emotional reactions generated by advertising, and their effects on the development of attitudes to brands over the years. They also fail to provide a conclusive answer to the question to what extent advertising, which does not cause short-term attitude shifts, might nevertheless be effective in the long-term, in that it succeeds in influencing positively the image (associative network or knowledge structure) of brands in the longer term. The research on which this book is based is, in fact, the least revealing about how advertising works in the longer term for the megabrands in product categories which everyone has known since childhood. The Coca-Colas, Douwe Egberts, Campbells, Heinekens, PG Tips and all the other brands which are linked with products which large groups of the population use every day and which have been going strong, almost unchanged, for years.

We have seen how many different factors influence how advertising works. And it will be clear that the question of how advertising works is almost impossible to answer in general terms. Advertising for what? What kind of advertising? What exactly do we mean? The answers to these questions will determine whether we can say anything about how advertising works. Or how it ought to work.

26.1 Communication objectives

An essential part of advertising planning is to determine what effects should be aimed at in the given, specific situation. Ultimately, there are nearly always three objectives:

- to establish brand recognition and to increase brand awareness;
- to stimulate trial purchases; and
- to stimulate and safeguard brand loyalty (share in individual consumers purchases).

If advertising is to help us to achieve these three goals, it must succeed in:

1. getting attention;
2. communicating a message (including an emotional message);

3. contributing to improving attitude to the brand;
4. reinforcing an already positive attitude to the brand;

and in a society which is encountering an ever-growing communication overload, a fifth criterion can be added:

5. obtaining a reader's or a viewer's liking for the message and/or execution of the advertising.

We have seen that all kinds of advertising attributes contribute in very different degrees to these effects. Admittedly, all five effects are important in every situation, but not equally important.

And we now also know that choice of a certain basic form or of certain execution attributes inevitably means that one objective is better served than the other. So good advertising planning requires us to make clear priorities as regards the effects we wish to achieve. In that context two criteria apply:

1. the *relationship between user and product*, and the concomitant market attributes, as described in chapter 11;
2. the *brand position*, as discussed in the final chapters.

They are summarised in the following two tables, the first of which indicates the priorities which the author feels are most appropriate for each category. It is hard to avoid a degree of subjectivity and some simplification of the highly complex situation entailed in advertising planning.

Relationship between user and product, and advertising objectives

INSTRUMENTAL VALUES	−	+	−	'+
SYMBOLIC VALUES	−	−	+	+
	1	2	3	4
HIGH PRODUCT INVOLVEMENT		* Message * (Believability) * Message likeability	* Feelings * (Identification) * Executional likeability	* Message + * Feelings (believability) + (identification) likeability
	5	6	7	
LOW PRODUCT INVOLVEMENT	* Awareness (recall) * Execution likeability	* Message * Awareness (recall) * Message likeability	* Feelings (conditioning) * Awareness * Execution likeability * (Identification)	

228

The second table, in which the former serves as a guideline, is intended to plot the priorities in target groups and objectives in a concrete case. It is based on analysis of purchasing behaviour in a specific market.

The priorities can be expressed in this table by any subjective means. The important thing is that decisions are being taken about the relative importance of the intended communication effects.

Target groups and communication objectives

Target group(s)	New product users	Repertoire buyers and short-term loyals of competing brands	Repertoire buyers of own brand	Loyal buyers of own brand
Target behaviour Communication objectives	Experimental purchases	Experimental purchases	Increase in buying frequency (at expense of competition)	Continuation of buying behaviour
* Brand awareness (attention, recall)				

* Likeability
  – message
  – execution				

* Communication response
  – cognitions (messages)
  – specific feelings				

* Brand associations
  – instrumental values
  – im/expressive values
  – central values				

* Brand attitude
  – development
  – reinforcement
  – consolidation				

26.2 Principles of communication

This book began with a review of developments in the amount of communication confronting people in the industrialised countries of the Western world at the end of the twentieth century. We have seen that, since 1950, that amount has doubled about every ten years, and that, as a result of current technological developments, it will increase even faster in the final decade of this century.

We have also examined the consequences for advertising:
- greater selectivity in perception;
- shorter exposure and premature breaking of contact;
- more superficial processing; and
- the supplanting of reading by viewing.

Spontaneous recall of television commercials has been seen to drop as a result – on average, 3% per 10 years. However, we have also seen that aided recall is managing to hold its own. Viewers do perceive commercials, but process them more superficially. Moreover, as we have discovered, this phenomenon does not only apply to television. The 'seeing' (recognition) of advertisements in magazines and newspapers is also declining, by about one per cent a year, on average. In addition, advertisements are rarely 'really read'. And lastly, advertising awareness is also on the decline – by about 1% a year.

In the long-term, these are serious developments for the effectiveness of advertising. However, for individual advertisers they are not, as yet, reasons to feel discouraged and to turn away from advertising. Test scores for recall, recognition and persuasion vary considerably from one communication to another. This means there is still great scope for most advertisers to improve effectiveness. In addition, competitors are also facing the same developments – so the key question is who will best succeed in addressing the issue.

We have shown the effects of the great variety of forms and aspects of advertising in an attempt to indicate its wide scope. As we said in the introduction, there are no magic formulas or golden rules for advertising success. But, at the same time, there are countless elements which greatly influence ultimate effectiveness, and which deserve more attention.

We are concluding this book with a concise summary of the principles which have become more important in the context of current developments in the communication society. None of them are new, but they do require more consistent application than in past decades. The author does not intend the following points to be used as a 'check-list'. No advertising can fully meet all the principles, nor are all principles equally relevant in all situations.

We cannot repeat too often that it is impossible to generalise on how advertising ought to work. It works slightly differently in each specific situation. And that is the context in which the following principles should be considered. It is advisable to examine, from one case to another, perhaps even from one advertisement to another, which effects should be aimed at and how they can best be achieved.

26.2.1 Value-linkage

The foremost factor for advertising effectiveness is the extent to which we succeed in developing associations with the brand and the product which represent values for the selected target group. It takes a good understanding of the value systems of groups of consumers and of the structure of the meaning (association network) of the product and the brand. The next thing is to establish which value associations have to be formed and which reinforced. That decision is a very long-term one. The formation and reinforcement of strong associations is more likely to take decades rather than years!

26.2.2 'Sense-making'

Communication overload is forcing advertising practitioners to focus a great deal, sometimes one-sidedly, on entertainment. Meaningfulness and personal relevance are, however, still the main criteria for liking or appreciation of advertising. Consumers want to be approached as intelligent human beings and to know why they should buy the advertised brand rather than another.

I should like to mention in this context the technique of 'message engineering', as described by Clancy and Schulman (1991). It amounts to the formulation of a large number of possible product attributes and benefits, their subsequent evaluation in terms of actual product performance, their persuasive capacity and the extent to which they are distinctive from competing brands.

Come what may, we should never lose sight of the product itself. It must be integrated properly into the situations and occurrences covered in the advertising, without any larger effort being needed to understand what the advertisement or commercial is about.

26.2.3 Simplification

In view of the avalanche of communication reaching consumers every day, strict simplification is an absolute necessity, more than ever before. It means that we must restrict ourselves to the bare essentials. We must concentrate on one message, make that important, and try to convey it very effectively. We should omit the rest or limit it to what is absolutely necessary. The less we have to communicate, the better we can do it. In television advertising that also means limiting the number of pictures and scenes which are not logically connected.

26.2.4 Acceleration

In print advertising we must try to get the central message across in only a few seconds. That mainly means that the message must be understood in fractions of a second. The visual and the headline must do the job together. If we put the central message in the body copy, it cuts advertising effectiveness dramatically. We cannot afford complicated detours. Moreover, we must try to avoid everything that can slow communication down. So, eliminate any superfluity, and give important matters extra emphasis.

Generally speaking, the less copy the better. Long copy no longer belongs in ads in mass media. And if longer copy cannot be avoided, we use typographical elements to guide readers through the essential information.

In television commercials we must try to interest viewers from the very first second. If we still have not managed to interest them after five seconds, we risk losing their undivided attention. The same applies to television as to print advertising: avoid anything that takes considerable attention to understand. So no purely verbal monologues, but only copy which supports the visual. And omit anything that can distract attention from the central message.

26.2.5 Visualisation

We must try to communicate visually, first and foremost. If at all possible, the visual element in print advertising should be functional in conveying the central message, and the headline should provide suspense and support. The picture should show what the headline says, if possible, and the headline pick up what the picture shows. If there is a discrepancy between visual and headline, it must be possible to solve it in fractions of a second. For pictures proximity, expressiveness and vividness are important. They should not be 'puzzles', but not dull, ordinary or uninteresting either.

Television is primarily a visual medium. Television pictures should be simple and direct, easy to follow and to understand. So avoid visual, meaningless videographic terror. A worthwhile test is what is communicated when the sound is turned off? In television commercials as well, unique and exciting visuals are needed to break through communication overload.

26.2.6 Humanisation

We must also try to communicate in a 'human' way, which entails attempting to reflect the role the products in question play in the lives and dreams of real people. If possible we should use interesting people, situations and events, with which readers and viewers can identify. We might also call this aspect 'dramatisation'. We endeavour to avoid aloofness and abstractness.

26.2.7 Emotionalisation

We should activate the 'receivers' feelings more. Positive feelings, in particular, like interest, cheerfulness, warmth, happiness, trust or pride. Sometimes starting off with the evoking of discomfort, shock or fear. This has always been important for brands and products which meet emotional needs. But it has also become important to create an emotional context in order to convey rational arguments. 'Cool' information is no longer enough. An emotional context ensures that consumers can identify with the users of the product and the brand.

26.2.8 *Conditioning*

Advertising can also work at a lower level of processing. If the brand is constantly linked to the same type of stimuli, strong associations come about with images, feelings and/or cognitions. They add 'inner images', meanings and, especially, emotional experiences to the brand. Effective use of this principle necessitates the development of strong, unambiguous, vivid stimuli, which are used consistently over the years.

26.2.9 *'Refreshment'*

Once 'receivers' have processed the message, a commercials persuasive power drops. We must assume that when a person is confronted with an ad which he has seen before, his level of attention will also drop. Campaigns focusing on conscious processing of the message and direct persuasion, will need to have the concomitant advertising refreshed regularly and in good time. If the same ads are used for too long it will detract from advertising effectiveness in this case.

26.2.10 *Branding*

More than ever, the brand will have to be an integral part of the advertising. This can be achieved in all kinds of ways. Clearly, we should make sure that the brand name itself is dominant on the eyes scanning route. But we can also use strong signals, which consumers learned to associate with a brand in the past. A specific colour, a trademark, a tune, a melody, familiar personalities, and other striking, distinctive elements of form. However, these principles only work if they have been adhered to consistently for many years, so that they have become inextricably associated with the brand in question.

The sooner the brand can be identified, the better. The later that happens, the greater the risk that the right brand linkage will not be made. And then it is essential to end with a very powerful branding device. As far as television commercials are concerned: the sooner it is clear what brand is involved, the better. In addition, it is vitally important that the creative idea be linked properly with the brand. So not a feature film with a 'sender', but an idea from which the brand is indivisible, or in which it plays a key role. More than ever before we shall have to develop a strong and distinctive brand identity, by means of which readers and viewers can recognise us immediately.

26.2.11 *Entertainment*

This principle is mentioned expressly towards the end of the list. Not because it is the least important. Entertainment can be extremely effective in obtaining attention and activating a receiver's interest. But entertainment tends to be seen as the panacea for all problems which confront advertisers. And it is certainly not a panacea.

If pure brand awareness is the dominant factor in a consumer's choice process, and humour fits in with the feelings associated with the product and the brand, it can be a powerful tool. At other times, entertainment should primarily be subservient to communication of the central message. It must not distract attention from that.

Humour and other forms of entertainment, which are used solely to attract attention and amuse people, but have no fundamental connection with the product or the brand, do not belong in an advertising policy which is spearheaded by persuasion by means of communication of a message.

26.2.12 Lastly: consistency

Communication over the years has always been an important mainstay for the success of many megabrands – at least, consistency in the values with which the brand is linked. As well as in the brand identity, which is reflected in the consistent use of brand-related signals, the specific brand style and tone of voice.

For many of those brands the basic advertising idea has also been adhered to for decades. New versions were usually adapted carefully to the changing spirit of the times. Every country has examples of brands which have become stronger and stronger because they have 'remained themselves' over the years, without becoming boring or outdated.

At the end of the twentieth century these principles are more important than ever. At a time when people are inundated with a never-ending stream of communications, when their selectivity is growing accordingly, and their attention is becoming more superficial, it is even more important to be recognized fast. As well as to ensure that the associations with attributes, images and feelings which distinguish a brand from its competitors are constantly being confirmed and reinforced.

References

12 jaar NIPO TV-Impactonderzoek, 1986: FHV/BBDO.

Aaker, D.A., Bruzzone, D.E., 1981: Viewer perceptions of prime-time television advertising, Journal of Advertising Research, Vol. 21, No. 5.

Aaker, D.A., and Bruzzone, D.E., 1985: Causes of irritation in advertising, Journal of Marketing, Vol. 49, Spring.

Aaker, D.A., Stayman, D.M., and Hagerty, M.R., 1986: Warmth in Advertising: Measurement, Impact, and Sequence Effects, Journal of Consumer Research, Vol. 12.

Aaker, D.A., Stayman, D.M., and Vezina, R., 1988: Identifying Feelings Elicited by Advertising, Psychology and Marketing.

Aaker, D.A., and Stayman, D.M., 1989: What mediates the emotional response to advertising? The case of warmth, in: Cafferata P., and Tybout, A.M., Cognitive and Affective Responses to Advertising, Lexington Books.

Aaker, D.A. and Stayman, D.M., 1990: Measuring Audience Perceptions of Commercials and Relating them to Ad Impact, Journal of Advertising Research, Vol. 30.

Abernethy, A.M., 1990: Television Exposure: Programs vs. Advertising, Current Issues and Research in Advertising, No. 2.

Adams, A.J., and Henderson Blair, M., 1992: Persuasive Advertising and Sales Accountability: Past Experience and Forward Validation, Journal of Advertising Research, Vol. 32, No. 2, March/April.

Advertising and Research Issues, How different Media Work, How Advertising Works and Promotions Work, Esomar, Amsterdam, 22nd-24th April.

Agres, S.J., 1987: Rational, Emotional and Mixed Appeals in Advertising: Impact on Recall and Persuasion, Annual Conference of the American Psychological Association, New York, August.

Allwit, L.F. and Mitchell, A.A., 1985: A description of television at home, in: "Psychological processes and advertising effects; Theory research and applications", Erlbaum.

Alpers, H.,1976: Anzeigen Post Tests, Gruner und Jahr Schriftenreihe bd 20.

Alsem, K.J., Leeflang, PSH, en Reuyl, J.C., 1991: Media in beweging, Bedrijfsfonds voor de pers.

Anderson, D.R., Alwitt, L.F., Lorch, P. a.o 1979: Watching children watch television, in: Hale, G.A., and Lewis, M. Attention and cognitive development, Plenum Press.

Andresen, T., "Guck" "doch mal hin!" "Anzeigenkontakten in der Werbewirkungsforschung, GfK Jahrbuch der Absatz- und Verbrauchsforschung."

Andresen, T., 1987: "Anzeigenkontakt und Informationsüberschuss", Inauguraldissertation, Nürnberg.

The ARF Copy Research Validity Project 1990: Likability plus a few other things, Marketing Review.

Assael, H., Kofron, J.H., and Burgi, W., 1967: Advertising performance as a function of print ad characteristics, Journal of Advertising Research, Vol. 7.

Axelrod, J.N., Attitude Measures That Predict Purchase, Journal of Advertising, Vol. 8, No. 1.

Baker, W.E., and Lutz, R.J., 1988: The relevance-accessibility model of advertising effectiveness, in: Hecker, S and Stewart, D.W., Nonverbal communication in advertising, Lexington Books.

Barnard, N.R., and Ehrenberg, A.S.C.,1990: Robust Measures of Consumer Brand Beliefs, Journal of Marketing Research, Vol. 27, November.

Barry, T.E., 1987: The development of the hierarchy of effects, An historical perspective, Current Issues & Research in Advertising, Vol. 10, No.2.

Barry, T.E., and Howard, D.J., 1990: A review and critique of the hierarchy of effects in advertising, International Journal of Advertising, Vol. 9.

Barwise, T.P., and Ehrenberg A.S.C., 1985: Consumer beliefs and brand usage, Journal of the Market Research Society, Vol. 27.

Batra, R., 1991: How Ad-Evoked Emotions Influence Processing of Information in the Ad, paper presented at "Tears, cheers and fears conference", MSI.

Batra, R., and Ray, M.L., 1986: Affective Responses Mediating Acceptance of Advertising, Journal of Consumer Research, Vol. 13, September.

Beattie, A.E., and Mitchell, A.A., The relationship between advertising recall and persuasion: an experimental investigation, in: Alwitt, L.F. and Mitchell, A.A., Psychological processes and advertising effects: theory, research and application, Lawrence Erlbaum.

Beentjes, H., en Voort, T. van der, 1987: De invloed van televisiekijken op het lezen van de jeugd, Masscommunicatie, No. 2.

Berlyne, D.E., 1970: Attention as a problem in behaviour theory, in: Mostofsky, D.I., Attention: Contemporary theory and analysis, Appleton Century Crofts.

Berlyne, D.E., 1960: Conflict, arousal and curiosity, McGraw Hill.

Beijk, J., Raay, W.F., van, 1989: Schemata; Informatieverwerking, beïnvloedingsprocessen en reclame. Pre-advies aan de VEA.

Biel, A.L, 1990: Love the Ad, Buy the Product? ADMAP, September.

Biel, A.L., and Bridgwater, C.A., 1990: Attributes of Likable Television Commercials, Journal of Advertising Research, Vol. 30, June/July.

Bock, de, H., en Sikkema, P., 1992: Op het juiste moment, Blad dossier, No. 4, June.

Bogart, L., and Lehman, C. 1983: The case of the 30-second commercial, ADMAP, July/August.

Bogart, L., and Stuart Tolley, B.S., 1988: The search for information in newspaper advertising, Journal of Advertising Research, Vol. 28, April/May.

Bogart, L., Stuart Tolley, B.S., and Orenstein, F., 1970: What one little ad can do, Journal of Advertising Research, Vol. 10, No. 4. August.

Bogozzi, R., and Silk, R., 1983: Recall, recognition and the measurement of memory for print-advertising, Marketing Science, Spring.

Borden, N.H., The Economic effects of advertising, Irwin, Homewood, Illinois.

Bornstein, R.F., 1989: Exposure and Affect: Overview and Meta-Analysis of Research, 1968-1987, Pschycological Bulletin, Vol. 106, No. 2.

Bornstein, R.F., Leone, D.R., and Galley, D.J., 1987: The Generalizability of Subliminal Mere Exposure Effects: Influence of Stimuli Perceived Without Awareness on Social Behavior, Journal of Personality and Social Psychology, Vol. 53, No. 6.

Brandt, C., 1990: Zapping, scriptie Universiteit van Amsteram, vakgroep Communicatie-wetenschappen.

Broadbent, D.E., 1977: The hidden preattentive processes, American Psychologist, Vol. 32, No. 2.

Broadbent, S., 1988: Measuring advertising effects: American practice and lessons for Brits, ADMAP, June.

Broadbent, S., 1991: Introduction in: How advertising works, Esomar Seminar, Amsterdam, 22nd-24th April.

Broadbent, S., and Burnett, L., 1991: The shifting base, ADMAP, March.

Broadbent, S., and Colman, S., Advertising effectiveness: across brands, Journal of the Market Research Society, Vol. 28, No. 1.

Brown, G., 1986: Monitoring Advertising Performance, The link between ad content and sales effects, ADMAP, March.

Brown, G., 1988: Facts from tracking studies – and old advertising chestnuts, ADMAP, June.

Brown, G., 1991: Response modelling advertising awareness, Journal of the Market Research Society, Vol. 33, No. 3, July.

Brown, G., 1991: "Why established brands behave as they do – more research evidence", in: Breakthrough marketplace advertising research for bottom line results, transcript proceedings, ARF Marketplace advertising research workshop, New York, Hilton Hotel, November.

Brown, G., and Brown, M: How advertising works – some new thinking in the light of modern evidence.

Brown, G., and Brown, M., 1991: Modelling advertising awareness, ADMAP, April.

Brown, S.P., and Stayman, D.M., 1992: Antecedents and Consequences of Attitude toward the Ad: A Meta-analysis, Journal of Consumer Research, Vol. 19, June.

Buck, S., and Yates, A., 1986: Television viewing, consumer purchasing and single source research, Journal of the Market Research Society, Vol. 28, No. 3.

Bullmore, J., 1985: Getting explicit about the implicit, ADMAP, October.

Burke Marketing Research, 1986: Day after recall, Television commercial testing,

Burke Marketing Research, 1990: TV recall isn't what it used to be.

Burnett, L., 1947: Checklist for a succesful advertisement, Memorandum to creative staff.

Busnel, G.T., How people look at pictures: a study of the psychology of perception in art, University of Chicago-press, Chicago.

Cantor, J.R., and Venus, P., 1990: The effect of humour on recall of a radio advertisement, Journal of Broadcasting, 24, (1980) 1. pp. 13-22.

Castleberry, S.B., and Ehrenberg, A.S.C.,1990: Brand Usage: A Factor in Consumer Beliefs, Marketing Research, June.

Cazeneuve, J., 1974: Television as a Functional Alternative to Traditional Sources of Need Satisfaction, in: The Uses of Mass Communication, Blumer, J.G., and Katz, E.

Cermak, L.S. and Craik, F.F.M., 1979: Levels of Processing in Human Memory, Lawrence Erlbaum, pp. 321.

Chattopadhyay, A., and Basu, K.,1990: Humor in Advertising: The Moderating Role of Prior Brand Evaluation, Journal of Marketing Research, Vol. 27, November.

Chattopadhyay, A., and Nedungadi, P., 1992: Does Attitude toward the Ad Endure? The Moderating Effects of Attention and Delay, Journal of Consumer Research, Vol. 19.

Cebuco, 1985: Dagbladen binnen bereik, (samenvatting).

Clancy, K.J., Ostlund, L.E., and Wyner, G.A.,1979: False Reporting of Magazine Readership, Journal of Advertising Research, Vol. 19, No. 5, October.

Clancy, K.J., and Schulman, R.S., 1991: The marketing resolution: A radical manifesto for dominating the marketplace, Harper Business.

Clark, E., 1988: The Want Makers, Hodder & Stoughton.

Colman, S., and Brown, G., 1983: Advertising tracking studies and sales effects, Journal of the Market Research Society, Vol. 25, No. 2.

Copy Testing Sales Validity, 1992: transcript proceedings of an ARF-open forum.

Coulson, J.S., 1989: An investigation of mood commercials, in: Cognitive and affective responses to advertising, Lexington Books.

Craik, F.I.M., and Lockhart R.S., 1972: Levels of Processing: A Framework for Memory Research, Journal of Verbal Learning and Verbal Behavior, Vol. 11.

Craik, F.I.M., 1979: Levels of Processing: Overview and closing comments, in: Levels of Processing in Human Memory. Lawrence Erlbaum Ass. Hillsdale, New Jersey.

Cronin, J.J., and Menelly, N.E., 1992: Discrimination vs. Avoidance: "Zipping" of Television Commercials, Journal of Advertising, Volume 21, No. 2.

Cuilenburg, J. van, 1992: On-Line Informatie: Tussen Vraag en Aanbod, On-line Conferentie Nederland.

Cuilenburg, J. van, Haaren, H. van, Haselhoff, F., en Lichtenberg L., 1992: "Tussen krantebedrijf en mediaconcern; Een beleidsessay over pers en persbedrijf."

Danke, R., 1986: Die qualitatieve Bedeutung von Anzeigen, In Anzeigen-copytests; Erkentnisse aus 10 Jahren Argus, Gruner + Jahr, Die Stern Bibliothek.

Denon, L., 1985: Understanding Television Audience Behaviour; the Italian Test-bed, ADMAP, September.

Dervin, B., 1984: A theoretical perspective and research approach for generating research helpful to communication practice, in: Public Relations Research and Education I.

Doorn, van, L.J., and Stapel, J., 1991: NIPO's Brand Monitor and How Advertising Works, in: Esomar Seminar, How advertising works and how promotions work, Amsterdam, 22nd-24th April.

Duin, van, E.M., en Papousek, D.A.P., 1990: Humor in reclame, Doctoraalscriptie Universiteit van Amsterdam, vakgroep communicatienetenschapper.

Duncan, C.P., 1979: Humor in Advertising: A Behavioral Perspective, Journal of the Academy of Marketing Science, Vol. 7, No. 4.

Edell, J., and Chapman Moore, M., 1991: The Effect of Feelings on Attitude Toward the Ad and Brand Beliefs, Paper presented at ibid.

Ehrenberg, A.S., 1974: Repetitive advertising and the consumer, Journal of Advertising Reseacrh., Vol. 14, No. 2.

Eigenständigkeit und Markenbezug als Erfolgskriterien bei Spots, 1992: W&V No. 12, 20th March.

Elliott, J., 1987: Campaign evaluation, in Cowley, D., How to plan advertising.

Estes, W.K., 1978: Handbook of learning and cognitive processes: ed. by W.K. Estes, Hillsdale, Erlbaum.

FCB: Day-after-recall cheats emotion, 1981: Ad Age, May.

Feldwick, P., 1991: The Longer and Broader Effects of Advertising: Some Observations and Recent Evidence, Esomar seminar, How advertising works and how promotions work, Amsterdam.

Feldwick, P., Carter, S., and Cook, L., 1991: How valuable is the Awareness Index, Journal of the Market Research Society, Vol. 33, No. 3.

Feldwick, P., Cook, L., and Carter, S., 1991: Ad effectiveness and ad awareness, ADMAP, March

Ferguson, 1989: The Aquarian Conspiracy, Paladin, London.

Fernsehspots büssen zunehmend an Erinnerungswert ein, 1992: W&V No. 8/21.

Finn, A., 1988: Print Ad Recognition Readership Scores: An information processing perspective, Journal of Marketing Research, Vol. 25.

Flechsig, R.G., 1988: What's happening to differential length commercial scores? An update, Electronic media and research technologies, ARF conference, Hilton Hotel, New York, 6-7th December.

Friedman, R., and Zimmer, R., 1988: The role of psychological meaning in advertising, Journal of Advertising, Vol. 17, No. 1.

Friestad, M., and Thorson, E., 1986: Emotion-eliciting advertising: effects on long-term memory and judgment, Advances in Consumer Research, Vol. 13.

Gaag, A. van der, 1991: Een derde tieners zapt bij reclameblok, Adformatie No. 22.

Gardner, M.P., Mitchell, A.A., and Russo, J.E., 1985: Low Involvement Strategies for Processing Advertisements, Journal of Advertising, Vol. 14, No. 2.

Garner, W.R., The Processing of information and structure, Lawrence Erlbaum Associates, Hillsdale, N.Y.

Gates, F.R., 1986: Further comments on the miscomprehension of televised advertisements, Journal of Advertising, Vol. 15, No. 1.

Gelb, B.D., and Pickett, C.M., 1983: Attitude toward the ad: Links to humor and to advertising effectiveness, Journal of Advertising, Vol. 12, No. 2.

Gelb, B.D., and Zinkhan, G.M., 1986: Humor and Advertising Effectiveness After Repeated Exposures to a Radio Commercial, Journal of Advertising, Vol. 15, No. 2.

Ghorpade, S., 1986: Agenda Setting: A Test of Advertising's Neglected Function, Journal of Advertising Research. Vol. 26, August/September.

Gibson, E., and Rader, N., 1979: Attention as performer, in: Attention and cognitive development, Hale, G.A. and Lewis, M., (Eds) Plenum Press.

Gibson, L.D., 1983: Not Recall, Journal of Advertising Research, Vol. 23, No. 1.

Glass, A.L., and Holyoak, K.J., 1986: Cognitions, McGraw Hill.

Green, L., 1990: Does Award winning advertising sell? Presentation for I.A.A. congress, June.

Greenberg, B.S., 1974: Gratifications of Television Viewing and their Correlates for British Children, in: The Uses of Mass Communications, Blumer, J.G., and Katz, E. Sage Publications.

Greene, W.F 1992: Observations: What drives commercial liking? Journal of Advertising Research, Vol. 32, March/April.

Greenwald, A.G., and Leavitt, C., 1984: Audience involvement in advertising: Four levels, Journal of Consumer Research, Vol. 11, June.

Greig, I.D, 1991: Quant pretesting; Preferences and image shifts, ADMAP, June.

Greig, I.D., 1991: Advertising Pretesting; What is Important?, How advertising works and how promotions work, Esomar seminar, Amsterdam, 22nd-24th April.

Häcker, T.W.F., en Verhallen, T.M.M., 1988: Het voorkomen van merkverwarring: Adverteert u voor uw concurrent, Tijdschrift voor Marketing, December.

Haley, R.I., and Baldinger, A.L., 1991: The ARF Copy Research Validity Project, Journal of Advertising Research, Vol. 31, April/May.

Hansen, F. 1984: Towards an alternative theory of the advertising communication process, International Journal of Research in Marketing.

Heeter, C., and Greenberg, B.S., 1985: Profiling the zappers, in: Journal of Advertising Research, Vol. 25, No. 2.

Hell, D., 1992: Beelden zijn snelle schoten in het brein, Adformatie No. 13, March.

Henderson Blair, M., Kuse, A.R., Furse, D.H., and Stewart, D.W., 1987: Advertising in a New Competitive Environment: Persuading Customers to Buy, Business Horizons, Vol. 30, No. 6, November/December.

Henderson Blair, M., 1988: An empirical investigation of advertising wearin and wearout, Journal of Advertising Research, Vol. 27, No. 6.

Henderson Blair, M., 1991: How to make our quarterly numbers with advertising, Marketing management workshop, Research System Corporation, 22nd August.

Hendon, D.W., 1973: How Mechanical Factors Affect Ad Perception, Journal of Advertising Research, Vol. 13, No. 4.

Hess, E.M., 1976: Analysen zum Werbemittelkontakt im Werbeträgensumfeld, Esomar-seminar 3.

Higie, R.A., and Sewall, M.A., 1991: Using recall and brand preference to evaluate advertising effectiveness, Journal of Advertising Research. Vol. 23, No. 2.

Hillebrand, K., 1992: Erfolgsvoraussetzungen und Erscheinungsformen des Humors in der Werbung – dargestellt am Beispiel von Low-Involvement Produkten, Diplomarbeit im Fach Marketing, Münster.

Hofstede, P., 1990: in Zapping, Brandt, C., stageverslag FHV/BBDO.

Holbrook, M.B., and Batra, R., 1988: Toward a standardized emotional profile useful in measuring responses to the nonverbal components of advertising, in: Nonverbal communication in advertising, Hecker, S., and Stewart, D.W., Lexington Books.

Holbrook, M.B., and Lehmann, D.R., 1980: Form versus Content in Predicting Starch Scores, Journal of Advertising Research, August, Vol. 20, No. 4.

Holloway, P., 1991: Maximising Communicational Effectiveness, How Research can Help, Esomar seminar, Amsterdam, How advertising works and how promotions work, 22nd-24th April.

Holman, R., and Hecker, S., 1983: Advertising Impact: Creative Elements Affecting Brand Saliency, Current Issues and Reserach in Advertising.

Homer, P.M., and Yoon, S.G., 1992: Message Framing and the Interrelationships Among Ad-Based Feelings, Affect, and Cognition, Journal of Advertising, Vol. 21, No. 1.

Homer, P.M., 1990: The Mediating Role of Attitude Toward the Ad: Some Additional Evidence, Journal of Marketing Research, Vol. 27, February.

Horsbey, C., 1986: A quantified study on what people do during commercial breaks, in: Esomar congress, Helsinki.

Horton, D.L., and Bergfeld Mills, C., 1984: Human learning and memory, Annual Review Psychology.

Houson, F.S., and Scott, D., 1984: The determination of advertising page exposure, Journal of Advertising, Vol. 13, No. 2.

Houston, M.J., Childers, T.L., and Heckler, S.E., 1987: Picture-Word Consistency and the Elaborative Processing of Advertisements, Journal of Marketing Research, Vol. 24, November.

How advertising works: analyses of 400 Behaviorscan cases, IRI 1991.

Hoyer, W.D., Srivastava, R.K., Jacoby, J., 1984: Sources of Miscomprehension in Television Advertising, Journal of Advertising, Vol. 13, No. 2.

Hulst, T., van 1992: Factoranalyse statements, Reclame reaktie onderzoek Admedia (unpublished).

Jacoby, J., Hoyer, W.D., and Zimmer, M.R., 1983: To Read, View, or Listen? A Cross-Media Comparison of Comprehension, Current Issues and Research in Advertising, August.

Jacoby, J., and Hoyer, W.D., 1987: The comprehension and miscomprehension of print communications, Advertising Educational Foundation.

Jacoby, J., and Hoyer, W.D., 1989: The Comprehension/Miscomprehension of Print Communication; Selected Findings, Journal of Consumer Research, Vol. 15, No. 4.

Janiszewski, C., 1990: The Influence of Print Advertisement Organization on Affect Toward a Brand Name, Journal of Consumer Research, Vol. 17, No.1, June.

Jeck-Schlottmann, G., 1987: Visuele Informationsverarbeitung bei wenig involvierten Konsumenten – eine impirische Untersuchung zur Anzeigenbetrachtung mittels Blick-aufzeichnung, Dissertatie, Saarbrücken.

Jewler A.J., 1981: Creative Strategy in Advertising; What the copywriter should know about the creative side of the business, Wadsworth Publishing Company.

Johar, J.S., and Sirgy, M.J., 1991: Value-Expressive Versus Utilitarian Advertising Appeals: When and why to use which appeal, Journal of Advertising, Vol. 20, No. 3, September.

Jones, J.P., 1991: Over-Promise and Under-Delivery, How Advertising Works, in Esomar conference: How advertising works and how promotions work, Amsterdam, 22nd-24th April.

Joyce, T., 1991: Models of the advertising process, in Esomar seminar, How advertising works and how promotions work, Amsterdam, 22nd-24th April.

Joyce, T., 1991: Models of the Advertising Process, Marketing and Research Today, November.

Keitz, B., von, 1985: Symposium zur Kommunikations-Forschung, Saarbrücken, 28th June.

Kelly, J.P., and Solomon, P.J., 1975: Humor in Television Advertising, Journal of Advertising, Vol. 4, No. 3.

Khan, F., and Light, L., BBDO, Copy Testing, Communication vs. Persuasion? (unpublished).

Kiss, T., und Wettig, H., 1973: Die Anzeigenwirkung in abhängigkeit von Wirkungsfaktoren der Zeitschriften, in: The application of market and social research for more efficient planning, Esomar/Wapor Congress, special groups, Budapest, September.

Klein, P.R., 1976: The Influence of Executional Elements on Commercial Effectiveness (Ad*Vantage Act, Executional Analysis I), (unpublished paper), Presented at the 1976 Advertising Research Foundation, New York, McCollum Spielman Worldwide.

Klein, P.R., 1989: Advertising Research: Does it Pay? Paper presented at Market Research Society of Australia, Conference.

Klein, P.R., 1990: Will the creative approaches of the 80's work in the 90's? Paper presented at the 36th Annual Conference of the Advertising Research Foundation, Hilton Hotel, New York, April.

Klein, P.R., 1991: Image/mood television advertising and the multiple exposure of test stimuli: A philosophical and empirical overview, McCollum Spielman Worldwide, June.

Klein, P.R., 1991: What's happening with advertising and advertising research globally, How to increase advertising productivity, (unpublished paper), presented at the ANA Seminar: Marketing for the 21st century, McCollum Spielman Worldwide, October.

Klein, P.R., and Musiol, K.G., 1990: Validation: Results from the United States and Europe, Paper presented at Copy Research Workshop of the ARF, OMNI Park Central Hotel, 11-12th July.

Klein, P.R., and Tainiter, M., 1983: Copy research validation, The advertiser's perspective, Journal of Advertising Research, Vol. 23, October/November.

Knecht, J. 1990: Advertising tracking, Reclame en Onderzoek, Vol. 2, No. 1.

Knulst, W., Kalmijn, M., Beek, P., van, 1988: Van woord naar beeld?, Sociaal en Cultureel Planbureau.

Koeppler, K., 1974: Werbewirkungen definiert und gemessen, Heinrich Bauer Stiftung.

Koeppler, K., 1987: Agenda setting bringt mehr, VJH 1/87.

Korgaonkar, P.K., Moschis, G.P., and Bellenger, D.N., 1984: Correlates of succesful advertising campaigns, Journal of Advertising Research, Vol. 24, February/March.

Kosaris, G., 1985: Anzeigenerfolg nicht dem Zufall überlassen, Konsequenzen aus copytests mit Blikaufzeichnung, in: Symposium zur Kommunikationsforschung, Institut fur Kommunikationsforschung, Von Keitz, Saarbrücken, March.

Kraay, W.F., 1991: Scannen en focussen, Blad dossier, No. 2.

Kraaykamp, G., en Knulst, W., 1992: Stijgend scholingsniveau afnemende belezenheid; verschuivingen in het gebruik van media tussen 1955-1990, January.

Kroeber-Riel, W., 1984: Werbung, die nicht wirken kann, Marketing Journal, No. 3.

Kroeber-Riel, W., 1984: Zentrale Probleme auf gesättigten Märkten; Auswechselbare produkte und auswechselbare Werbung und ihre Uberwindungen durch erlebnisbetonte Marketingstrategien, No. 3, August.

Kroeber-Riel, W., 1985: Weniger Information, mehr Erlebnis, mehr Bild, Absatzwirtschaft, No. 3.

Kroeber-Riel, W., 1987: Hört der Konsument noch zu? Strategien der Werbung unter heutigen Kommunikationsbedingungen, Universität des Saarlandes, Saarbrücken.

Kroeber-Riel, W.,1987: Informationsüberlastung durch Massenmedien und Werbung in Deutschland, DBW 47, No. 3.

Kroeber-Riel, W., 1987: Weniger Informationsüberlastung durch Bildkommunikation; Zur Verwendung von Bildern in Kommerziellen Kommunikationssystemen, WiSt No. 10, October.

Kroeber-Riel, W., 1987: Laut Schreien um gehört zu werden, Copy 23.

Kroeber-Riel, W., 1988: Kommunikation im Zeitalter der Informationsüberlastung, Marketing ZFP, No. 3.

Kroeber-Riel, W., 1990: Strategie und Technik der Werbung; Verhaltenswissenschaftliche Ansätze, Kohlhammer.

Kroeber-Riel, W., Prof. Dr., 1992: Ich mache Kreatieven keine Vorschriften, W&V No. 11/13, March.

Kroeber-Riel Aussagen bleiben heftig umstritten, 1992: W&V No. 18/30, April.

Kroeber-Riel, W., and Barton, B., 1980: Scanning Ads-Effects of Position and Arousal, Potential of Ad Elements, Current Issues and Research in Advertising.

Krugman, H.E., 1975: What makes advertising effective? Harvard Business Review.

Krugman, H.E., 1986: Low recall and high recognition of advertising, Journal of Advertising Research, Vol. 26, February/March.

Kuse, A.R., 1990: Continuing Useful Validation into the 1990's, ARF Key Issues Workshop, The Omni Park Central Hotel, 11th July.

Lachman, J.L., and Lachman, R., 1979: Comprehension and Cognition; A State of the Art Inquiry, in: Levels of processing in human memory, Cermak, L.S., and Craik, F.I.M., Lawrence Erlbaum Ass. Hillsdale, New Jersey.

Lang, A., Involuntary attention and physiological arousal evoked by structural features and emotional contact in tv commercials, Communication Research.

Lannon, J., 1992: Asking the right questions, ADMAP.

Laufer, J., 1986: Erkentnisse aus 10 Jahren Argus, in: Anzeigen-copytests; Erkentnisse aus 10 Jahren Argus, Gruner + Jahr, Die Stern Bibliothek.

Leavitt, C., 1970: A Multidimensional Set of Rating Scales For Television Commercials, Journal of Applied Psychology, Vol. 54, No. 5.

Leckenby, J.D., and Plummer, J.T., 1983: Advertising measurement and assessment research: A review of advertising testing methods, Current Issues and Research in Advertising.

Leven, W., 1983: Die Blickfangwirkung der Aufmerksamkeit beim Betrachten von Werbeanzeigen, in; Jahrbuch der Absatz – und Verbrauchersforschung, 29, No. 3.

Leven, W., 1992: Forschungs-Ergebnisse, May 1992, W&V No. 22/29.

Levine, J., 1990: The last gasp of mass media? Forbes, September.

Lloyd, D.W., and Clancy, K.J., 1991: Television Program Involvement and Advertising Response: Some unsettling implications for copy research, The Journal of Consumer Marketing, Vol. 8, Autumn.

Lodish, Dr. L.M., 1991: Key findings from the "How advertising works" study, in: Transcript proceedings Breakthrough marketplace advertising research for bottom line results, ARF, New York.

Lukeman, G., 1988: How recall scores come about; The underlying structure from a 700 commercial study, ARF 34th Annual Conference, New York, Hilton, 7-9th March.

Lukeman, G., 1989: No attention, no recall: Getting it and losing it. Copy Research Workshop ARF, New York, 22nd May.

MacInnis, D.J., and Jaworski, B.J., 1989: Information processing from advertisements: toward an integrative framework, Journal of Marketing, Vol. 53, October.

MacKenzie, S.B., and Lutz, R.J., 1989: An Empirical Examination of the Structural Antecedents of Attitude Toward the Ad in an Advertising Pretesting Context, Journal of Marketing, Vol. 53.

Madden, T.J., and Weinberger M.G., 1982: The effects of humor on attention in magazine advertising, Journal of Advertising, Vol. 11, No. 3.

Madden T.J., and Weinberger M.G., 1984: Humor in Advertising: A Practitioner View, Journal of Advertising Research, Vol. 24, No. 4, August/September.

Mandler, G., 1982: Mind and Emotion, chapter 3, Robert E. Krieger Publishing Company.

McCollum Spielman, 1980: Liking and sales effectiveness: a hypothesis, Topline, Vol. 2, No. 1, February.

McCollum Spielman, 1982: Focus on Funny, Topline. Vol. 3, No. 3.

McCollum Spielman Worldwide 1991: Analyse van copy-test-resultaten van 251 tv-commercials in 6 produktcategorieèn.

McCollum Spielman Worldwide, 1991: The Comparative Advertising Demonstration: A Review of McCollum Spielman Worldwide Ad*Vantage/ACT Copy Testing Experience, (unpublished paper), July.

McCollum Spielman Worldwide, 1991: Does commercial liking matter?; An empirical investigation of the relationship of liking/disliking to Ad*Vantage/Act, Topline, December.

McDonald, C., 1986: Advertising effectiveness revisited, ADMAP, April.

McEwen, W.J., and Leavitt, C., 1976: A way to describe tv commercials, Journal of Advertising Research, Vol. 16, No. 6.

McGuire, W.J., 1968: Selective exposure: A summing up, in: Abelson, P., e.a., Theories of Cognitive Consistency, A sourcebook, Rand McNally & Company.

McGuire, W.J., 1976: Some internal psychological factors influencing consumer choice, Journal of Consumer Research, Vol. 2, March.

McGuire, W.J., 1978: An Information-Processing Model of Advertising Effectiveness, in: Davis, H.L., and Silk, A.J.,: Behavioral and Management Science in Marketing, Wiley.

McQuarrie, E.F., and Munson J.M., 1992: A Revised Product Involvement Inventory: Improved Usability and Validity, Advances in Consumer Research, Vol. 19.

McQueen, J.,1990: The different ways ads work, Journal of Advertising Research. Vol. 30, August/September.

McQueen, J., 1991: Important learning about how advertising works in stimulating long-term brand-growth, in: Transcript proceedings Breakthrough marketplace advertising research for bottom line results ARF, New York.

McQueen, J., 1991: Measuring the Subtlety of Emotions: Leo Burnett's Lexicon, Paper presented at "Tears, cheers and fears" conference, MSI. May

McQueen, J., 1992: How advertising works, Stimulating long-term brand growth, ADMAP, April.

Mediamarkt, 1988: Video-experiment toont geringe aandacht voor tv-commercials, June.

Mehr Sender, mehr Werbung – weniger Werbewirkung W&V No. 12, 1992.

Merz, G., 1989: Humor in der Werbung, Freie wissengeschaftliche Arbeit zur Erlanging des akadem ischen Grades Nürnberg.

Metzger, R.L., and Antes, J.R., 1983: The Nature of Processing Early in Picture Perception, Psychological Research, Vol. 45.

Meyer-Hentschel, G: "Erfolgreiche Anzeige; Kriterien und Beispiele zur Beurteilung und Gestaltung."

Meyer-Hentschel, G., 1992: Print ist nicht schnell genug, W&V No. 20.

Miller, C., 1992: New Study Downplays 'likeability' as major factor in ad succes, Marketing News, Vol. 26, No. 8.

Miniard, P.W., Bhatla, S., Lord, K.R., Dickson, P.R. a.o., 1991: Picture-based Persuasion Processes and the Moderating Role of Involvement, Journal of Consumer Research, Vol. 18, June.

Mitchell, A.A., 1983: The Effects of Visual and Emotional Advertising: An Information-Processing Approach, in: Percy, L., Woodside, G., Advertising and Consumer Psychology, Lexington Books.

Mittal, B., 1990: The relative roles of brand beliefs and attitude toward the ad as mediators of brand attitude: A second look, Journal of Marketing Research, Vol. 27, May.

Moldovan, S.E., 1984/1985: Copy factors related to persuasion scores, Journal of Advertising Research, Vol. 24, No. 6.

Molen, M. v.d., en Robben H., 1991: Meettechnieken, Blad dossier, VNU Tijdschriftengroep/Admedia.

Molen, M. v.d., en Robben, H., 1991: Reclame Reactie Onderzoek, Blad dossier, No. 2, September.

Moore, D.L., and Hutchinson, J.W., 1983: The Effects of Ad Affect on Advertising Effectiveness in: Advances in Consumer Research, Vol. 10.

Moran, W.T., 1990: Brand presence and the perceptual frame, Journal of Advertising Research.

Moriarty, S.E., 1983: Beyond the Hierarchy of Effects; A Conceptual Framework, Current Issues and Research in Advertising, No. 1.

Munzinger, U., Sind Commercials, die gefallen, wirksamer? Hauptabteilungsleiter Werbeforschung GfK Marktforschung, (unpublished paper).

Munzinger, U., und Musiol, K.G., 1986: Superstar contra Unbekannt, W&V No. 34, August.

Munzinger, U., 1992: "Analyse van de effecten van 'likeability' van 965 tv-commercials", getest door GfK Marktfurschung, Duitsland.

Murphy, J.H., Cunningham, I.C.M., and Wilcox, G.B., The Impact of Program Environment on Recall of Humorous Television Commercials.

Murray, H., So You Know How Advertising Works, Management Decision, Vol. 17.

Nakra, P., 1991: Zapping Nonsense: Should Television Media Planners Lose Sleep Over It? International Journal of Advertising, Vol. 10.

Nederlanders besteden hun tijd: hoofdrol voor de beeldbuis, 1988: Mediamarkt, November.

Neibecker, B., 1987: Werben mit Bildern, Marketing Journal, No. 4.

Nelson, D.L., 1979: Remembering Pictures and Words: Appearance, Significance, and Name, in; Cermak, L.S., and Craik, T.I.M., Levels of Processing in Human Memory, Erlbaum.

Newspaper Advertising Bureau Inc: Recall of last television commercial, 1965-1990, New York.

Newspaper Advertising Bureau Inc, 1990: TV recall isn't what it used to be, New York.

Noordhoff, J., 1986: Die Anzeigen-Nutzung in Tageszeitungen, Viertel Jahreshefte fur Mediaplanning.

Norris, C.E., and Colman, A.M., 1992: Context Effects on Recall and Recognition of Magazine Advertisements, Journal of Advertising, Vol. 21, No. 3, September.

Nur Sport und News können die Zuschauer noch faszinieren, 1992: W&V No. 17/24, April.

Ogilvy, D., and Raphaelson, J., 1982: Research on advertising techniques that work and don't work, Harvard Business Review. Vol. 60, July-August.

Ogilvy Center for Research & Development, 1985: Does likeable tv-advertising help sell the product? September.

Olney, T.J., Holbrook, M.B., and Batra, R., 1991: Consumer responses to advertising: The effects of ad content, emotions, and attitude toward the ad on viewing time, Journal of Consumer Research, Vol. 17, March.

Olson, D.W., 1984: Validation of copytesting measures based on in-market performance: an analysis of new product ads, in: Esomar symposium Methodolique Advances in Marketing Research, In Theory and Practice.

Olson, D.W., 1985: Guidelines to better new product advertising, Leo Burnett Co., internal document, March.

Olson, D.W., 1985: The characteristics of high-trial new-product advertising, Journal of Advertising Research, Vol. 25, No. 5, October.

Opaschowski, H.W., Herausforderung Freizeit. Band 10 der Schriftenreihe zur Freizeitforschung, B.A.T. Freizeitforschungsinstitut.

Page Jr., T.J., Daugherty, P.J., Eroglu, D., a.o., 1988: Measuring Emotional Response to Advertising: A Comment on Stout and Leckenby, Journal of Advertising, Vol. 17, No. 4.

Percy, L., 1983: A Review of the Effect of Specific Advertising Elements upon Overall Communication Response, Current Issues and Research in Advertising.

Philips, D., 1991: Press towards a deeper understanding of readership, advertising and research issues, How advertising works and how promotions works, Esomar seminar, Amsterdam.

Pieters, R., 1990: Een fijn contact, gevoelens bij reclame en hun funktie in communicatie, Presentatie Zandvoort, June.

Pieters, R., 1990: EPM, een positioneringsmodel, Publikatie Vakgroep Economische Sociologie en Psychologie, Erasmus Universiteit, Rotterdam.

Pieters, R., en Warmerdam M., 1990: Structure in Ad-Evoked Feelings; Its relationship with attitudes and advertising recall, September, (unpublished paper).

Pieters, R., en Warmerdam M., 1990: Feelings at Contact, Paper presented at Conference of Applied Psychology, Kyoto, Japan.

Pincus, J.D.R., 1992: Interpreting Perceiver Reactions to Emotional Stimuli, University of Connecticut, Advances in Consumer Research, Vol. 19.

Poiesz, T.B.C., and Verhallen, T.M.M.,1989: Brand Confusion in Advertising, International Journal of Advertising, Vol. 8.

Poiesz, T.B.C., 1989: Het voorkomen van merkverwarring (2), Tijdschrift voor Marketing, February.

Polsfuss, M., and Hess, M., 1991: Liking Through Moment-To-Moment Evaluation; Identify Key Selling Segments In Advertising, Advances in Consumer Research, Vol. 18.

Pompe, E., en Verhoeven, I: Reklame reaktie onderzoek, Wat is het en wat zijn de mogelijkheden? Admedia.

Presser, R., 1986: Reclame-effectiviteit (hoe) meten we die?, Reclameherinnering: symposium Samsom, 14th January.

Preston, I.L., 1982: The association model of the advertising communication process, Journal of Advertising, Vol. 11, No. 2.

Preston, I.L., and Thorson, E., 1984: The expanded association model: Keeping the hierarchy concept alive, Journal of Advertising Research, Vol. 24, No. 1.

Prue, T., 1987: Where is the scientific method in the measurement of advertising effect? ADMAP.

Prue, T., 1991: Recall or response? Ad effectiveness monitoring, the real issues, ADMAP, June.

Quatresooz, J., 1990: Correlates of advertising impact in newspapers and magazines, in: Brown, M., Dear reader; some readership measurements questions and some answers, Research Service Ltd.

Raay, W.F., van, 1989: How consumers react to advertising, International Journal of Advertising, No. 8.

Raay, W.F., van, 1991: Hoe gaat de consument om met reclame? Blad Dossier, No. 1, pp. 7-25.

Rao Unnava, H., and Burnkrant, R.E., 1991: An imagery-processing view of the role of pictures in print advertisements, Journal of Marketing Research, Vol. 28, May.

Raskin, V., 1985: Semantic mechanisms of humour, Dordrecht.

Reeves, R., Reality in Advertising, Alfred A. Knopf.

Rehorn, J., 1989: Gröse zahlt sich aus; Zur Werbe-Wirkung unterschiedeicher Anzeigen-Formate, Marketing Journal, No. 2.

Reid, L.N., and Soley, L.C., 1980: Levels-of-Processing in Memory and the Recall and Recognition of Television Commercials, Current Issues and Research in Advertising.

Research Alert, 1991: At our leisure: how Americans spend their free time, Vol. 9, No. 14, 20th December.

Research Systems Corporation, 1985: Vanderbilt study, Basic Research, Evansville, Indiana.

Research Systems Corporation, 1990: Validation and Advertising Elasticity, April.

Roper, B.W., 1990: What people really think about television, ANA Television Workshop, New York, February.

Rosenberg, K.E., Arnold, R., and Capetta, P., 1991: Heart strings to purse strings, Paper presented at the congress "Tears, cheers and fears", the role of emotions in advertising, Marketing Science Institute, 14-15th February.

Ross Jr, H.L., 1982: Recall Versus Persuasion: An answer, Journal of Advertising Research, Vol. 22, February/March.

Rossiter, J.R., 1981: Predicting Starch Scores, Journal of Advertising Research, October, Vol. 21, No. 5.

Rossiter, J.R., 1987: Comments on consumer beliefs and brand usage and on Ehrenberg's model, Journal of the Market Research Society, Vol. 29, No. 1.

Rossiter, J.R., and Percy, L., 1980: Attitude change through visual imagery in advertising, Journal of Advertising, Vol. 9, No. 2.

Rossiter, J.R., Percy, L., and Donovan R.J., 1991: A Better Advertising Planning Grid, Journal of Advertising Research, Vol. 13.

Rothbart, M.K., and Pien, 1977: Elephants and marshmallows: a theoretical synthesis of incongruity-resolution and arousal theories of humor, It's a funny thing humour, Oxford.

Russell, D.A., and Starkman, D.L., 1990: Measuring the emotional response to advertising, BBDO's emotional measurement system and emotional photodeck, No. 1, (unpublished paper).

Saegert, J., 1979: A Demonstration of Levels of Processing Theory in Memory for Advertisements, in: Advances in Consumer Research, Vol. 6.

Saupe, C., 1992: 'Likeability' und 'Werbewirksamkeit'; Freie wissenschaftliche Arbeit zur Erlangung des Akademischen Grades 'Diplomkaufman', Nürnberg.

Schlechte Werbe-Erinnerung ist nicht nur ein tv-problem, W&V No. 11, 1992.

Schlinger, M.J.,1979: A profile of responses to commercials, Journal of Advertising Research, Vol. 1, No. 2.

Schor, J.B., 1991: The overworked American; the unexpected decline of leisure! Basic Books.

Schweiker, A., 1987: Advertising testing measuring recall and persuasion, Esomar Marketing Research Congress Montreux, September.

Schwoerer, J., 1987: Measuring advertising effectiveness: Emergence of an international standard? European Research, Vol. 15, No. 1.

Sheth, J.N., Newman, B.I., and Gross, B.L., 1991: Why We Buy What We Buy: A Theory of Consumption Values, Journal of Business Research.

Shimp, T.A., 1981: Attitude Toward the Ad as a Mediator of Consumer Brand Choice. Journal of Advertising, Vol. 10.

Shimp, T.A., and Gresham, L.G., 1983: An information-processing perspective on recent advertising literature, Current Issues and Research in Advertising.

Singh, S.N., Rothschild, M.L., and Churchill Jr., G.A., 1988: Recognition Versus Recall as Mesaures of Television Commercial Forgetting, Journal of Marketing Research, Vol. 15.

Smith, A., 1983: The effect of advertising on those who are brand loyal, ADMAP.

Smith, R.E., and Buchholz, L.M., 1991: Multiple Resource Theory and Consumer Processing of Broadcast Advertisements: An Involvement Perspective, Journal of Advertising, Vol. 20, No. 3.

Smith, R.E., and Swinyard, W.R., 1988: Cognitive Response to Advertising and Trial: Belief Strength, Belief Confidence and Product Curiosity, Journal of Advertising, Vol. 17, No. 3.

Smith, R.S., 1991: An introduction to the 'How advertising works'– study: a landmark analysis of advertising effectiveness, in: Transcript proceedings: Breakthrough marketplace advertising research for bottom line results, ARF conference, November.

Snyder, M., and DeBono, K.G., 1985: Appeals to Image and Claims About Quality: Understanding the Psychology of Advertising, Journal of Personality and Social Psychology, Vol. 49, No. 3.

Sola Pool, I. de, Inose, H., Takasaki, N., and Hurwitz, R., 1984: Communications Flows, A census in the U.S. and Japan, North Holland Publishing Company.

Speetzen, R., 1990: The value of media exposures, in: Brown, M., Dear reader; some readership measurement questions and some answers, Research Service Ltd.

Stapel, J., 1970: Back of head photographs reconsidered, Journal of the Market Research Society, Vol. 12, No. 3.

Stapel, J., 1971: Sales Effects of Print Ads, Journal of Marketing Research, No. 3.

Stapel, J., 1972: Reclameresultaten meten voor marketing, Samson Uitgeverij N.V.

Stapel, J., 1974: Konfrontatie = zelf-perceptie, al was het maar heel vluchtig, Adformatie, 30th May.

Stapel, J., 1975: Intention-to-Buy Statements and the Short-Term Effects of Advertising, ADMAP, March.

Stapel, J., 1975: Er zijn veel meer leuke dan irritante televisiespots, Adformatie, No. 12, 6th March.

Stapel, J., 1976: Waarom mensen pagina's openslaan maar niet bekijken, Adformatie, 18th November.

Stapel, J., 1990: Monitoring advertising performance, ADMAP, July/August.

Stapel, J., 1991: "Like the ad...but does it interest me?" Ad effectiveness, ADMAP, April.

Stappers, J.G., en Reijnders, A.D., en Möller, W.A.J., 1990: De werking van massamedia, een overzicht van inzichten, De Arbeiderspers, Amsterdam.

Starch, D., 1966: Measuring advertising readership and results, New York.

Starch Tested Copy, 1989; Vol. 1, No. 1, February.

Starch Tested Copy, 1989. Vol. 1, No. 5, June.

Starch Tested Copy, 1989: Vol. 1, No. 9, October.

Starch Tested Copy, 1990: Vol. 2, No. 3, April.

Starch Tested Copy, 1990: Vol. 2, No. 8, September.

Stayman, D., 1991: Two Perspectives on the Role of Affect in Influencing Brand Associations, Paper presented at the conference "Tears, cheers, and fears", The role of emotions in advertising, MSI.

Stayman, D.M., and Batra, R., 1991: Encoding and retrieval of ad affect in memory, Journal of Marketing Research, Vol. 28, May.

Sternthal, B., and Craig, C.S., 1973: Humor in Advertising, Journal of Marketing, Vol. 37.

Steurer, K., 1985: Was leisten Anzeigen in Trend und Profil, Vierjahreshefte für mediaplanning.

Stewart, D.W., 1986: The moderating role of recall, comprehension and brand differentiation on the persuasiveness of television advertising, Journal of Advertising Research, Vol. 26.

Stewart, D.W., 1989: Measures, methods, and models in advertising research, Journal of Advertising Research, Vol. 29, June/July.

Stewart, D.W., Koslow, S., 1979: A replication, Journal of Advertising Research, Vol. 19, No. 2.

Stewart, D.W., Pechmann, C., Ratneshwar, Methodological and Theoretical Foundations of Advertising Copytesting: A Review, in Current Issues & Research in Advertising 1985, Graduate School of Business Administration, The University of Michigan.

Stewart, D.W., and Furse, D.H., 1986: Effective television advertising, Lexington Books, Toronto.

Stewart-Hunter, D. 1985: Humor in television advertising: the search for a golden rule, ADMAP, May.

Stockman, L., 1991: Het tv-publiek is er niet altijd met de gedachten bij, Nieuwstribune, Week 3, 17th January.

Stout, P.A., and Leckenby, J.D., 1986: Measuring emotional response to advertising, Journal of Advertising, Vol. 15, No. 4.

Stout, P.A., and Leckenby, J.D., 1988: The Nature of Emotional Response to Advertising: A Further Examination, Journal of Advertising, Vol. 17, No. 4.

Sutherland, M., and Galloway, J., 1981: Persuasion or Agenda Setting? Journal of Advertising Research, Vol. 21, No. 5.

Sylvester, A., 1992: What works. What doesn't; Practical applications of the AdWorks material, ADMAP, March.

Thorson, E., 1989: Processing Television Commercials, in: Rethinking Communication, Davin, B., a.o., Sage Publications, Vol. 2.

Thorson, E.,1990: Consumer Processing of Advertising, Current Issues & Research in Advertising, Vol. 12, No. 2.

Thorson, E., 1991: Emotional Flow During Commercials, Paper presented at the conference "Tears, cheers and fears"; the role of emotions in advertising, MSI.

Thorson, E., and Friestad, M., 1985: The Effects of Emotion on Episodic Memory for TV Commercials, Paper presented at the Advertising and Consumer Psychology Conference, Needham-Harper-Steers, Chicago, May.

Tiempo/BBDO 1990: Zapping, Onderzoek, October, (unpublished paper).

Tranberg, H., and Hansen, F., 1986: Patterns of Brand Loyalty: Their Determinants and Their Role for Leading Brands, European Journal of Marketing, No. 20.

Treisman, A., 1979: The Psychological Reality of Levels of Processing, in; Levels of Processing in Human Memory, Cermak, L.S., and Craik, F.I.M., Lawrence Erlbaum, Hillsdale, New Jersey.

Tucker, C., 1991: Synopsis of the presentation from the ARF Copy Research Workshop, Presented at the ARF Copy Research Validation Conference, 11th September.

Twivy, P., 1987: Humour in Advertising: A Blessing and a Curse, Campaign, 30th January.

Twyman, T., 1984: Assesing the validity of pre-testing: Part 1, ADMAP, February.

Twyman, T., 1984: Assesing the validity of pre-testing: Part 2, ADMAP, March.

Unilever Plan for Good Advertising, 1988: Marketing Division Unilever.

Validity of Consumer Predicting Variables Used in Marketing Research, León, J.L., and Olábarri, Esomar Congress.

Verhallen, Th. M.M. en Pieters, R.G.M., Attitude theory and behavioral costs, Journal of Economic Psychology, No. 5.

Voort, T.H.A., van der, 1991: Television and the decline of reading, Poetics, Vol. 20.

Vorstenbosch, R., 1992: Analyse consumenten-koopstrategieèn voor de uitbouw van de consumerfranchise, Nieuwstribune, week 22.

Walker, D., 1990: Beyond validation: Advertising research for the 1990's, presentation at ARF 7th Annual Copy Research Workshop, 11th July.

Walker, D., 1991: Efficiency and Effectiveness: Calibrating Copy Research to Sales, 8th Annual ARF Copy Research Workshop, Hilton Hotel, New York.

Walker, D., and Dubitsky, T., 1991: Do they like it? Does it matter? Presented at the 36th Annual Conference of the Advertising Research Foundation, New York.

Walker, D., and Eaton, H., 1991: Persuasion, Recall, and Liking Measures, Paper presented at the conference "Tears, cheers and fears", the role of emotions in advertising, MSI.

Ward, J., and Gadis, W., 1990: Metaphor in Promotional Communication: A Review of Research on Metaphor Comprehension and Quality, in Advances in Consumer Research, Vol. 17.

Waring, P.A., 1986: Copytests in den USA: Ansätze zur Verbesserung der Werbewirksamkeit von Anzeigen, in: Laufer, J., Generelle Erkentnisse aus 10 Jahren Argus, Gruner + Jahr, Die Stern Bibliothek.

Weinberger, M.G., and Spotts, H.E., 1989: Humor in U.S. versus U.K., TV Commercials, A Comparison, Journal of Advertising, Vol. 18, No. 2.

Wells, W., 1964: EQ, son of EQ and the reaction profile, Journal of Marketing, Vol. 28, No. 4.

Wells, W.D., Recognition, recall, and rating scales, Journal of Advertising Research.

Wells, W.D., Leavitt, C., and McConville, M., 1971: A reaction profile for tv commercials, Journal of Advertising Research, Vol. 11, No. 6, December.

Westbrook, R.A., 1991: An Overview of Emotions, Paper presented at the Conference "Tears, cheers and fears", The role of emotions in advertising, Marketing Science Institute, report No. 91-112, May.

Whipple, T.W., and Courtney, A.E., 1981: How Men and Women Judge Humor, Current Issues and Research in Advertising.

Windahl, S., Signitzer, B., and Olson J.T., 1992: Using Communication Theory, Sage Publications.

Woodside, A.G., and Wilson, E.J., 1985: Effects of consumer awareness of brand advertising on preference, Journal of Advertising Research, Vol. 25, No. 4, August/September.

Zebrowitz McArthur, L., What grabs you?; The role of attention in impression formation and causal attribution in: Higgins, E.T., Herman, C.P., and Zanna, M.P., Social Cognition, The Ontario Symposium, Vol. 1.

Zeitunglesen: Vom grosen zum kleinen Element, 1991: W&V No. 44/31.

Zeldenrust, D., 1990: Waarom weer een nieuw reclamemodel? Reclame en Onderzoek, jaargang 2, No. 1.

Zinkhan, G.M., and Gelb, B.D., 1986: What starch scores predict, Journal of Advertsing Research, August/September.

Zinkhan, G.M., and Gelb, B.D., 1987: Humor and advertising effectiveness reexamined, Journal of Advertising, Vol. 16, No. 1.

Index